LITERARY COPYRIGHT REFORM IN EARLY VICTORIAN ENGLAND

The Framing of the 1842 Copyright Act

Talfourd's first copyright bill was presented in 1837, and the public and parliamentary controversy it provoked is reflected in contemporary pamphlets, correspondence and hundreds of petitions presented to parliament, as well as in the changing aims of the bill itself. In addition to the expected debate as to the nature of literary property and the economic effects on the publishing trade, discussion of copyright law raised broader questions: the relative values of literature and science, the importance of public education, the dangers of monopolies and the nature of public interest. In a period of social, political and technological upheaval, these were incendiary matters. Talfourd audaciously demanded not only a considerable extension of copyright term, but also international protection. This book explores and sets in context the making of this crucial Act, using it to illuminate enduring issues and difficulties in the legal concept of intellectual property.

CATHERINE SEVILLE is director of studies in law at Newnham College, Cambridge.

CAMBRIDGE STUDIES IN ENGLISH LEGAL HISTORY

Edited by
J. H. BAKER
Fellow of St Catherine's College, Cambridge

Recent series titles include

Sir William Scott, Lord Stowell
Judge of the High Court of Admiralty 1798–1828
HENRY J. BOURGUIGNON

Sir Henry Maine
A study in Victorian jurisprudence
R. C. J. COCKS

Roman canon law in Reformation England
R. H. HELMHOLZ

Fundamental authority in late Medieval English law
NORMAN DOE

Law, politics and the Church of England
The career of Stephen Lushington 1782–1873
S. M. WADDAMS

The early history of the law of bills and notes
A study of the origins of Anglo-American commercial law
JAMES STEVEN ROGERS

The law of evidence in Victorian England
CHRISTOPHER ALLEN

John Scott, Lord Eldon
ROSE MELIKAN

Literary copyright reform in Early Victorian England
CATHERINE SEVILLE

Engraving of Thomas Noon Talfourd
(reproduced from the author's collection)

LITERARY COPYRIGHT REFORM IN EARLY VICTORIAN ENGLAND

THE FRAMING OF THE 1842 COPYRIGHT ACT

CATHERINE SEVILLE

CAMBRIDGE
UNIVERSITY PRESS

CAMBRIDGE UNIVERSITY PRESS
Cambridge, New York, Melbourne, Madrid, Cape Town,
Singapore, São Paulo, Delhi, Tokyo, Mexico City

Cambridge University Press
The Edinburgh Building, Cambridge CB2 8RU, UK

Published in the United States of America by Cambridge University Press, New York

www.cambridge.org
Information on this title: www.cambridge.org/9780521174503

First published 1999
First paperback edition 2011

A catalogue record for this publication is available from the British Library

ISBN 978-0-521-62175-5 Hardback
ISBN 978-0-521-17450-3 Paperback

FOR J. S. & A. H. S.

CONTENTS

ACKNOWLEDGEMENTS

I owe a substantial debt of gratitude to Bill Cornish, whose work and teaching first sparked my interest in copyright. As my supervisor he encouraged what must at first have seemed an unlikely project, and his support continues. I am also very grateful to Gill Sutherland: her rigour, patience and encouragement have been invaluable. Others have helped in other ways, particularly Tom Kass, who first suggested that I study law.

I have been privileged to work in Newnham throughout this time.

1

INTRODUCTION

The subject of this book is Serjeant Talfourd's back-bench attempt to reform the law of copyright, an attempt which eventually produced the Copyright Act of 1842. The idea of reform is potent in the history of England in the nineteenth century. It would be impossible to write a general history of the period without giving an account of the major constitutional reforms concerned with popular representation, which eventually transformed parliament. Yet other contemporary legislative reforms are arguably as striking, both in terms of their volume, and in terms of the changes which resulted. The many attempts to improve the law and its mechanisms make this period a significant one for legal history. In the decade following the 1832 Reform Act, approaches to government in the widest sense were re-examined and transformed. This process had protean qualities: striking though the direction and velocity of the immediate changes could be, they often represented only the first phase of lengthy trajectories.

Nevertheless, it would be foolhardy (and unduly Whiggish) to regard these changes as inevitable; they were the product of many complex and conflicting forces. Although nineteenth-century legislators did create a battery of significant reforms, the antecedents and characteristics of individual measures varied considerably. To take the example central to this book, the changes to copyright law which resulted from the 1842 Copyright Act were not overtly typical of a reforming brief. However, the efforts to promote the various copyright measures (which began in 1836) were profoundly affected by the prevailing mood of reform, and the methods and mechanisms associated with it. Talfourd had originally envisaged a thoroughgoing consolidation of all aspects of copyright, an aim which might have been thought consistent with general reforming objectives. Such an assumption ignores the complex and varied character of reforming activity at this time. Copyright instead became characterised as harmful by a significant body of popular opinion, and a campaign of resistance was organised. After a lengthy battle, the bill's sponsors were forced to settle for the compromise effected by the 1842 Act.

Although it is possible to reduce the principle of reform to little more than a Benthamite slogan, this is to ignore the subtlety and pervasiveness of the concept. The Great Reform Act of 1832 has (and had) a well-developed popular image as the keynote reform of the period. Its symbolic importance was certainly considerable. In terms of practical results, however, the 1832 Act's reputation bears only limited examination: later reform Acts, and related legislation, were arguably more significant.[1] Inevitably, the close link between the legislative and constitutional aspects of parliamentary reform ensured ample publicity for any statutory changes in this area. This should not be allowed to obscure the many other social and economic reforms of the period, which often required implementing legislation.[2] In addition, there were deliberate attempts to render the law itself more coherent and accessible; specific legislative reforms covered many aspects of practice and procedure.[3]

[1] For details of these see, for example, John Cannon, *Parliamentary reform, 1640–1832* (Cambridge, 1973); Michael Brock, *The Great Reform Act* (1973); Norman Gash, *Politics in the age of Peel* (1953); Francis B. Smith, *The making of the second Reform Bill* (Cambridge, 1966); Norman Gash, *Pillars of government and other essays on state and society, c. 1770–c. 1880* (1986); Andrew Jones, *The politics of reform: 1884* (Cambridge, 1972); Martin D. Pugh, *The making of modern British politics, 1867–1939* (1982).

[2] For example, the Municipal Corporations Act 1835 began a process of local government reform which continued throughout the century. In another sphere, the New Poor Law Amendment Act 1834 made controversial changes intended to reduce expenditure. Other measures addressed a range of issues including public health and education, and also dealt with more general matters such as financial and administrative efficiency. Geoffrey B. A. M. Finlayson, 'The politics of municipal reform, 1835', *English Historical Review* 81 (1966), 673–92; Gillian Sutherland (ed.), *Studies in the growth of nineteenth-century government* (1972); Derek Fraser (ed.), *The new poor law in the nineteenth century* (1976).

[3] For example Peel's Acts, which consolidated the criminal law and reduced the use of capital punishment. A considerable programme of reforms resulted, both before and after the 1832 Reform Act. For confirmation see Holdsworth's catalogue of statutory changes (vol. XIII, ch. 4) which details an extraordinary list of interventions, large and small. Sir William Holdsworth, *A history of English law*, 16 vols. and index (1903–52); Leon Radzinowicz, *A history of English criminal law* (1948); William R. Cornish and Geoffrey de N. Clark, *Law and society in England, 1750–1950* (1989).

The notion of law reform is certainly not peculiar to the nineteenth century. It has always been necessary for the law to respond to society's needs, sometimes willingly, sometimes under pressure. Nevertheless, this period provides a unique presentation of this process. We are repeatedly offered a vision of reform as the 'spirit of the age', with conscious emphasis on utility, efficiency and humanitarianism. Such generalisations are in some ways helpful, yet can become parodic if attention to detail is lost. On a more technical level, it should be observed that the governments of this period were ground breaking in their extensive resort to statute law. The job of developing and adapting the law to a changing society had previously been left largely to the courts, which had gone about their task with subtlety and quiet skill. The process of legal reform by judicial precedent is a slow but constant process, usually gradual, and necessarily piecemeal. In this it is quite different from statute, which can change the face of the law in an afternoon. For grand schemes of consolidation or codification, statute law is essential. Talfourd's plans for copyright reform were, therefore, dependent on the passage of a bill.

The legislative history of literary copyright in England may be summarised fairly briefly. The sixteenth-century licensing system was born of Tudor desires to control the press. In 1557 Mary granted the Stationers' Company a charter, which allowed its members an effective monopoly on legal printing.[4] The system was remarkably resilient, and even survived throughout the Civil War, in form if not in fact. In 1662 Charles II restored the licensing system to strength, again with a view to maintaining Crown power over the press, but let it lapse in 1679. After a brief revival under James II, in 1695 parliament finally refused to extend the life of the licensing system, and chaos in the book trade was threatened. After repeated trade efforts, in 1710 the first English copyright statute was passed, often referred to as the Act of Anne. Described as an 'Act for the Encouragement of learned Men to compose and write useful Books', this gave a fourteen-year

[4] An entry in the Stationers' Registerer originally indicated that the book had been properly licensed, but soon came to indicate a quasi-proprietary right to the 'copy'. Thus 'copy' came to mean the sole right of printing publishing and selling (hence 'copy-right'), although the word is also used to refer to the work incorporated in the manuscript, and to the physical copy. For a fuller account see John Feather, *A history of British publishing* (1988).

term to all books registered with the Stationers' Company, with an additional fourteen years if the author was still living at the expiry of the first term. Although the right was granted to 'authors and their assigns', in practice it was invariably held by the bookseller. It was at first thought that the Act of Anne offered rights which were supplementary to a perpetual common law right of literary property, but in 1774 the famous case of *Donaldson* v. *Beckett* decided otherwise. The decision was followed by a long period of stagnation, broken in 1814 by a new Copyright Act which set the term at twenty-eight years, or the author's life if this was longer. It was this Act that Talfourd sought to change.

It is easy enough to describe copyright reform in a way which would suggest a parallel with a general Whiggish trajectory of reform. It is possible to see the 1814 Act as a breakthrough in terms of the author's place in copyright law, because for the first time the author's lifespan is an important element in the calculation of term. On this line of reasoning, the 1842 Copyright Act provided further improvement, setting the term to the author's life plus seven years, providing this was not less than forty-two years in total. The 1911 Copyright Act, enacting the Berne Convention's minimum requirement of the author's life plus fifty years, might then be the pinnacle of a reform movement to provide author-centred copyright legislation, where entrepreneurs at last rate second to the creative individual. However, such an analysis would be dangerously wrong, revealing sharply the dangers of isolating the law from its context. The influence of the reform movement was powerful, but not so crude.

Certainly many of the mechanisms of protest used in the parliamentary and other reform struggles were used again in the copyright campaign; both sides sought to lobby MPs and other influential figures, newspapers and the periodical press provided publicity, and the use of petitions was crucial. Yet there were other, distinct, sources of pressure. It is important to realise that the resistance to the early copyright bills came largely from print workers and publishers, because the changes to copyright were perceived as a threat to the print trade. It took time for this simple trade dispute to escalate, but eventually the debate encompassed a wider and far more explosive mixture of issues, including taxes on knowledge, popular education and free trade. Some of these issues had been linked to copyright previously, notably copyright and censorship; other themes, at least in their presentation, were new.

As has been suggested, in some ways copyright law was an ideal target for reform. It was fragmented, incomplete, sometimes unclear, and it lacked the international dimension which was needed more and more urgently. The rapid changes in social and economic conditions were having a profound effect on the book trade. Markets were increasing significantly, but so was competition: the book trade had to adapt if it was to survive. Authors too were changing: their status increased as the popular market grew. Copyright was the bargaining counter which passed between the artist and the entrepreneur. A re-examination of copyright's aims and mechanisms might well have been timely.

Yet it is here that further parallels may be drawn between parliamentary reform and copyright reform. The process of parliamentary reform continued for decades, as different ideological models jostled for political primacy. Although a series of compromises were achieved, the concept of effective representation remained a matter of fierce disagreement. Similarly, there was no single goal for copyright reform, and even if agreement had been reached as to copyright's purpose, there was no obvious or guaranteed method of achieving this. Talfourd himself was certain that the author's role should be pre-eminent in literary copyright, and he tried to maintain this principled stance. Others disagreed fundamentally. Copyright was characterised by some as a state-sanctioned monopoly, and Talfourd's proposals came to be perceived as contrary to Benthamite doctrine. The complex and technical bill was judged largely on the single issue of copyright term, and the deeper issues of principle were put aside. Trade and radical interests were more numerous, more vocal and more organised than Talfourd's supporters, and they prevailed.

Talfourd argued indefatigably that genius should be prized above all else, and that the immeasurable, indefinable needs of culture should prevail over what he termed the 'freezing effects' of the radicals' position. In a post-reform parliament, few MPs felt able to argue for what was perceived as special treatment for authors, particularly in a trade-related matter. The bill's sponsors, caught in a storm of lobby groups, understandably salvaged the best compromise they could. It is arguable that Talfourd's vision

– of copyright as a recognition of cultural worth and not a commodity – deserved closer attention.

THE 1842 ACT – PASSAGE AND POSITION

The 1842 Copyright Act was the product of five years of heated public and parliamentary debate. It resulted in an extension of term: copyright was to last for the author's lifetime plus seven years, or for a minimum of forty-two years from the date of publication. The 1814 Copyright Act had provided for a twenty-eight-year term, or the author's lifetime if this was longer, so the change is now regarded as of little real significance. Brief histories of copyright often gloss over the 1842 Act altogether, although the introduction of a post-mortem term may be noted. Much more attention is paid to the eighteenth-century great cases, *Millar* v. *Taylor*, and *Donaldson* v. *Beckett*. Such treatments underestimate the historical significance of the 1842 Copyright Act, and in particular the circumstances surrounding its passing.

The struggle to pass a copyright Act began in 1837, when the first bill was introduced by Serjeant Talfourd. Versions of the bill were presented every year after this, under the gaze of two monarchs and two prime ministers, until 1842. The bill became hugely controversial, and provoked great public interest. It was perceived as being of great significance, as several influential groups became involved in either promoting or blocking its passage. Some of these groups included those directly affected by changes to copyright law, such as publishers, print workers and authors. However, the bill was also regarded as having considerable political significance, because of the wider issues raised. The various bills were therefore very heavily and noisily contested, both in and out of parliament. A striking feature of the campaign was the use of petitions, both mass petitioning to oppose the measures, and more selective petitions in support. Analysis of these, and other lobbying measures, reveals the contemporary mechanisms of popular protest.

A reassessment of the 1842 Act's place in copyright history is therefore overdue. The Act formed the basis of modern copyright law: it provided the groundwork for the domestic aspects of the 1911 Act, and this foundation was to a significant extent carried forward in the 1956 and 1988 Acts. In addition, there were consequences for the lobbying groups, and these, too, had an effect on the development of copyright, albeit rather more indirect.

That conventional approaches to copyright do not acknowledge the wider significance of the 1842 Act is in part due to their particular and limited aims. Standard copyright works, such as Copinger, have only brief space for history.[5] Understandably they focus on contemporary positive law, and its direct and practical consequences in case law. Feather's historical study of copyright in Britain provides a helpful narrative that does explore the circumstances surrounding copyright, in particular its interaction with the book trade.[6] However, this history, too, has limitations of space and dimension, imposed by the decision to cover copyright law from its origins to the current governing Act. The linearity of these approaches obscures the extent to which nineteenth-century domestic copyright interconnects with contemporary issues – and results in an underestimation of its importance.

Other accounts of copyright are provided by related historical disciplines, particularly the history of aesthetics. Here the focus on the author, and the imposition of a Romantic trajectory, can sometimes act to distort and simplify situations where obscurities and difficulties remain. The post-structuralist approach to authorship adds a further agenda, hostile to positivity and dominant meaning, which cuts across any familiar history of copyright law.

This book aims to provide a more rounded account of the 1842 Act, situating it in the many contexts in which it operated, and freeing it from the linearity imposed by standard accounts. This is achieved through a comprehensive analysis of a wide range of contemporary sources, a luxury permitted by the choice of a limited time period. The remainder of this introductory chapter presents the main themes and problems of copyright law during this period, and provides an overview of the bill's progress. The book is then structured to reflect the adversarial nature of the debate: the first half is concerned principally with opposition and opponents, the second half with those in favour of Talfourd's proposals. The bills themselves were long and detailed. Some of

[5] Edmund P. Skone James *et al.*, *Copinger and Skone James on copyright*, 14th edn (1998).

[6] John Feather, *Publishing, piracy and politics* (1994).

the clauses underwent considerable change as the bills developed, whether for political or legal reasons. Talfourd's original plans included revision and clarification of various matters which, although of practical and legal significance, were generally regarded as specialist and technical. These included some striking ideas (such as a 'fair use' clause), many still of interest and relevance today. A detailed account of these is given in Appendix II. However, attention was largely focused on a few of the most disputed clauses: as will be seen, these achieved a more general currency, both in debates and petitions. There is an extended discussion of the mechanisms available to and used by each side.

Mass petitioning was one of the main weapons used against the bill, provoked by the radicals' characterisation of copyright as a monopoly which acted as an intolerable fetter on the diffusion of knowledge. This technique is examined first in its parliamentary context. The petitions themselves are then explored in detail. These show that the book trade's hostility to copyright extension came from both print workers and publishers, and highlights the differences in their mechanisms of protest. The organised and well-established trade bodies proved to be of great importance. Analysis of the petitions also reveals a progressive widening of the debate beyond trade boundaries, adding to its political significance. Heavy-weight parliamentarians became more embroiled in the debate as a result. Contemporary newspapers provide reports of the proceedings and act as a benchmark of public opinion.

Authors did not have the ready-made organisational structures of the print trade, and had to rely on individual campaigners. However, the literary world was cohesive in its own way, and eventually roused itself to make full use of the levers available to it. Although discreet lobbying was preferred at first, authors helped to disseminate the debate through the printed word. As the stakes grew higher, they overcame their distaste for the public petition, and provided Talfourd with an array of petitions which rivalled the trade's for completeness, although not in number. The copyright issue drew the literary world together in a way not seen before.

The detailed narrative is important in itself, and allows consideration of how far the 1842 Act provided a resolution to the conflict between these two entrenched sides. Parliament was set a considerable task. The importance of copyright in the international context was becoming clearer, and the commercial implications of legislation were considerable for trade both at home and abroad. The links between copyright and wider topics such as free trade and education did not make the process of reconciliation any easier. Copyright became caught between those who valued intellectual property only prosaically and those who wished to associate its intangible qualities with the intangible in literature.

In addition, since Talfourd's Act had such influence on modern copyright law, it is appropriate to assess the legislative foundation it provided. In particular, it is necessary to consider what, if anything, the 1842 Act contributed towards a functioning and resilient rationale for copyright law. The book will conclude with an attempt to set this question in its theoretical context.

COPYRIGHT – ITS NATURE AND HISTORY

Copyright is a broad and flexible form of intellectual property. It covers, for instance, an enormous range of subject-matter. In the United Kingdom, contemporary copyright law protects what might be regarded as the 'conventional' forms of aesthetic expression – literary, dramatic, artistic and musical works – although these categories include some perhaps unexpected items, such as photographs and computer programs. Broadcasts, recordings, films and published editions are likewise protected. These additions reflect the acute sensitivity of copyright to certain areas of technology, particularly those which relate to recording and copying. This is to be expected, given copyright's nature and history.

The pressure for a general right to prevent the copying of works grew out of the development of the printing-press. Early demands came from printers and publishers, and not from authors. Rights to print tended to be granted by the Crown, and for individual works or types of work. The Crown could use these grants as a form of control, and clearly saw and exploited the possibilities of censorship. Eventually, demand by the Stationers' Company for a general right resulted in the Statute of Anne 1710. This gave the 'sole right and liberty of printing books' to authors and their assigns, for fourteen years from first publication; although if the author was still living at the expiry of this period, the right was 'returned' to him for a further fourteen years. These provisions reveal some of the drafting difficulties which arise in any attempt to frame a general copyright law: the subject-matter has to be determined, as does the term; and the definition of an infringing act has to be clear.

Without these basic parameters a right to prevent copying is of little use. The problem lies in the decisions made as to how to set them. The decisions taken depend on the view taken of the purpose and nature of copyright, a view which is in turn dependent on a sense of the place and worth of the artistic objects of protection. The answers to these questions are not uncomplicated, and broaden the context of the discussion to include contemporary issues and ideas. The Act of Anne's preamble appears to give a simple solution – 'the Encouragement of learned Men to compose and write useful Books' – but in fact the answer is much more complex.

The twentieth century has come to regard copyright as, broadly, an economic right. In fact, twentieth-century law is heavily based on nineteenth-century law, with the obvious changes needed to take account of developments in technology. The nineteenth century saw one of the fullest discussions of the problems of domestic copyright law, provoked by Serjeant Talfourd's repeated attempts to shepherd a comprehensive copyright bill through parliament. Talfourd was a key figure. This book will examine the process of evolution which eventually resulted in the Copyright Act 1842. It also aims to show how the wider social, economic and philosophical forces present in the first half of the nineteenth century changed the nature of copyright, transforming it from a parochial system of rather limited significance, into a highly prized economic right. This newly defined copyright would come to stand as the basis for twentieth-century copyright law, and helped to provide impetus for the discussion of international measures.

How, then, should copyright be defined? In a legal context, it is often helpful to consider the various elements of a right; its subject and duration, for instance. The initial definitional problem for any copyright law is its subject-matter. The Act of Anne refers only to books, whereas modern copyright statutes cover many forms of expression. In the eighteenth century, books remained the single most important product in this area, and there was little attempt to widen the range of copyright.

By the early nineteenth century, however, new technology was driving demand for new forms of protection. When it came, protection tended to be piecemeal; engravings, lectures, dramatic works and designs were protected by individual statutes. This diffusion of subject-matter blurred the focus of copyright somewhat, particularly as some of these processes had an industrial element which brought them closer to the field of patent protection than 'conventional' copyright material. Talfourd had hoped to consolidate the various domestic copyright laws into one single statute: his 1837 attempt to include some rudimentary international protection was blocked by the government by 1838.

The international dimension of copyright was to become of increasing importance. Early copyright laws usually protected only nationals of the relevant state or, at best, works first published in that state. An increase in the reading public coupled with advances in communications meant that it was worthwhile to publish 'continental' editions, for which a British author was entitled to nothing. Protection could only be obtained by bilateral treaties, slowly and painfully negotiated, or by informal agreements amongst the various publishers. The strength of feeling with regard to free trade had a direct impact on Talfourd's bill, as will be seen.

Even within the accepted boundaries of copyright, the subject-matter could be challenged. A modern copyright lawyer will be very familiar with the distinction between ideas, which (broadly) copyright law does not protect, and expression, which copyright does protect. As Pritchard J has said, the idea/expression dichotomy is probably the most difficult concept in the law of copyright:

> The difficulty, of course, is to determine just where the general concept ends and the exercise of expressing the concepts begins . . . There can be no general formula by which to establish the line between the general idea and the author's expression of the idea. The basic idea (or concept) is not necessarily simple – it may be banal. The way the author treats the subject, the forms he uses to express the basic concept, may range from the crude and simplistic to the ornate, complicated – and involving the collation and application of a great number of constructive ideas. . . . It is in this area that the author expends the skill and industry which (even though they may be slight) give the work its originality and entitle him to copyright.[7]

[7] *Plix Products* v. *Frank M. Winstone* [1986] FSR 92, 93.

Talfourd, himself a lawyer, understood this dichotomy well, but his opponents often could not, or would not, accept that this line between idea and expression could be satisfactorily drawn. Popular access to education was a contentious and hotly debated issue during this period, and there were genuine fears that a strengthened copyright law would halt the dissemination of knowledge.

These concerns were based in part on another confusion – between patent and copyright. The rationale for the grant of a patent is relatively easy to grasp: an inventor incurs expense in developing an invention; if others are permitted to exploit the invention without having first incurred a share of the development costs, there will be no incentive to invent. Assuming that innovation is regarded as beneficial, this absence of motivation is unsatisfactory. Therefore, most legal systems protect a novel invention, by granting a patent which prevents competitors from using the invention without the inventor's consent. However, the monopoly is limited in time, after which the inventor is regarded as having had a sufficient head start, which should have enabled a reasonable reward to be extracted.

Thus a patent grant is firmly based in a system of economic reward, a system which is regarded as of benefit both to patentee and state. There is therefore no particular need to argue that the basis for protection is a moral one, as the practical and economic arguments are sufficiently convincing. The fact that patents are already restricted to a relatively short time period is also relevant: there would be little justification for curtailing a property right to an invention which was based on a moral entitlement.

In contrast, the rationale for copyright remains far from clear. There was certainly always an economic element: the demands for protection grew stronger as publishing markets enlarged, and the potential for exploitation grew with them. However, the aesthetic element could never be dismissed, although putting a value on this aspect of a work is extremely difficult. Historically, there was no attempt to protect ideas as such, as it was the expression, the product, which required protection. So the form of protection which naturally arose was a protection against copying, and not against use.

Talfourd made this point during one of the debates on the 1838 copyright bill, although the distinction is not one that seems to have been commonly made or understood: 'the law of literary property of necessity accommodates itself to the nature of its subject – when the work is properly a creation, leaving it preserved in its entirety – when it is mere discovery, rendering the essence of truth to mankind, and preserving nothing to its author but the form in which it is enshrined'.[8] It was therefore much easier to argue for a longer period of protection than was the case with patents: patents by definition resulted in a much stronger monopoly, preventing use even of an independently invented device.

The dispute as to the true basis of copyright is seen most clearly in the great eighteenth-century cases, *Millar* v. *Taylor*[9] and *Donaldson* v. *Beckett*.[10] There was division between those seeking to base copyright in a moral right to the fruits of one's own labour, and therefore demanding a perpetual copyright, and those who regarded it purely as a privilege granted by statute.

Both cases involved disputes between rival booksellers. London booksellers enjoyed powerful control over distribution and sales, reinforced by various long-standing trade practices. For instance, a system of customary cooperation allowed the owners of each title to print without competition from other booksellers. The mutual benefits which ensued ensured that the London trade was generally glad to maintain the scheme, and English provincial booksellers lacked the power to challenge it. However, the Scottish booksellers were not so hampered, and gradually began to send more and more reprints south of the border, in flagrant breach of the customary London privileges.

The London booksellers responded with legal action both in Scotland and in London.[11] These preliminary legal skirmishes were inconclusive, although the Scottish courts were noticeably hostile.[12] The first result was to come in 1769, when the London bookseller Andrew Millar sued Robert Taylor in the Court of King's Bench, for having published and offered for sale James Thomson's *The Seasons*. Millar had bought the copyright from Thomson in 1729: it had been legally assigned to him, and duly

[8] *Hansard, Parliamentary debates* (3rd series), xlii, 566 (25 April 1838).

[9] (1769) 4 Burr 2303. [10] (1774) 2 Bro PC 129.

[11] This account draws on Feather, *Publishing*, ch. 3; Mark Rose, *Authors and owners: the invention of copyright* (1993), chs. 5 and 6.

[12] For a helpful account of these see Richard S. Tompson, 'Scottish judges and the birth of British copyright', *Juridical Review* 37 (1992), 18–42.

registered at Stationers' Hall. Taylor's edition appeared in 1763, well past the twenty-eight-year statutory protection of the Act of Anne. In *Millar* v. *Taylor* the majority, including the lord chief justice, Lord Mansfield, found that the author did have a common law right of property in his works. Lord Mansfield relied on a Lockean argument: 'it is just, that an author should reap the pecuniary profit of his own ingenuity and labour', and doubted whether the abrogation of the common law right could be implied into the Act of Anne.[13] There was, however, a strong dissent from Yates J who considered that only the statutory copyright was available once a work was published.[14] His view was later to prevail in *Donaldson* v. *Beckett*.

Donaldson v. *Beckett* again involved an 'unauthorised' edition of Thomson's poetry. Millar's copyrights had been sold on his death in 1769, and *The Seasons* had been divided up between several London booksellers. A preliminary injunction was obtained against Donaldson, then made permanent in 1772. Donaldson appealed to the House of Lords. The case caused unprecedented interest; the spectators apparently included various literary figures, and hundreds were turned away from the House. Five questions were put to the twelve law lords for their opinions, although these were not binding on the House. Lord Mansfield, although present in the House, remained silent throughout. On the crucial question, as to whether the Act of Anne had abrogated the author's common law right of printing, Lord Mansfield's silence resulted in a majority decision that the statute prevailed.

The reasons for Lord Mansfield's silence have been much discussed.[15] It was generally attributed to a heightened sense of delicacy in what was in effect an appeal from his own judgment in *Millar* v. *Taylor*. Further complications arise from Rose's assertion

[13] (1769) 4 Burr 2303, 2398.

[14] The decision in *Millar* v. *Taylor* was predictably unpopular in Scotland, where many doubted that a right of literary property existed there apart from statute. This was confirmed by the Court of Session in *Hinton* v. *Donaldson* (1773). Thus, for a time, literary property was perpetual in England, but of limited term in Scotland.

[15] Tompson observes that the appeal was against a Chancery decree, and not (technically) against a judgment of Lord Mansfield's. His tentative hypothesis is that *Millar* v. *Taylor* might have involved collusion which Mansfield did not wish to expose: Tompson, 'Scottish judges'. Rose's conjecture is that Mansfield lacked the spirit for further bruising conflict with Lord Camden, a fierce political opponent and a powerful legal figure: Rose, *Authors and owners*.

that, on the same crucial question, there is 'good reason to believe that the clerk of the house of Lords made an honest error in recording the opinion of one of the judges'.[16] This would have made the decision six to five *in favour* of the common law right, or even seven to five with Mansfield's silent voice. It is very possible that this would have affected the votes of the eighty-four lay peers present. There appears to have been no formal division, but in what was probably a voice vote, the House of Lords decided to reverse the judgment granting Beckett an injunction against Donaldson.

Thus the dramatic decision in *Donaldson* v. *Beckett*, with all its attendant complications, ended the perpetual common law right of literary property. It was a very close contest, and it was quite understandable that Serjeant Talfourd felt able to revisit the issues. In the nineteenth-century debate, those opposed to an extension to the copyright term argued for equality of treatment between patents and copyrights. This type of argument highlights the strong differences of opinion as to the 'correct' basis of copyright privileges. Although it is possible to see Talfourd's reliance on moral and aesthetic arguments as old-fashioned and idealist, or even irrelevant after *Donaldson* v. *Beckett*, Talfourd's rationale cannot be dismissed in this way. The fact that the copyright issue became controversial at all is an indication that it was affected by even deeper currents of thought than Talfourd probably envisaged when he brought the bill forward. The relatively limited question of authors' rights to literary property was quickly set in a national (and later global) context.

Notwithstanding *Donaldson* v. *Beckett*, the rationale of copyright was in many ways still fluid, and the discussion that Talfourd's bill provoked had a profound effect on it. Very wide terms of reference were eventually set as the context for the debate. The question is perhaps whether this was helpful. Although parliament was offered the freedom to reach a sound and broadly based conclusion, the contextual issues, such as free trade and education, were of such magnitude that it proved impossible to keep the main issue in focus: the opportunity was to some extent thrown away.

[16] Rose, *Authors and owners*, p. 99 and App. B. The judge was Nares J. See also H. B. Abrams, 'The historic foundation of American copyright law: exploding the myth of common law copyright', *Wayne Law Review* 29 (1983), 1120–91.

TALFOURD AND HIS AIMS

Talfourd's persistence in bringing forward copyright bills in the teeth of all the opposition was remarkable. It can be attributed to a combination of enthusiasm and character. Literary copyright stood at the intersection between Talfourd's two main interests, law and literature, which he combined throughout his life. Born in Reading in 1795, he was a promising student, publishing a volume of poetry while still at school. He chose law as a profession, apparently at the suggestion of Brougham, and became a pupil of the celebrated Joseph Chitty. He funded himself with literary work, of which the most famous was 'An attempt to estimate the poetical talent of the present age'.[17] Talfourd was a close friend of Lamb, knew Godwin, Leigh Hunt, Wordsworth, Coleridge and many other writers. His criticism was based on a genuine love of literature, and his continual praise of contemporary poetry was thought by many to have been instrumental in bringing it to eventual popularity.

Once Talfourd's pupillage had expired he became a special pleader, but continued his literary work, particularly for the *London Magazine* and the *New Monthly*. He was called to the Bar in 1821, where he was a member of the Oxford Circuit, and married Rachael Rutt the following year. He became a serjeant in 1833, and was elected member for Reading in 1835. His literary activity continued: his tragedy *Ion* was printed for private circulation in 1835, and was played at Covent Garden with Macready in the title role. The play was one of the brilliant successes of the 1836 season, Macready attributing this to his acting, and Talfourd to the play itself. Talfourd was certainly inordinately proud of *Ion*, and could not bear to hear anything against it. Most of his friends regarded this as an isolated vanity, although some (notably Mary Russell Mitford and William Macready) were less generous.

The play reflects the florid eloquence for which Talfourd was known, both as an advocate and as a friend. He was very sociable, loved societies, dinners and company. His name appears often in literary letters and diaries of the period, and he is almost always spoken of fondly. He seems to have been considered generous and full of heart, more solid than sparkling, but a good friend. A

[17] *Pamphleteer* 5 (1815).

similar description applies to his advocacy. He seems to have had an efficient, although not brilliant, understanding of the law, and although eloquent and earnest, he was 'above all chicanery. . .and neither would nor could puzzle an honest witness in cross-examination'.[18] This is said to have limited his practice. However, he became a judge in the court of common pleas in 1849, and died on the bench at Stafford in 1854, while delivering a charge to the grand jury.

Literary interests and friendships were Talfourd's first love, and this probably explains his taking up the copyright question. He was certainly encouraged by Wordsworth, although there is no evidence that it was originally Wordsworth's idea. Talfourd would have liked to be the instrument through which justice (as he saw it) was achieved for authors. He would also have felt himself an important author, following the success of *Ion* the previous year: he wrote two more tragedies during this period. On a more practical note, Talfourd was unusually well qualified to speak on both literary and legal matters. His genuine belief in the cause, and his stubbornness of character, allowed him to continue bringing the matter before the House even when things seemed hopeless. It was easy for the radicals to mock Talfourd's idealism and flowery language, and, although he returned for more punishment, the onslaught took its toll. His journal for the beginning of 1842 reveals how downcast he felt: 'For five years I have worked the Copyright Bill in the House of Commons – to see it thrown out in one night by Macaulay.'[19] Given Talfourd's early hopes for copyright legislation, his misery is easy to understand.

Talfourd had originally planned a grand, consolidated scheme, and the 1837 bill reflected this. He wanted to make a fresh, considered approach, and to replace the existing statutes which had been enacted piecemeal.[20] Not only did he intend to bring the various types of subject-matter under one single statute, he also sought to provide some sort of international dimension to copyright. However, there was strong government resistance to this ambitious plan: international copyright was regarded as a matter

[18] 'The late Mr Justice Talfourd', *Law Magazine* 51 (1854).

[19] Quoted in Vera Watson, 'The journals of Thomas Noon Talfourd', *Times Literary Supplement*, 8 February 1957, p. 88.

[20] For instance, Engraving Copyright Acts 1734 and 1766 (and further enactments in 1777 and 1836), Dramatic Copyright Act 1833, Lectures Copyright Act 1835.

of foreign policy and unsuitable for back-bench treatment. By 1838 Talfourd had been forced to confine himself to literary copyright.

Even within this limited remit, Talfourd was determined to rationalise and improve. The existing system of registration and assignment had grown up from the old privileges of the Stationers' Company, and had defects. The number of deposit copies associated with the registration had long been controversial: already in the nineteenth century it had been the focus of a bad-tempered debate in which Edward Christian was one of the leading figures.[21] The 1836 Act had cleared the air considerably, but the reopening of this issue was possible.[22]

The subject-matter of copyright needed proper definition: even if paintings and engravings were to be separately treated, problems had arisen regarding the ownership of the copyrights of periodical and encyclopaedia articles, and of part-works. It was not always clear what constituted infringement, abridgements being a controversial case in point. The growth of the publishing markets had made the resolution of these questions essential, and clearly the answer given would depend on the perceived nature of copyright. Appropriate penalties also had to be devised. The existing system of fines, laid down in the Act of Anne, was effectively worthless; the question of damages was dependent on case law.

However, the aspect of Talfourd's bill which was most discussed, and which came to be regarded as its identifying characteristic, was his attempt to increase the *term* of copyright from the existing twenty-eight-year term, to last for the author's life and then sixty years after death.[23] By the time that the 1842 Copyright Act was finally passed, it was widely regarded as a single-issue

[21] For reasons of control, the Act of Anne had required that nine copies of new books, or new editions of old books, should be sent to Stationers' Hall, from where they were deposited in various named libraries. The predictable reluctance of the book trade led to very poor observance of the provision. See Feather, *Publishing*, ch. 4; Robert Partridge, *The history of the legal deposit of books* (1938).

[22] 6 & 7 Wm. 4 c. 110.

[23] The 1814 Act (15 Geo. 3 c. 53) gave a twenty-eight-year term at the outset, and extended it for the remainder of the author's life if still living on the original term's expiry. The Act of Anne had granted a fourteen-year term (from publication), which was 'returned' to the author for another fourteen years if still living at the end of the first term.

piece of legislation. The other details of the bill were scarcely considered, and the coherence (or otherwise) of Talfourd's original plan became of secondary importance.

CONFLICTING RATIONALES

It was perhaps inevitable, given the complex and technical matters addressed, that the ideas in the bill should become stereotyped and simplified during parliamentary and public discussions. Nevertheless, this process can be seen as fatal to any serious discussion of the true basis of copyright. Talfourd's position was founded on a belief in the value of literary works to society in general. His arguments could be subtle, and were vulnerable to misrepresentation. Once the bill was perceived to turn solely on the question of the length of the term which would constitute an appropriate reward for an author's effort, the argument became largely economic.

Talfourd regarded the term as primarily something of symbolic importance, and not as a parameter to be determined by economic argument. At the heart of Talfourd's plan was the 'life-plus' element; the author was to have the right during his lifetime, and for a sixty-year period after that. This combination of variable and fixed elements was important. Firstly, the life term recognised each author as an individual creator, and a maturing one. The fixed period that followed acknowledged the author's natural desire to provide for his family and heirs, and to ensure the continuing integrity of his work. However, these aims were not universally accepted as desirable, or even as legitimate. The resulting discussions provoked many anecdotal accounts of authors' lives and habits, some of it damaging to Talfourd's cause, and all of rather doubtful evidential value.

Talfourd had seen the life plus sixty year term as a fundamental clause which expressed the concentrated weight of all the moral arguments for protecting authors' works. Instead, the 'appropriate term' came to be regarded as a point on a sliding scale, to be arrived at by compromise in the light of the prevailing economic considerations. The special role for authors, which Talfourd had argued deserved special recognition, was regarded as being of less importance than the 'objective' criteria of fairness and equality, and than the measurable, though often anecdotal, evidence of sales and profits.

The final decision as to the length of the copyright term was the result of a suggestion made in a parliamentary speech by Thomas Babington Macaulay. In over five years the House had seen eleven versions of the copyright bill, and was heartily sick of it. Macaulay's compromise plan of a forty-two-year term was welcomed with relief by the House, and adopted on the spot. Yet, although this was a solution of sorts, it provided no answers regarding the purpose of copyright. Talfourd had asked and answered this question with some consistency, and never denied that his aim was to increase the rewards available to authors. On one occasion he reaffirmed what he termed 'the principle of the bill': 'the present term of copyright is much too short for the attainment of that justice which society owes to authors, especially to those . . . whose reputation is of slow growth and enduring character'.[24]

Talfourd took particular pride in the fact that this was the first copyright bill to be devised unashamedly to reward authors, in contrast to previous bills driven by interest groups and publishers. He was unabashed in his idealism, and valued literature highly as a cultural essential. He saw copyright as the minimum reward that society should bestow on authors in recognition of their special contribution and abilities. He thought that copyright law's function should be to provide formal, legal recognition of a self-evident right to one's literary output, with the added justification of an indirect public benefit resulting from the products of authors' special talents. He therefore presented the bill as a claim to a right unwittingly revoked by the Act of Anne, an error not evident until the decision in *Donaldson* v. *Beckett*:

> In truth, the claim of the author to perpetual copyright was never disputed, until literature had received its first fatal present in the first act of Parliament for its encouragement – the eighth Anne, c.19, passed in 1709; in which the mischief lurked, unsuspected, for many years before it was called into action to limit the rights it professed, and was probably intended to secure.[25]

Talfourd knew that there was little to be gained in arguing for a statutory 'right perpetual' following *Donaldson* v. *Beckett*. In

[24] *Hansard, Parliamentary debates* (3rd series), xlii, 556 (25 April 1838).
[25] *Hansard, Parliamentary debates* (3rd series), xxxviii, 868 (18 May 1837).

settling for life plus sixty years, he felt he was achieving what he considered a fair balance of public and private interests, although he was still convinced that this was a compromise. Nevertheless, he still retained emotional sympathy for the perpetual right, and a sense that any qualification was a compromise. However, his proposal represented a significant advance on the 1814 Act, which gave at best a life term.

One disadvantage of the simple life term is that if the author does not write for immediate reward and the prevailing taste, then the financial penalties may be severe. For instance Wordsworth, who was widely regarded as having created the taste by which he eventually came to be appreciated, was lucky to be sufficiently long-lived to begin to reap the rewards of his own success. This is one reason why a long post-mortem term continued to be regarded as important. In justifying the longer term Talfourd highlighted the dangers to the integrity of works, in the form of abridgements and 'base intermixtures', in the absence of adequate protection. He also noted the injustice that resulted to authors from international piracies, and the cultural benefits that accrued to a society which acted nobly and granted the fair reward.[26]

Talfourd's opponents were much more interested in costs, both to the book-buying and book-reading public, and to the printing and publishing trades. There was extensive disagreement as to whether the longer copyrights would in fact be more valuable in the author's hands, or whether the author would still be forced to sell them for the same sum as a shorter right would command, leaving the publisher to reap a windfall reward. It was widely assumed that any extra cost to the publisher would anyway be passed straight on to the purchaser, and this was regarded with disfavour by several groups, some of whom lobbied actively.

For instance, those interested in wider public education were anxious to disseminate knowledge by any effective means, and cheap books were regarded as very important in this task. There were various important societies which existed for the purpose of promoting education, such as the Society for the Promotion of Christian Knowledge, and the Society for the Diffusion of Useful Knowledge. The SDUK was formed in 1827 with the help of Lord Brougham, who was to be a notable opponent of Talfourd's

[26] Ibid., 875–9.

bill. Brougham's pamphlet *Practical observations for the education of the people*, advocating 'the gospel of the alphabet', more cheap books and popular instruction, sold 50,000 copies in a few weeks and ran to twenty editions. The momentum generated was infectious and carried the SDUK into the 1840s.

Another group opposed to any increase in the price of books were those who had fought the newspaper stamp, and other 'taxes on knowledge' to such effect. These people, often radicals, regarded the extension of the copyright term as an additional 'tax on knowledge': some of the bill's most vehement opponents fall into this category, notably the parliamentary radicals Wakley, Warburton and Hume. The fight over the newspaper stamp had been a bitter one, and had only recently been brought under control, with the reduction of the stamp to 1d in 1836. Regardless of this concession, there were many who felt that even the 1d stamp was objectionable, and the arguments continued: several of those who were important figures in the stamp war were also active in the copyright debate.

Another strand was the utilitarian line of reasoning. Founded on Bentham's works, which posited an ideal for legislation of the greatest happiness of the greatest number, this position was enormously influential.[27] Bentham thought this a more helpful way of considering the advantages of any particular piece of legislation than arguing whether or not it was in accordance with nature. Another feature of utilitarianism was a great belief in the power of education in increasing the sum of happiness. Although the principle of utilitarianism could be made to function in a positive and sophisticated way, in certain hands it permitted only a crude and two-dimensional balancing of interests; it seemed impossible to take account of 'special' factors. Since Talfourd's argument was largely based on an assertion of the unique qualities of authors, mutual incomprehension was inevitable. The very dubious argument by analogy from patent to copyright was much favoured by those who espoused popular utilitarian methods; this misconception was extremely damaging, as well as being difficult to counter.

[27] Jeremy Bentham, *An introduction to the principles of morals and legislation*, in *Collected works*, ed. James H. Burns (1970), p. 11. For doubts as to Bentham's actual influence on legislation, see Christopher Allen, *The law of evidence in Victorian England* (Cambridge, 1997).

Those directly concerned in the publishing and printing of books were likewise strongly opposed to any extension to the copyright term. The fear was that presses would grind to a halt, and that books would become very scarce and expensive. This might reasonably have been predicted, given the trade's previous reaction to similar issues. However, the speed, strength and coordination of the response was extraordinary. Within days of the first reading of the bill there were dozens of petitions against, representing hundreds of signatures, and this pressure was maintained.

Those lobbying were members of diverse branches of the book trade; master printers, compositors, press men, binders and gilders, for instance. Nevertheless, there was remarkable cohesion of opposition, at least for the early years of the campaign. Printers and publishers were later to be reconciled to the notion of an extended copyright term; their change of heart was due partly to their being bribed with the omission of the hated 'retrospective' clause from Talfourd's bill, and partly by their realisation that the new law would result in economic benefits for them. In fact, by the end of the period in question, they were lobbying actively for an international copyright law. Given this rather changeable attitude, it is important to consider whether the trade position was ever based on any specific objections to copyright, or whether the resistance was a reflex reaction to any potential threat.

Naturally enough, newspapers and periodicals covered the argument in detail. Given the interests and issues involved, the stance taken was, in some cases, easy to predict. There was strong feeling on both sides, but certain periodical articles were given added zest by the knowledge that those writing the articles were set to benefit directly from Talfourd's bill, whereas those who owned and published the periodical (often being book publishers also) might well regard themselves as losers. Newspapers and periodicals were extremely influential, and represent an important source of research material.

Those who remained outside all of these camps were nevertheless likely to be affected by the much more general debate concerning free trade, and the linked question of political economy. The corn laws had been controversial from the outset, 1815, when the landed interests in parliament succeeded in getting the first protectionist measure passed, in the face of riots by the London mob. Most political economists (with the exception of

Malthus) had demanded complete free trade in corn, arguing that the landlords' selfishness should not be permitted to damage the interests of the country as a whole. Social discontent and unrest continued. The corn issue remained very controversial, in spite of the Liverpool government's liberalising reforms. Although the harvests had been good between 1832 and 1836, by 1837 the economy was under severe strain. Unemployment was considerable and although there were glimmers of improvement in 1838 and 1839, the recession continued through 1842.

During these hard times the middle-class merchants and manufacturers – with an increasingly high public profile – argued for changes to national economic policy, for instance through the Anti-Corn Law League, founded in 1838. Farmers, also, had particular grievances and their own demands on parliament. Working-class misery and discontent found expression in the Chartist movement, representing a further pressure on parliament. These intractable conflicts of interest continued over a decade, until people had become very familiar both with the arguments and also with the related discontent and unrest. Dislike of monopolies was not new, but the view of monopolies as harmful and corrupt gained fresh resonance in these debates. It is therefore understandable that when Talfourd suggested the extension of an exclusive right to publish a work, it should have been challenged as an extension of an undesirable monopoly.

The most inflexible advocates of the free market advocated its unmitigated application to the market for books, which they understood to imply that copyright protection should not exist. This refusal to distinguish between the work and the book, or to accord literary products any special place, had startling implications. The radical Wakley, for instance, demanded to know 'why a distinction was made between the mere bookwright and the producer of other inventions', and poured scorn on authors who 'had so far miscalulated their own powers, or the taste of the public, as to have engaged in pursuits which had turned out so unprofitably'.[28]

This was a point of view which alarmed the literary world. One of the arguments for an extended post-mortem copyright term was that important works were not always given tangible

[28] *Hansard, Parliamentary debates* (3rd series), lxi, 1378 (6 April 1842).

recognition by the book-buying public until some time had elapsed. There was also concern for the general public taste, and a feeling that it was not necessarily beneficial to either public or author to give the public what it wanted; education of taste was regarded as important.

In this context the intangible nature of intellectual property was a severe disadvantage, as the standard notions of possession and ownership simply did not apply. Talfourd was sharply aware of this frustrating difficulty: 'Is the interest itself so refined – so ethereal – that you cannot regard it as property, because it is not palpable to sense or feeling!'[29] It seemed impossible for Talfourd adequately to refute the arguments that books were a commodity like any other, or that, even if it were to be admitted that literary work deserved special treatment, the dangerous 'monopoly' should be very limited in time, just as it was for patents. It is here that the distinction between the literary work and the book in which it is contained becomes important: it is the work itself which is the subject of copyright, and the many books in which it is copied are the 'commodity'. This point was made in parliament by Disraeli, who agreed that monopolies should be tightly controlled, but asked the House to convert a monopoly for the publishers into a property for authors.[30]

The relationship between the copyright and the resulting book is more complex than was appreciated by Talfourd's opposition. This relationship cannot be reduced to a simple economic equation, and particularly not to one which demonstrates a linear relationship between the term of copyright and the price of books. The issues of copyright and its nature as property had been very fully explored in *Donaldson* v. *Beckett*. However, the court's decision that the Act of Anne had limited the right perpetual rendered any further jurisprudential discussion theoretical rather than practical, since the statute had priority.

Nevertheless, the argument that copyright represented the legal expression of a natural right to the products of one's labour could still be put forward in a parliamentary context, where the aim was (arguably) to provide a functioning rationale for copyright which reflected a balance of public and private interests. Although it

[29] *Hansard, Parliamentary debates* (3rd series), xlv, 927 (27 February 1839).
[30] *Hansard, Parliamentary debates* (3rd series), xlii, 575–8 (25 April 1838).

would have been fruitless to argue that a perpetual copyright still existed, the natural law argument still had persuasive value, and often served to counterbalance the cruder opposition arguments. In addition, in a post-reform context, the claim to the fruits of one's own labour now had resonances of Chartist thinking quite removed from the natural law arguments expounded in *Donaldson* v. *Beckett*.

ALTERNATIVES TO COPYRIGHT – A PROFESSION OF AUTHORSHIP?

Given the breadth of the issues involved in the copyright question, it is perhaps surprising that so little consideration was given to alternative solutions. Even those who were the most violently opposed to Talfourd's bill seemed to accept, even if grudgingly, that some form of copyright was necessary. But if one of copyright's purposes is regarded as being to ensure authors a reasonable livelihood, then there are various alternatives, of which patronage is perhaps the most obvious.

In the early nineteenth century, however, patronage was a much less common form of support than it had been a century earlier. Partly this was due to the wider range of money-making opportunities available to authors, notably in journalism and periodical literature, and later as a result of the circulating libraries. The growth in the reading public had naturally resulted in a larger market for books, enabling publishers to buy more manuscripts and to pay more for them: thus authors looked to these sources and less to patrons. There was a reaction in parliament against the whole notion of patronage, linked to a wider struggle against the abuse of influence. Macaulay was one of the few who explicitly addressed the subject of authors and patronage, and he rejected patronage with striking vehemence.

In 1837 the Civil List Act provided for the grant of pensions, and sometimes 'bounties', to deserving authors. However, these were not always regarded appreciatively by their intended recipients: many felt that such grants compromised their independence, or that they were in some way demeaning. There was some parliamentary feeling about the issue. Those arguing that pensions were the appropriate means of reward were regarded as insensitive and backward by those who could see the system's drawbacks. Talfourd might have been expected to appreciate authorial sensitivities, having funded his own literary career through his legal work.

Thomas Spring Rice was, with Talfourd, one of the sponsors of the 1837 bill. As chancellor of the exchequer, he would have been close to the lobbying which inevitably preceded the actual grants: these usually lay in the prime minister's gift – if he was sufficiently interested. Spring Rice expressed strong criticism of the system of civil list pensions: 'No such case had been under his cognaisance without his feeling, when the Crown was doling out the bounty which Parliament placed at its disposal for such purposes, that a much more liberal provision than could be thus afforded, would have been secured to them as a matter of right, if the law of copyright had been just in its operation.'[31] Macaulay was to make a similar point in his scathing dismissal of public and private patronage.[32] The prevailing feeling was that patronage was unacceptable, and there were constructive attempts to improve existing mechanisms.

However, there were other sources of income for authors. For instance, there were many private organisations which were quite clearly charitable in nature. For some authors, these organisations combined all the defects of patronage with the demeaning aspects of charity: there was certainly great partiality reflected in many of the grants, plenty of which were the result of influential lobbying. Sometimes there was an insistence that the author's personal moral standards should be acceptable: drunkenness, or a 'marriage' that was not properly solemnised, could disqualify an author, regardless of the hardship caused.

The beginnings of a profession of authorship can be seen in the reaction to these issues. The status of authors was still far from settled. Although Talfourd may have held them in the highest regard, others retained the notion that only gentlemen could or should write literature, and that they should not do so for money. Authors who wrote for a living were often regarded with

[31] *Hansard, Parliamentary debates* (3rd series), xxxviii, 880 (18 May 1837).

[32] 'I can conceive no system more fatal to the independence and integrity of literary men, than one under which they should be taught to look for their daily bread to the favour of ministers and nobles': *Hansard, Parliamentary debates* (3rd series), lvi, 347 (5 February 1841). The implication was that the author should not be forced to look to public taste either.

ambivalence (witness Macaulay himself) and sometimes with contempt: Talfourd's opponents would frequently raise the image of the foolish and feckless scribbler of worthless drivel. Thus those writers who engaged in the debate on Talfourd's side could expect to feel exposed and vulnerable, particularly if, like Wordsworth and Carlyle, they enjoyed a high public profile.

There was no existing system of cooperation for authors, for instance via guilds or trade associations. There were various attempts to remedy this, such as Campbell's Literary Union Club (founded 1831) and the Dramatic Authors' Society (founded 1833), but these tended to be clubs and societies, with the focus on social contact. Dickens had visions of mutual cooperation when he helped to found the Guild of Literature and Art in 1851; yet many authors, notably Thackeray, were ferociously at odds with its ambitions and methods.

Although there were many potential modes of funding authors, there was very little parliamentary discussion of the alternatives to copyright. It was fairly widely accepted by politicians that the law of copyright was unsatisfactory, and that the solution was to modify it. Few argued seriously for the abolition of copyright. Even those such as Macaulay, who disapproved of some of the characteristics of copyright, thought it less objectionable than patronage. There were some calls for a modification of the civil list system, mostly from the most ardent opponents of Talfourd's plans: these usually advocated measures which could reasonably be regarded as even more demeaning to authors than the worst possible system of patronage.

Only one serious rival plan was ever put forward. This stemmed from the argument that individual instances of injustice did not warrant an alteration to the entire system. In particular it was felt that the general changes advocated would have an extremely adverse effect on the public at large, and would not in fact achieve the purported benefits. Therefore, it was argued, a discretionary approach was more appropriate, and the suggestion was that the Judicial Committee of the Privy Council should be empowered to grant an extension to particular copyrights in special circumstances.

This idea was put forward at the second reading of the 1838 bill by the attorney-general, Sir John Campbell.[33] He reminded the

[33] *Hansard, Parliamentary debates* (3rd series), xlii, 586 (25 April 1838).

House of Commons that the Judicial Committee already had the power to extend the patent monopoly in deserving cases. He advocated the grant of a similar power, to be used in what he called the 'analogous' case of copyright. Perhaps regrettably, Talfourd did not explore the limits of the 'analogy' between patent and copyright at this point. The idea continued to find favour in some quarters: Lord Brougham sought to increase support for it by introducing a bill which would have put it into effect. Although the bill had not the slightest chance of becoming law, being introduced in the House of Lords just before the end of the 1838 session, this was further unwelcome opposition.

It was a characteristic of Talfourd's opponents that they were well organised and well disciplined. To a large extent this was because Talfourd's proposals angered existing groups, which turned their attention to fighting proposals, making use of machinery that was already available. There is little evidence that brand-new alliances were formed to oppose the copyright bill. The trade groups certainly had meetings and formed committees to monitor the progress of the bill, but similar methods had been used before, for instance over the apprentice question.[34]

So Talfourd was facing a variety of determined lobby groups. What forces could he marshal himself? There was not even a remotely equivalent trade force. The 'profession' of authorship was still forming, and even the extent to which it had already done so was conceptual and social rather than practical. Even within the literary world there were divisions: for instance, one might distinguish between the purely imaginative writers, historical or scientific writers, periodical writers, reviewers, journalists, writers of popular novels or of children's books, or those writing works intended for self-help and education. Talfourd therefore had to recruit his supporters one by one, his only advantage being that some writers were important and influential figures, perhaps already in parliament – such as Bulwer Lytton, Disraeli, Gladstone, Spring Rice and Monckton Milnes. Probably his single most important supporter was William Wordsworth, who was a conscientious and well-connected lobbyist.

[34] Apprentices were a source of cheap labour for printers, and journeymen sought to control their number to protect their own livelihoods: Ellic Howe and Harold E. Waite, *The London Society of Compositors* (1948).

Another difficulty was lack of numbers. By the second reading of the 1838 version of the bill there were ninety-seven petitions against, representing 4,700 signatures. There was not a single petition in favour. This was in part due to the acute sensitivities of prominent authors, who did not like to be seen to petition on their own behalf. The other reason was that it would simply have been impossible to find thousands of people actively interested in supporting Talfourd's alterations to the copyright law. By 1839 some notable petitioners for the bill had emerged, such as Thomas Carlyle, Thomas Arnold and Hartley Coleridge, as well as, eventually, Wordsworth himself. However, the opposition was quick to make capital out of, for instance, petitioning periodical writers such as Archibald Alison; his writings and arguments were publicly ridiculed. Petitioning cannot have been a very pleasant prospect.

Talfourd could count on some staunch support in parliament, however. The other original sponsors were Thomas Spring Rice, Lord Mahon and Sir Robert Inglis. When Spring Rice was elevated to the House of Lords (as Lord Monteagle) in 1840, Gladstone took his place as sponsor, and became the source of valuable tactical advice. Bulwer Lytton was already known as a supporter of an improved copyright law, and the young Disraeli also spoke in favour of the changes.

Yet there was also formidable parliamentary opposition. The radicals, particularly Warburton, Wakley and Hume, had strong objections to any strengthening of copyright; they regarded it as an indefensible extension to a monopoly already of doubtful justification, which would raise the price of books and favour the undeserving at the expense of the general public. In addition, since this was not a party issue, senior parliamentary figures were free to vote as they thought fit, and Talfourd failed to persuade some crucial members of the virtues of his claims. Perhaps the three most damaging voices against were those of Lord John Russell, Peel and Macaulay.

Lord John Russell waited until the committee stage of the 1838 version of the bill to make his views known. His arguments were not particularly original, and some of his points could have been dealt with by appropriate drafting. His opposition was totally unexpected and extremely damaging, coming from a very senior Whig who was himself a writer. Talfourd could reasonably protest at the suddenness and timing of the intervention, particularly from a member of his own party: it would certainly have been courteous to signal any objections earlier.

Talfourd was first elected to parliament in the general election which took place at the beginning of 1835. Although the Conservatives hung on to power a little longer, Peel's first ministry collapsed completely in the spring: he was not to become prime minister again until 1841. Peel's views on copyright were evidently still fluid in 1838, when Wordsworth corresponded with him on the subject. The letters contain detailed consideration of the issues. Having failed to persuade Peel himself, Wordsworth asked Gladstone to try to overcome Peel's specific objections. However, Peel remained unconvinced, and was afraid 'of being charged with favouring *monopoly* if he gave it his support'.[35] It took Macaulay's oratory to change Peel's mind.

Macaulay could be regarded as Talfourd's single most damaging opponent. He had a reputation as a brilliant literary man, as well as being known for his personal political independence and integrity. In 1834 he went to India as member of the Supreme Council of India, where he had became head of the Law Commission. Although his absence coincided with the first part of Talfourd's campaign, Macaulay was back in England early in 1839. He was returned to parliament as member for Edinburgh in May, and in September was offered the secretaryship of war and a seat in the cabinet. The copyright bill did not even progress to committee stage in 1840, and there is no evidence of particular interest on Macaulay's part. However, in 1841 he intervened in the debate on the second reading, with devastating results for the bill. He characterised copyright as a monopoly, whose evil effects were in direct proportion to its length, whereas its good effects were not. The damage was irreparable. Talfourd lost the division, and could only protest at the lateness and ferocity of the intervention.

Macaulay continued to be interested in the subject. In the next session another show-stopping speech had the effect of radically altering the bill, which was already much curtailed in that it sought a term of the author's life plus only twenty-five years, with a twenty-eight year minimum. Macaulay objected to the 'life-plus'

[35] Wordsworth, *The letters of William and Dorothy Wordsworth*, 2nd edn, ed. Alan G. Hill (Oxford, 1969–88), VII, p. 214 (10 July 1841) (italics in original).

term, on the grounds that it was a lottery which incidentally gave juvenilia longer protection than mature works. His suggestion was for a life term or, alternatively, a term of forty-two years, whichever was the longer. Inglis pointed out that this proposal ignored any possibility of provision for the author's family, so Peel's compromise solution of life plus seven years, or forty-two years, was finally adopted.

Although he was outvoted, Macaulay continued to believe in a fixed term. Such a solution stood in complete opposition to the principle on which Talfourd sought to base the bill; a lengthy life-plus term was essential to him. Did the final result represent the triumph of one principle over another? Or was it the product of utter boredom with the issues, leaving the House desperate for a face-saving resolution? In a letter to Talfourd, Macaulay remarked that: 'the settlement which has been made has excited no violent discontent in any quarter. I do not remember to have seen a case in which a compromise has been so welcome to all parties. Something must be attributed to the fear entertained by members that, if this opportunity were lost, they might have to pass their Wednesday afternoons during many Sessions in the house.'[36] If this is true, it is at least arguable that the peace was dearly bought. The final debate focused exclusively on the question of the term and not on the basis or purposes of copyright.

However, it is also possible that little could in fact have been achieved in the circumstances. There was perhaps more than a grain of truth in Macaulay's light-hearted quip to Talfourd regarding the interest of members in resolving the issue to save themselves the pain of further discussion. Their fatigue is understandable: five full years were needed to effect any change to the copyright law. Talfourd had had to face many difficulties, some due to ill luck and others due to determined opposition. He had been forced to modify his bill dozens of times, in ways which altered it very significantly. It seems remarkable that Talfourd continued to bring the bill forward.

[36] *The Letters of Thomas Babington, Baron Macaulay*, ed. Thomas Pinney (Cambridge, 1974–81), IV, p. 33 (30 April 1842).

2

PETITIONS AND COPYRIGHT

Almost 500 petitions against the copyright bills were presented in the House of Commons between 1838 and 1840, amounting to over 30,000 signatures. Only thirty-seven petitions were received in favour of the changes, representing 341 signatures in total, a figure in the order of only a hundredth of the popular opposition. Before this discrepancy can be understood, an understanding of the petitioning process, and of these particular petitions and petitioners, is essential.

PETITIONING – PARLIAMENTARY HISTORY AND BACKGROUND

The first edition of Erskine May notes that petitioning is the means 'by which the people are brought into communication with the Parliament', and acknowledges it as 'a fundamental principle of the constitution'.[1] Certainly the right of any aggrieved person to present a petition to parliament was of long standing. At first petitions sought redress for private grievances, and they were received and tried in a way which was more judicial than legislative; but, as parliament lost much of its remedial jurisdiction to the courts of equity, petitions took on the nature of private bills, and thus assumed a more legislative character.

Presentation of petitions differed in the two Houses. Few petitions were addressed to the House of Lords, and there was no comprehensive system for recording their contents. However,

[1] Thomas Erskine May, *A treatise upon the law, privileges, proceedings and usage of parliament* (1844), p. 300. On petitions generally see ch. XIX. Blackstone does not address the subject of petitioning (except for private bills): see Sir William Blackstone, *Commentaries on the laws of England* (Oxford, 1765–70).

when a petition was introduced, there was no time restriction on any resulting debate. This had also been the practice in the House of Commons. However, in the 1830s, when petitions began to arrive in huge numbers, the procedural conventions associated with their presentation threatened to halt legislative business.

Petitions enjoyed priority over all other ordinary business, on order days and others. Ministers were expected to attend for the presentations, which took place at the beginning of the sitting. Whereas an ordinary motion, once voted on, could not be reintroduced in the same session, petitions could be used again and again to renew debate on a topic. The member presenting the petition was allowed four chances to speak, and so by judicious collaboration could force a debate: 'With these advantages, [petitions] became the standard means of political agitation, offering an excuse for holding public meetings in the country, and repeated discussion in the House.'[2]

This opportunity was repeatedly exploited by the parliamentary radicals, as it provided them with a power to harass the government which was out of all proportion to their numbers in the House. This provoked Peel into action: in May 1832 he moved the appointment of a select committee to look into the presentation of petitions, a proposal which was welcomed by both Whigs and Tories.[3] The restraints on speaking which had allowed the system to operate before the Reform Act had broken down. It was widely recognised that unless debates on petitions were given defined limits, public business would come to a standstill. Although the committee's report was not received until shortly before the election, Althorp was determined that its recommendations should be put into effect in the new parliament.[4]

This was done, at least in part. Members were given only two

[2] Peter Fraser, 'The growth of ministerial control in the nineteenth-century House of Commons', *English Historical Review* 75 (1960), 444–63 (p. 450).

[3] Colin Leys, 'Petitioning in the nineteenth and twentieth centuries', *Political Studies* 3 (1955), 44–64 (p. 48).

[4] Election petitions presented a different problem. These challenged the validity of election returns on the grounds of bribery or other illegal practices, and were used as a political weapon with great freedom. Although most petitions were either withdrawn or lapsed, even a validly elected candidate might prefer to give way rather than fight: the process was very costly for both sides. See Norman Gash, *Politics in the age of Peel: a study in the technique of parliamentary representation 1830–50* (1953), p. 133.

opportunities to speak on presentation, and the Select Committee on Public Petitions was created. Peel had suggested that petitions be received by a standing committee of the whole House, to meet (with no quorum) on certain days a week under the chairmanship of one of the members present. This would technically have preserved the inviolability of the right to present petitions to the whole House, but would in fact have removed the reception of petitions from its full sittings (with the speaker in the chair). Althorp did not go this far, and instead instituted morning sittings.

This still infuriated William Cobbett and Daniel O'Connell, who chose to present the issue as one of constitutional principle. However, the scale of petitioning rather worked against them: even though nine hours a week were set aside for the reception of petitions, the arrears of unpresented petitions grew alarmingly. The extensive use of parliamentary time was much resented, and in fact became so inconvenient for all parties that the radicals stopped forcing the issue. From 1834 it was possible to place petitions in the hands of the Committee on Petitions without any formal presentation, and the 'morning' sittings were abandoned in 1835. From about 1836 it became the practice to allow a member to put down a motion arising out of a petition (which there was a chance might be moved), but this had the effect of preventing any debate on presentation.

Although this 'gag' rule was vigorously challenged by various radicals in 1839, memories of the inconveniences caused by its absence were strong, and it was endorsed. It was in theory still possible to read out a petition on presentation, but the member who attempted this would first face efforts to drown him out with howls and noise, and would then address empty benches. So after 1839 debate upon presentation was not permitted, except in certain special circumstances.[5] At the beginning of the 1842 parliament, Wallace tried once more to reverse the system, by rescinding the sessional orders which gave it effect: he failed.[6] Later in the session

[5] Such as petitions for private bills, or those involving an urgent personal grievance requiring immediate remedy. Erskine May, *Treatise*, p. 307.

[6] Robert Wallace, MP for Greenock. He argued that the people did not wish to see their petitions 'lying in hundreds on the table and crammed into a bag, while not the slightest attention has been paid to their contents'. His motion was defeated by 237 votes to 50. Patrick J. F. Howarth, *Questions in the House: the history of a unique British institution* (1956), p. 104.

the gag rule was enshrined in a standing order, when the two main parties cooperated to prevent further minority challenges.

Thus the vast majority of petitions were referred to the Committee on Public Petitions for classification and analysis. The Committee's reports were printed twice a week, listing the name of each petition, the number of signatures to it and its general object. Within each heading, the running total of petitions and signatures was also recorded. Certain petitions were printed in full in the Appendix, which was 'accessible to the public at the cheapest rate of purchase'.[7] The choice was based on either general importance of the petition (and presumably of its signatories), and on the particular arguments or facts stated. These reports provide the only consolidated record of popular reaction in this form, and have led to the survival of material which was never published elsewhere.

PETITIONS – FORMS AND FORMALITIES

At the time of Talfourd's bill, various formalities were still required.[8] Petitioners had to use the prescribed form of address (to the relevant House). They were required to give a general designation of the parties to it: this was used by the Committee on Public Petitions in their regular reports. The body of the petition had to conclude with the 'prayer', which summarised the petitioners' aims (for instance, that the copyright bill might not pass into a law). Without a 'prayer' the document could not be regarded as a petition, and 'remonstrances' were not received.

Petitions had to be written rather than printed, and considerable attention was paid to the nature of the signatures.[9] At least one

[7] Erskine May, *Treatise*, p. 308. [8] Ibid., p. 303.

[9] This requirement occasionally provided lucrative work for Robert Chambers, the elder of the two famous Edinburgh bookselling brothers. They created their business from scratch, and Robert supplemented his income with commissions for caligraphy on visiting-cards, books, etc. William Chambers gives this account of his brother's side-line: 'The writing of "petitions" was the most profitable of this kind of work, only it did not come very often. On one occasion we see an entry [in Robert Chambers' accounts] of a pound for "writing a petition", the profit on which is candidly set down at nineteen shillings and sixpence': William Chambers, *Memoir of William and Robert Chambers*, 13th edn (Edinburgh, 1884), p. 181.

signature was supposed to be on the same sheet of paper as the petition itself: some of the copyright petitions do not observe this rule, and are nevertheless recorded, although with a note of the irregularity. Signatures (or marks) had to be originals rather than copies, nor could they be signatures of agents on behalf of others. If a public meeting was held to discuss a particular petition, the chairman could sign on behalf of those assembled. However, this was only counted as the petition of that one individual 'because the signature of one party for others cannot be recognised'.[10] This device was used during the campaign against copyright extension, and in fact results in an underestimate of those against the bills, because it adds just a single signature to the total.[11] Corporations could petition under common seal, and this was likewise done for the copyright bills.[12] If any forgery or fraud was detected either in preparation of the petitions or in the signatures themselves, this was treated very seriously, and punished as a breach of privilege.

The character and substance of a petition was similarly controlled: its language was supposed to be 'respectful and temperate, and free from offensive imputations upon the character or conduct of Parliament', and no reference to debates in either House was permitted.[13] They had to be presented by a member of the House to which they were addressed, to whom they could be posted free of charge. Members had a duty to read the petitions presented by them, to check for any violations of these rules.

PETITIONS – VOLUME AND SUBJECTS

It has already been noted that the number of public petitions presented to parliament during the 1830s threatened to bring business to a standstill. In the five years ending in 1789, the number of petitions was 880. By the end of a similar period ending in 1831 the number was 24,492, rising to 70,369 in the five years ending in 1841. Leys attributes this striking increase to

[10] Erskine May, *Treatise*, p. 304.

[11] For an example, see petition 5,953, signed by Dr George Birkbeck as chairman of a public meeting. See ch. 4, pp. 91–2.

[12] For example, petition 6970, from the lord provost, magistrates and council of the City of Edinburgh, presented 1 May 1839.

[13] Erskine May, *Treatise*, p. 304.

'general conditions of rapid economic change and agricultural unrest, popular radicalism, and incipient working-class organization', and explains that 'petitions as a political instrument, like public meetings and the circulation of political literature, enjoyed an unprecedented boom'.[14]

Further, Leys's analysis of the subjects that attracted over 10,000 signatures shows a heavy preponderance of causes which were of central importance in radical politics. During 1837 to 1842, the years of Talfourd's bills, the particular issues which dominated were the franchise and the ballot, corn laws, and 'taxes on knowledge'.[15] In 1839 the Convention of Industrious Classes drew up a petition with 1,200,000 signatures, and in 1842 over 3 million people signed a petition against the poor laws which called for universal suffrage. Leys notes that these petitions were organised by people whose supporters were largely unrepresented in parliament, and thus were unable to use parliamentary party politics as a means of applying pressure: 'it seems reasonable to infer that the collection of signatures to petitions continued to recommend itself as being as good a way as any (and better than most) of building up and maintaining the popular support on which extra-parliamentary politics depend'.[16] Furthermore, the number of petitions presented was closely related to the amount of parliamentary time available to the radicals, at least until the gag rule was imposed.

These petitioning practices have implications for the copyright question. Copyright was an issue which attracted tens of thousands of signatures, mostly collected and presented by radical MPs. It is clearly regarded by them as an issue which threatened radical interests. This supports the contention that copyright came to be characterised as a tax on knowledge. Once included in this category, one of central concern on the radical agenda, the well-oiled machine of radical protest was brought into action to oppose it. This is one explanation for the volume and type of

[14] Leys, 'Petitioning', p. 47.

[15] Ibid., p. 58. The poor laws, municipal government, and factory legislation were also the subjects of extensive petitioning in the 1830s and 1840s, although not so markedly during the copyright struggle. Smaller but significant numbers of petitions were concerned with postage, chimney sweeps and the opium trade with China.

[16] Ibid., p. 59.

protest that Talfourd's bills faced, which cannot be accounted for simply by the opposition of the printing trades: the petitions themselves reveal a much wider base of support than this.[17]

Helpful though it may be in the context of the copyright debate, this explanation takes for granted the existence of the mechanism of protest: one question that should be raised is that of the nature and functioning of radical protest. A high level of organisation must have existed, if tens of thousands of signatures could be collected and presented to parliament, on many radical issues. In so far as copyright was a typical radical issue, analysis of the petitions may provide some insight into the organisation of popular radical pressure.

Further, the pressure was at least partially successful: the bill was severely delayed and significantly modified. It is harder to determine whether this was due to radical objections to taxes on knowledge, or to trade defence of trade interests. The answer would perhaps indicate something about the effectiveness of these radical efforts, and thus whether or not these extensive popular protests were worth the paper they were written on.

[17] It was certainly a level of organisation which those in favour of the copyright bills could not emulate.

3

CRITICS IN PARLIAMENT

THE RADICAL NEXUS

Talfourd faced considerable and diverse opposition within parliament. In a time when party discipline was not strong, and on a superficially non-political issue, such as copyright, members were in principle free to vote as they wished. Nevertheless, some subgroups are apparent, particularly the radicals, but also the law officers, as well as some high-profile individuals.

The most vociferous voices against the bill were those of Joseph Hume, Henry Warburton and Thomas Wakley. Politically, all three were radicals, as was Grote, also an opponent.[1] Henry Ward, Edward Baines and Edward Strutt, who also spoke strongly against an extension of copyright, were liberals with some radical sympathies. All of them presented many petitions, and were essential in the orchestration of the mass petitioning effort. Important though the radical inheritance was, it would be incomplete and misleading to explain their stance as an inevitable one given the 'radical' label. It is rather in the individual interests of these men that the roots of the radical opposition to copyright are revealed.

The war against the unstamped press, waged first by Viscount Sidmouth and the Tories, but maintained by the Whigs, represented a deliberate attempt to prevent the dissemination of radical political opinions.[2] This was only partially successful, and the

[1] See for example: Simon Maccoby, *English Radicalism* (1935–61); Gillian Sutherland (ed.), *Studies in the growth of nineteenth-century government* (1972); William Thomas, *The philosophic radicals* (Oxford, 1979).

[2] For a detailed history see the following: Collet Dobson Collet, *History of the taxes on knowledge, their origin and repeal* (1899); Patricia Hollis, *The pauper press* (1970); M. C. Moore, 'The history of the agitation against the stamp duty on

explosion of radical frustration during the Reform Bill crisis brought mounting popular protest and disorder in the early 1830s. The concessions of 1832 did not halt the radical momentum; the campaign against the 4d newspaper stamp continued, since this forced the price of newspapers above an affordable level for the working class, and thus reduced significantly the possibilities of expressing the radical point of view – legally, at least.

Although 1836 had seen the reduction of the stamp to 1d, this incomplete victory had not satisfied the most hard-line radicals. These men, such as Francis Place, George Roebuck and Robert Watson, saw a direct link between legislative measures such as the Stamp Act and the libel laws, and restrictions on their political freedom. Paper duties were likewise seen as a repressive burden, and it is therefore not surprising that copyright, once characterised as a tax on the public, would be regarded with hostility. Hume, Warburton, Wakley and Grote had been prominent in the campaign against the stamp, and their opposition to the copyright bill can be seen as a simple continuation of the war against the 'taxes on knowledge'. Yet for all of these men there were other, individual, motivating forces.

Hume (1777–1855) was a seasoned political campaigner: well accustomed to parliamentary lobbying, he valued parliamentary exposure.[3] Always concerned for press freedom, he and Place had been instrumental in the fight against taxes on knowledge. Hume had corresponded with Brougham, then lord chancellor, on the subject; a meeting with Spring Rice had followed. Although criticised by Place for being too soft in his demands, Hume had continued to fight for the total abolition of the stamp. In 1836 he started the moderately reformist newspaper, the *Constitutional*, to advance working-class knowledge and to combat anti-reformist views.

Grote (1794–1871) is now remembered for his *The history of Greece*.[4] In parliament he was perhaps best known for his continued work for the secret ballot, but he also had a strong interest in education. He was one of the founders of the City of London

newspapers 1830–55' (unpublished M.A. thesis, King's College, London, 1935); Joel H. Weiner, *The war of the unstamped* (Ithaca and London, 1969).

[3] Valerie Chancellor, *The political life of Joseph Hume, 1775–1855* (1986).

[4] Martin Lowther Clarke, *George Grote* (1962); Harriet Grote, *The personal life of George Grote* (1873).

Literary and Scientific Institution, and he had been an active member of the council of University College. London. His opposition to taxes on knowledge was well known: this had been one of the platforms of his original election address in 1832, and he had taken a leading role in the fight against them.

Wakley (1795–1862) had entered parliament in 1835, backed by Cobbett and Hume, but he was already very well known in medical circles.[5] The son of a farmer, he had been apprenticed to various medical men. Because of his background he lacked both the money and connections required to enter the medical profession as a surgeon or physician, and had been forced to become a general practitioner. Wakley was always alert to abuses of patronage and position, and was particularly anxious to ensure standards and availability of medical training; this was only available on payment of various fees, which could be very high.[6]

In 1823 Wakley founded the *Lancet*. The first number promised to publish the substance of Sir Astley Cooper's lectures on surgery, which Wakley had attended, and to report important recent case histories. The aim was to make this information freely available, thereby 'adding to the stock of useful knowledge of every individual in these realms'. Interested opposition was expected, as the *Lancet* was priced at 6d, whereas lectures could cost £5 per session per student. The medical societies also considered that they held the copyright of the reports of their proceedings; these were published at length by Wakley, particularly if they involved discussion of malpractice or poor administration.

A far greater problem was copyright in the lectures. Sir Astley Cooper had a sufficient reputation that his classes were undiminished, and he had ceased to object to publication provided that his name was removed.[7] Nevertheless, concern remained that the

[5] John Hostettler, *Thomas Wakley: an improbable radical* (Chichester, 1993); Samuel Squire Sprigge, *The life and times of Thomas Wakley* (1897).

[6] For a full account see M. Jeanne Peterson, *The medical profession in mid-Victorian London* (1978).

[7] For one version of this story see Henry Curwen, *A history of booksellers* (1874), p. 371. Since Wakley was only one of many taking notes in Cooper's lectures, it had been impossible to prevent the publication of the text. Nevertheless, Curwen explains, Wakley had evidently aroused the lecturer's suspicions: 'Cooper could not, however, bring the charge home till he hit upon the device of calling at midnight at [Wakley's] lodgings and asking to see the "doctor" upon urgent medical business, when he surprised him red-handed correcting a proof-sheet of a lecture. The discovery was so sudden and so undeniable that neither could

lectures were reproduced verbatim and not edited, and also that the lay press had developed the practice of reprinting the lectures in a non-medical context. In 1824 Mr Abernethy, senior surgeon at St Bartholomew's hospital, applied to Chancery for an injunction to restrain the publishers and printers of the *Lancet* from issuing his lectures.[8] Abernethy argued that he alone had property in his lectures, which were delivered 'as from writings' composed by him, and remained unpublished.

The publisher's name was Hutchinson, and his defence rested on two claims. Firstly, that similar lectures had previously been given at St Bartholomew's Hospital as part of a course of surgical lectures, attendance at which was required for those seeking the diploma of the Royal College of Surgeons. No other surgeon had ever published such lectures, nor had they claimed property in them, nor had any conditions been imposed on students as to how they should use the knowledge gained. Secondly, the defendants claimed that the lectures were delivered extempore, and were substantially derived from the principles of a previous surgeon, John Hunter. Since there was no right of property in ideas and language not reduced into writing, Mr Abernethy's lectures were not protected.

Although he described it as 'a question of mighty importance', Lord Eldon felt unable to decide the question of property in the lectures:

> In *Millar* v. *Taylor* there is a great deal said with respect to a person having a property in sentiments and language, though not deposited on paper, but there has been no decision upon that point yet. And as it is a pure question of law, I think it would be going further than a Judge in equity should go, to say, upon that, that he can grant an injunction upon it, before the point is tried.[9]

Instead, he considered the questions of express and implied contract, and implied trust. On the basis of implied contract, he concluded that pupils could not publish a lecture for profit.

refrain from laughter; and eventually Cooper, not ill-humouredly, offered to allow his lectures to appear if the proofs were first sent him for revision. Consequently, Cooper, though often criticised in the *Lancet*, never received a nickname, as did most of the other medical celebrities of the day.'

[8] This story is given by Sprigge, *Wakley*, pp. 89–100. His account is helpful, although not always accurate. The best report is [1825] LJ Ch (OS) 209. An abridged version (1 H & Tw 28) appears in the *English Reports* 47, p. 1313.

[9] [1825] LJ Ch (OS) 217.

Although on the facts there was insufficient evidence to establish an implied contract between the parties, it was clear that the lectures 'must have been procured in an undue manner from those who were under a contract not to publish for profit'.[10] Publication at a profit would thus be a fraud on a third party and the court would not allow such publication. Lord Eldon therefore granted an injunction restraining sale of the lectures. In spite of this setback, Wakley continued to use the *Lancet* as a controversial but very effective tool, both to reform medical practice and to disseminate medical information. The *Lancet* was financially successful and stable by the time Wakley entered parliament.

Aside from his medical interests, Wakley was pledged to the main radical doctrines, and he was a strenuous free trader. Once in parliament, as the proprietor of a periodical, and as one with radical friends, his motion for the total repeal of the newspaper stamp was entirely in character.[11] His *Letter to the people of England, on the new project for gagging the press* (1836) also attacked the newspaper stamp, which he regarded as a direct fetter on political freedom: 'Until the duty on newspapers is totally abolished, the press will not, cannot, become free.' As might be expected, Wakley had strong views about Lord Brougham's 1835 bill which sought to give lectures copyright protection. This perhaps had extra poignancy for Wakley: Brougham had been one of the defending counsel when Abernethy had sued the *Lancet*.

Wakley's spirited opposition to Talfourd's bill was thus inevitable. He was assiduous in his collection and presentation of petitions to the House of Commons. He also mobilised support from the British Medical Association – not the familiar modern institution but the original London-based BMA – 'which was founded in 1836 and subsequently died'.[12] He presented two petitions from the president and council of this organisation, expressing anxiety that an extended term would deny the public access to cheap publications, particularly scientific ones.[13]

Wakley's own argument was partly an anti-monopoly one, but he also relied heavily on a direct and inappropriate parallel with lectures, arguing that literary and artistic productions were in the

[10] Ibid., at 215.
[11] *Hansard, Parliamentary debates* (3rd series), xxxii, 335 (March 1838).
[12] Peterson, *Medical profession*, p. 23.
[13] For full details see ch. 4, p. 91.

same sense public works. As Wakley's biographer, Sprigge, observed: 'Wakley's view of the copyright question was certainly inspired by his close acquaintance with one side of it only.'[14] In one notorious parliamentary speech, Wakley's mocking treatment of Wordsworth's poetry brought reproaches and unfavourable comment both from parliamentary colleagues and the press.[15]

Similar newspaper connections can be seen for several of the Whigs with radical sympathies who opposed Talfourd. Henry George Ward (1797–1860), the wealthy ex-diplomat MP for Sheffield, owned the *Weekly Chronicle*, which he used as a platform for the political polemics for which he was famous. Priced at 3d by its original owners (the radicals Henry Cole and Charles Buller), it had lost 'hundreds of pounds'.[16] Ward had been forced to raise the price to 4d, and then 6d, and circulation had suffered as a direct result. Another newspaper man was Edward Baines (1774–1848). Nominally a liberal but a close friend of Cobden's, Baines was the very influential editor of the *Leeds Mercury*. He was also interested in education, especially local education, and helped to found the Leeds Mechanics' Institute.[17]

Some of the radical opposition was known for utilitarian views, often coupled with a great interest in political economy. Of these, Henry Warburton (1784?–1858) was perhaps the best known. One of the philosophic radicals, he was regarded as a clever scholar and man of science, elected FRS in 1809. A member of the Political Economy Club from its inception, he was a close friend of David Ricardo (the principal founder of the classical school of political economy). He was involved in the foundation of University College London, and was a member of its first council. In addition, he worked with Grote and Roebuck to found the Society for the Diffusion of Moral and Political Knowledge. In parliament

[14] Sprigge, *Wakley*, p. 326.

[15] *Hansard, Parliamentary debates* (3rd series), lxi, 1374–90 (April 1842). Richard Monkton Milnes's speech in reply brought him much distinction; according to Lady Blessington, he should have been voted a piece of plate. The newly founded *Punch* published several merciless satirical 'examples' of 'medical poetry' from 'Mr Wakley, the Modern Orpheus' – Wakley having claimed that he could write Wordsworth by the mile: *Punch* (1842), pp. 161, 172, 193.

[16] Quoted in Thomas, *Philosophic radicals*, p. 335.

[17] Edward Baines, *The life of Edward Baines* (1851); Donald Read, *Press and people, 1790–1850: opinion in three English cities* (1961), pp. 78–9, 108.

he tended to work closely with other radicals, especially Hume, Buller, Grote and Molesworth.

Other opponents, much less radical than Warburton, were known for their interest in political economy – such as George Pryme and Edward Strutt. Pryme (1781–1868) was a noted classical scholar, and a successful barrister. A Cambridge undergraduate, he later returned there to live, and began a course of private lectures in political economy. He was regarded with deep suspicion by the heads of houses at first, but he was made a professor in 1828. He shared the representation of Cambridge with Thomas Spring Rice. Edward Strutt (1801–80) knew Bentham, and both James and John Stuart Mill. His other main interests were free trade, law reform and education.

Given the weakness of contemporary party discipline, and the comparative disunity of the radical element in parliament, it is quite plausible that the individual interests of these men would have been relevant to their stance on Talfourd's copyright bill. However, the result is a united radical front. This in turn suggests that the copyright question raises problems and issues on which these very disparate men found it possible to agree. It is arguable that, at least for those with radical sympathies, the issues raised are strongly reminiscent of those raised in the past – first in the reform struggle, and most recently in the war against taxes on knowledge. It is this history which, when overlaid onto the copyright question, produces this extraordinary cohesive force.

These recurrent problems and issues appear in various forms during the 1830s, disguised or even hidden. It is nevertheless possible to isolate certain characteristic essentials. Acting as a defining foundation was the belief that political repression followed from the suppression of knowledge, in particular (but not exclusively) political knowledge. The view that an educated people would be better able to play a responsible political role develops naturally from this position. The education of the working class thereby became a priority for good government, with cheap books classified as an essential. This stance had a reciprocal: any government intervention which hindered the education of the working man became something to be strongly condemned and resisted. The most striking example of this theory in practice was the war against what came to be known as 'taxes on knowledge' – primarily the newspaper stamp and paper duties, but also the various libel laws.

These interlinked and interdependent strands proved extraordinarily flexible in their application. The language of free trade was easily grafted onto the original stock: under a principle of non-intervention all duties risked characterisation as an unacceptable tax on the public. It is the articulation of these arguments in an analysis of copyright which led to the radicals' rejection of the suggestion that the term of copyright should be increased.

In these terms, then: since an extended term would give the copyright owner an even longer period of control over the protected work, its price was thought likely to rise, and the risk that a work would be withheld from the public was perceived to increase directly in relation to the length of the extra term. Any increase in the price of books would discriminate against the working man, restricting his chances of self-education, and thereby denying him his rights in the political sphere. Even worse, the mechanism for this extension would be a legislative act, an act of government. Once characterised as a tax on knowledge, any increased burden on the public could only be justified in terms of a putative benefit to the public which could be offset against the extra-ordinary imposition. The radical position was that there were no such benefits, and that the extension was therefore indefensible.

That these ideas influenced the copyright debate is not a matter of supposition: in the parliamentary speeches made by Talfourd's radical opponents, there is evidence of several of these strands. Hume described the bill as 'a measure calculated to produce a great evil – that of increasing the price of books'.[18] Similarly, Grote thought the bill 'replete with mischief' and 'felt satisfied that [it] would have the effect. . .of narrowing the circle of the public amongst whom literature would circulate'.[19] Baines 'had no hesitation in saying that it would be difficult for the House to adopt a measure more calculated to be injurious to the spread of knowledge than the present'.[20]

Other comments confirm that copyright was regarded as a tax

[18] *Hansard, Parliamentary debates* (3rd series), xlii, 569 (25 April 1838).
[19] Ibid., 585.
[20] *Hansard, Parliamentary debates* (3rd series), xlv, 935 (27 February 1839).

on knowledge, and highlight the connection with free trade and anti-monopoly feeling. Responding to Mahon's contention that extended copyright would lower the price of books, Strutt retorted that 'since the time of Adam Smith, [he] thought it had always been considered, that monopoly was the parent of scarcity and dearness. If they admitted the noble Lord's principle, that monopoly was a cause of cheapness, then they must reform their entire commercial legislation.'[21] The repression/suppression argument was put by Warburton in its most bare form:

> Under the bill as it stood a Government adverse to popular rights might prevent the diffusion of political information, and he did not hesitate to say, that if such a measure were to pass into a law, the public would be deprived of many advantages arising from literature and science which they had long enjoyed, and which of late years they had much improved by means of cheap publications, but, according to some hon. Members who had taken a part in the present discussion, those cheap publications were a great evil, and nothing was more to be desired than that books should become dearer than they were at present.[22]

For all those with radical sympathies, then, there was a link between publishing freedom and political freedom; a copyright bill which operated to reduce the period during which a work could be freely published was bound to raise hackles. Legislation had been used in the past to suppress the political opinions of working men, who were reliant on cheap books and newspapers for the most basic education. Coming as soon as it did after the newspaper stamp controversy, Talfourd's bill rekindled a fire from embers that were still glowing. The radical reaction may not have been predicted, but it could certainly be explained. Copyright was no longer a simple matter of rewards for authors, it was a deeply political issue which touched raw political nerves: these aspects of the nineteenth-century copyright debate have not previously been fully explored.

POLITICAL CROSS-CURRENTS

While the printers turned openly to the radical MPs for help with their petitions, the publishers used more subtle methods of

[21] *Hansard, Parliamentary debates* (3rd series), lii, 415 (19 February 1840).
[22] *Hansard, Parliamentary debates* (3rd series), xlv, 939 (27 February 1839).

applying pressure: these disguise their targets somewhat. It seems likely that they raised the copyright issue with every MP with whom they could manoeuvre communication. There is evidence of several such interviews, and these are merely representative examples of what would have been a widespread practice. More concrete evidence of support for the publishers can be found in the parliamentary debates, and in the list of those presenting the publishers' petitions. Others, notably Lord Brougham and Macaulay, but also Lord John Russell and Peel, do not act for any single interest group: they opposed Talfourd's plans for more complex reasons. Their various reactions worked to modify the grand consolidated scheme first envisioned by Talfourd in 1837, and the 1842 Act was a product of these various pressures.

Yet it is hard to assess the practical effect of any of these interventions, or of the lobbying that provoked them. Even though it had emerged from over five years of debate, the 1842 bill was not allowed to pass unaltered: the realities of the parliamentary debating system produced a compromise measure, brokered at speed and under pressure on the floor of the House. The years of careful positioning had become almost irrelevant to a House that wanted to be rid of the problem. It can be argued that both sides hit their primary targets eventually: authors won an extension and the publishers disposed of the retrospective clause. During the campaign, however, the outcome could not have seemed likely to be so tidily reflective of the various lobbying efforts.

In terms of petitioning volume, non-radical MPs were heavily under-represented. Only a dozen or so presented petitions against the bill, and then no more than one or perhaps two petitions each: this pattern suggests that they were perhaps responding to individual constituency interests. Some names are striking nevertheless. Poulett Thomson, who had introduced the International Copyright Bill in March 1838,[23] presented two early petitions, from print workers in London and in Manchester.[24] Peel also presented a printing trade petition, from forty-seven compositors at Baldwin's shop.[25] Such non-radical petitions as there were came largely in 1838.

[23] *Hansard, Parliamentary debates* (3rd series), xli, 1096.
[24] 4,633 and 4,634 (App. 391), presented 11 April 1838.
[25] 5,183, presented 30 April 1838.

Several lawyers spoke against Talfourd's bill, although they form a group of only the loosest sort. Two were government law officers; the attorney-general, Sir John Campbell, and the solicitor-general, Robert Monsey Rolfe.[26] The others, Sir Edward Sugden and Sir J. Frederick Pollock, were Tories.[27] The attorney-general presented two petitions, one signed by 727 Edinburgh letterpress printers, the other from sixty-seven publishers, booksellers, printers, etc.[28] His stated view was that individual cases should not form the basis of legislation, and that the solution was a power in the Judicial Committee of the Privy Council, by analogy with the Patent Act.[29] The solicitor-general argued that the copyright term was already sufficiently long, and that the imposition of a tax on knowledge was indefensible. He presented one of the few petitions of 1839.[30] Sir Edward Sugden stated crudely that Talfourd's purpose was evidently to extend the copyright of valuable works about to expire, and though he regretted the case in question he felt that the public interest should be regarded. He did, however, indicate that he would tolerate a life term plus five or seven years.[31] By the committee stage the alliances with the publishers were no longer concealed: the attorney-general said that he objected to many clauses, citing the case of the Edinburgh publisher, Black, as his reason. However, the lawyers' opposition was not sustained: they did not speak

[26] 'It was said of [Rolfe's] contributions in the House of Commons that he remained, as he had begun, entirely ineffective, the government never dreaming of utilising him in the day of battle': John L. J. Edwards, *The law officers of the Crown* (1964), p. 48. As Lord Cranworth, however, he became a successful lord chancellor.

[27] Sugden was the author of two famous treatises, *The law of vendors and purchasers* (1805), and *Practical treatise on powers*. He built a hugely successful Chancery practice and became a highly regarded judge. A. W. Brian Simpson (ed.), *Biographical dictionary of the common law* (1984), p. 495.

[28] 4,747 and 4,748, presented 25 April 1838, App. 404.

[29] *Hansard, Parliamentary debates* (3rd series), xlii, 586.

[30] Ibid., 570. 7,254, from 'authors and others interested in the diffusion of literature and science', presented 7 May 1839, App. 688.

[31] *Hansard, Parliamentary debates* (3rd series), xlii, 590–2. When Wordsworth heard of these exchanges he wrote to Henry Crabb Robinson, who had qualified as a lawyer: 'The gentlemen of your quondam Profession, with their fictitious rights, their public rights, their sneers at sentiment and so forth, & the Sugdenian allowance of 7 years, after the death of the Authors, have indelibly disgraced themselves': *The letters of William and Dorothy Wordsworth*, 2nd edn, ed. Alan G. Hill (Oxford, 1969–88), VI, p. 580 (May 1838).

against the bill after 1838, probably because the retrospective clause was dropped.

Apart from the lawyers and radical MPs, the only other person to speak against the bill was Lord John Russell: as leader of the House of Commons his support was vital. Although he acknowledged that the bill was very important, he counselled 'ample and mature deliberation'. His fear was that the bill would damage public interests, and 'the general interests of literature, and the progress of information and knowledge': he also had particular concerns about the suppression of works.[32] Russell had apparently not signalled to Talfourd his intention to speak against the bill. Talfourd's side was understandably furious, particularly as this active opposition represented a change of position. Russell had been the target of a lobbying visit by Tom Longman in late May. Russell's surprise change of heart on 6 June seems to indicate that Longman was very persuasive.[33]

By the end of June 1838 Talfourd's plans were in shreds. Although his bill was already much less ambitious than the 1837 version, he had been forced to concede the retrospective clause to the publishers and he was still being opposed by a senior figure in his own party. Russell, as leader of the House, had influence over the use of parliamentary time, and thus was in a position to help or hinder the bill. Even worse, in July Lord Brougham introduced his rival copyright bill in the House of Lords. This sought to give the Judicial Committee of the Privy Council the power to grant extensions to individual copyrights in deserving cases. There is little direct evidence of Brougham's motives in bringing forward this plan, which at first seems to be an embodiment of the attorney-general's earlier proposal. However, Brougham's motives were rarely so simple: his interests in copyright, and in the Judicial Committee of the Privy Council, were of long standing.

BROUGHAM

Brougham was such a complex and changeable political figure that his reaction could never be predicted with any certainty. Nevertheless, his educational credentials and his repeated flirtations with

[32] *Hansard, Parliamentary debates* (3rd series), xliii, 556–8.

[33] See ch. 5, p. 122.

radical politics and popular issues might have suggested that resistance to a copyright bill would be likely. However, his contribution to the copyright debate cannot be characterised with such readiness. Brougham adopted a stance which was highly individual and uniquely isolated. It bore the stamp of his earlier political life and interests, and also reflected some of the bitterness and eccentricity which marked the end of his political career.

Brougham's talents had been recognised very early. He was heavily involved in the early *Edinburgh Review*, and was known for his sharp-edged contributions. His Whig politics making it hard for him to succeed at the Tory-dominated Scottish Bar, Brougham moved to London in search of political success. There he cultivated both Tory and Whig friendships, and also won popular acclaim with his defence of the mercantile interest in the trade war between Britain and France. Elected MP in 1810, he worked from the far left of the Whig party for various popular causes, such as the anti-slavery campaign, and again fought for trade interests in the Anglo-American trade war. He revealed an early interest in press freedom by defending the Hunt brothers in a notorious libel action.[34]

Out of parliament for a brief time, Brougham concentrated on his legal practice and the *Edinburgh Review*, but maintained his reforming interests. He had been introduced to Bentham, and others in that group, and found a common interest in education. In 1811 Brougham helped James Mill and others to found the Royal Lancastrian Society, which aimed to provide cheap education for working-class children in London. Brougham was to maintain this very practical involvement with the provision of education for his entire political career. He was a founder of the British and Foreign School Society which provided non-denominational religious instruction. Once back in parliament he introduced a bill intended to prevent the abuse of charitable funds intended for educational purposes. Another concrete expression of his commitment to education was his generous contribution to the fund which launched the London Mechanics' Institute in 1823.

An article on popular education followed. Although certainly

[34] This followed an article in the *Examiner* condemning flogging in the army. See Edmund Blunden, *Leigh Hunt's* 'Examiner' *examined* (1928) .

intended to advertise the London Mechanics' Institute, thereby encouraging other such institutes, it also set out the main tenets and arguments of those lobbying for cheap publications: the article's full title, *Practical observations on the education of the people, addressed to the working classes and their employers* (1825), indicates his area of concern. Brougham's claim was that attempts at self-improvement, and the efforts of those who sought to encourage such attempts, were being hampered by the lack of cheap good elementary texts. He objected to the high price of books in Great Britain when compared to continental prices, attributing this to the lack of mechanisation in the trade, and to paper duties, as well as to the customary wide margins and quality paper. Of these, he considered paper duties the most obnoxious: 'the tax on paper, which is truly a tax upon knowledge, and falls the heaviest upon those who most want instruction'.[35]

This very early use of the phrase 'tax upon knowledge' is noteworthy: only after 1830 did this become a widely used slogan of the campaigners against the newspaper stamp.[36] *Practical observations* also contains a hint about the embryonic Society for the Diffusion of Useful Knowledge: 'I am not without hopes of seeing formed a society for promoting the composition, publication, and distribution of cheap and useful works.'

Brougham's pamphlet was enormously successful, and was reprinted many times. Brougham built on this momentum in two very direct ways; with his connections with what became the University of London, and with the Society for the Diffusion of Useful Knowledge. In 1825 Brougham hosted a dinner at which Thomas Campbell, James Mill and Joseph Hume planned the foundation of a new, secular university: University College London was founded later that year, with its inaugural lecture in 1828. The SDUK stemmed from a committee formed in November 1826, which included Birkbeck and Grote: the nature and extent of the publishing venture which resulted has already been described. The importance to the SDUK project of Brougham's energy and interest should not be underestimated. He used his influence to assemble an exceptional committee, and led from the

[35] *Works of Henry, Lord Brougham*, 11 vols. (Edinburgh, 1872), VIII, p. 419.

[36] Courtesy of the front page of the *Examiner*. Edwin Chadwick is usually credited with coining the slogan, although Leigh Hunt is also claimed as a candidate for the honour.

front, producing dozens of articles himself, and (it was alleged) correcting SDUK proofs while in court. Although the SDUK did finally founder, it set an early example with its cheap publications, which other publishers were eventually to follow.

Brougham's efforts were not confined to educational matters. As lord chancellor he instituted a sweeping series of legal reforms, abolishing sinecures, improving the court system, and reforming the judicial functions of the Privy Council.[37] Before Brougham's bill in 1832, colonial appeals were heard by an ad hoc committee, and lay members were entitled to attend. Few appeals were even entered, because it was known that it sat only a few days a year. Brougham wanted to see a proper court, with a permanent bench and bar, with judges who specialised in colonial law. Although forced to make some concessions (chiefly to placate the then lord president, Lord Lansdowne), Brougham had secured improvements which increased the power and standing of the Privy Council's Judicial Committee. His continuing efforts on behalf of this Committee can be seen both in the details of his patent bill and, later, in his stance on the copyright question.

Brougham's patent bill was introduced in the House of Lords in June 1835. Various practical improvements were proposed: Brougham seemed well aware of the difficulties to be faced when defending a patent in court.[38] The most significant clause allowed the patentee to petition for an extension. The Judicial Committee of the Privy Council was to hear any petition, and was empowered to recommend an extension of up to seven years, with or without conditions. Brougham's Patent Bill received the royal assent in September.

During the same session Brougham had introduced a second bill with intellectual property as its theme, this time for preventing the publication of lectures without consent: it sought to grant authors and their assigns the sole right of publication. The reasons for Brougham's timing are unclear, but his 1824 defence of Wakley and the *Lancet* for the publication of Abernethy's lectures would have rendered him very familiar with the issues. The

[37] David Swinfen, 'Henry Brougham and the Judicial Committee of the Privy Council', *Law Quarterly Review* 90 (1974), 396–411 (p. 396).

[38] The first two clauses provide mechanisms for modifying the patent of a patentee who discovers that the specification is in some way faulty. There are also clauses to dissuade vexatious challenges, for instance by the award of treble costs.

scheme of the short bill draws heavily on the judgment in *Abernethy* v. *Hutchinson*.[39]

The bill passed the House of Lords without discussion. In the House of Commons, the objections of Wakley and Warburton – with hindsight – seem predictable. Wakley's complaint that the bill covered both public and private lectures can be traced directly to his experience in *Abernethy* v. *Hutchinson* and is of little importance. A more telling anxiety was that the bill might prevent objective appraisal of lectures: since admission was often charged, it was important that prospective students could look for an assessment in advance. Lord John Russell expressed the same concern, insisting that newspapers should be able to make extracts and to comment without fear of infringing copyright.[40] The complaints had no impact on the passage of Brougham's bill, which received the royal assent in August. It is only in retrospect that these reactions can be seen as significant for the copyright bills.

Brougham's reasons for introducing these two bills are a matter for conjecture. Both are in some ways characteristic of his many attempts to improve the everyday machinery of the law. In the patent bill, Brougham also created work for the Judicial Committee of the Privy Council, newly revitalised in his hands. There is an attempt to encourage invention, both by increasing the potential rewards, and by alleviating some of the difficulties arising from vexatious challenges to the patent grant. In the

39 Lectures publication bill (became the Lectures Copyright Act 1835). It was expressly stated that leave to attend a lecture did not carry with it a licence to print what was heard, and printers and publishers were rendered liable to penalties for publication without consent. Perhaps for reasons of proof, or for reasons of control, none of the provisions were to apply unless advance written notice of the lecture had been given to two local justices. By drafting a legislative instrument, Brougham was able to go further than Lord Eldon felt able to do on the question of property in lectures. Nevertheless, this is not styled a 'copyright' in lectures, presumably because of the absence of any fixed form of expression, but rather as a 'sole right of publishing'.

40 Wakley's suggested solution was to omit the clause which imposed liability on printers and publishers, but his motion was defeated. This would have left the law in the same state as following *Abernethy*'s case. There it was made clear that an action could be maintained against someone attending a lecture who later published it, and that an injunction could be granted to prevent the publication of a lecture obtained in this manner, but that no action could be sustained directly against the printer or publisher. *Hansard, Parliamentary debates* (3rd series), xxx, 953, 957.

lectures bill there is a clear educational thread: quite apart from his interest in *Abernethy*'s case, Brougham was involved with the organisation of educational lectures at various Mechanics' Institutes, and presumably baulked at the thought of their being published at a profit by a publisher with less laudable aims than those of the SDUK.

In addition, throughout the 1835 session, Brougham was actively campaigning against the newspaper stamp. His motivation for doing so is again uncertain. Speaking in support of one of the several petitions he presented, he indicated the breadth of the issue: the petition 'was not confined to the abolition of newspaper stamps, but to the taxes on knowledge of all descriptions, political, civil and scientific'.[41] In some ways his opposition to the stamp can be explained by his interest in the dissemination of cheap knowledge, but it is conceivable that he was at least partly driven by a desire to attack *The Times*.[42] To understand this vindictive streak, it is necessary to describe this stage of his political career, which proved to be its closing chapter.

Brougham's reforms and good works had previously brought him great popular support, although he was mistrusted (with good reason) by senior Whigs. Nevertheless, his power in the country had so far made him indispensable. Brougham's luck had begun to turn in 1834, when his intriguing over the Irish coercion bill, which brought down Grey's ministry, cost him the support of many, including the king.

Perhaps even more crucial was his breach with Thomas Barnes, the editor of *The Times*. Grey's ministry had been supported by *The Times* since 1830, but Barnes felt unable to endorse the Whig position on the new poor law. Barnes had previously relied on Le Marchant, Brougham's secretary, for inside government political information, and had made sure that Brougham's public and political efforts were highlighted and praised. But a disagreement, over what Barnes considered a deception by Le Marchant, brought the collaboration to an end. Barnes had also been unhappy with some of Brougham's activities, in particular his involvement with the Society for the Diffusion of

[41] *Hansard, Parliamentary debates* (3rd series), xxvii, 1125.

[42] As one indication, see the same speech for a barely concealed dig at *The Times*'s 'monopoly' of the London newspaper market.

Political Knowledge, and his proposals to take over Knight's *Companion to the Newspaper*. Also, Barnes and Brougham differed over the newspaper stamp, which put pressure on the cheap, popular press and thus worked to the advantage of the middle-class newspapers such as *The Times*.

The result was a complete rupture, not just with Brougham, but with the Whig party: government information now went to the *Morning Chronicle* and the *Globe*, and *The Times* attacked senior Whigs, particularly Brougham and Althorp.[43] Brougham went on an unprecedented publicity tour of the north, taking the Great Seal with him. His ill-considered speeches made him a public joke, while his indiscreet (and unfounded) claims that he had the ear of the king infuriated William IV. Several political colleagues thought that Brougham had actually gone quite mad.

In November 1834 a dispute, nominally about Althorp's successor as leader of the House of Commons, gave the king the opportunity to turn out Melbourne and to call Peel back from Italy to form a Conservative government. When Peel's unstable ministry fell in March 1835, Melbourne was returned to office. In spite of the pleas of Grey and Russell, Melbourne refused to consider having Brougham in his cabinet. His one concession was to put the Great Seal in commission: this had the effect of keeping Brougham under temporary control, in the hope that Melbourne would reconsider. But Lord Cottenham became the new lord chancellor at the end of the session, and Brougham learned of this humiliation only through the newspapers. Without hope of political office, there was no further reason for Brougham to follow a party line. He became ill, and played no part in the 1836 session, but resumed his seat in the House of Lords in 1837. There he paid court to the radicals for a while, perhaps hoping to become their leader. Although this ploy failed, Brougham remained an isolated and dangerous figure, always looking for a chance to attack the Whigs.

Against this background, Brougham's activities can be brought into focus. The patent bill and the lectures copyright bill both date, at least in part, from before his breach with Barnes. Both bills are sensible attempts to improve the law in this area. There is

[43] Althorp was chancellor of the exchequer, and responsible for a set of abortive budget proposals concerning the repeal of the newspaper stamp.

more vindictiveness in his efforts to abolish the newspaper stamp, although he had other reasons for promoting such a bill: he would not have avoided a natural opportunity to strengthen his radical credentials, even though he disliked the more extreme elements of the popular press, and intended the SDUK publications to serve as a replacement. Although Brougham had no hope of a cabinet seat, his influence was still extraordinary, and he retained the capability to embarrass the government.[44] In relation to the copyright question, it is therefore important to consider whether his reaction seems to be of a piece with his earlier position in this field, or whether it bears the marks of his political struggles.

One final piece of background material reveals that even as early as 1831 Brougham had been considering the ways in which literature could be encouraged by the government, and had written to ask Southey's opinion on the matter.[45] An astonished and suspicious Southey proposed an academy, with salaries for thirty-five members, although his strongest plea was for changes to the law of copyright. Southey was under no illusions that his suggestions would be implemented, but perhaps Brougham took note of Southey's discomfiture with the existing system. Their exchange may even have sparked Brougham's own plans for copyright reform, although these did not emerge in public until well after Talfourd's scheme had been aired.

Brougham had no opportunity to debate the early copyright bills, since none of them passed the House of Commons until 1842. However, in the speech introducing his rival plan in the House of Lords in 1838, he described Talfourd's bill as 'liable to very great objections'.[46] His own bill was modelled closely on his 1835 Patent Act: authors, or their assignees, were to be able to apply to the Judicial Committee of the Privy Council for an extension of their expiring copyrights. Citing the satisfactory model provided by the success of the system in the patent field as evidential support, Brougham argued that his scheme would do greater justice to authors without sacrificing the interests of the public.[47] Brougham also claimed to have the approbation of many

[44] Notably over Durham's handling of Lower Canada.

[45] See below, p. 157.

[46] *Hansard, Parliamentary debates* (3rd series), xliv, 701–2 (27 July 1838).

[47] Not everybody thought the model successful: Greville complained that 'Since this Patent Bill we have got very noisy between percussion guns and piano-

individuals of the legal profession, and of some judges: the attorney-general had proposed a similar solution during the second reading of Talfourd's 1838 bill. Even so, Brougham's plan was not adopted, and the bill did not proceed any further.

This was not the end of Brougham's involvement in the copyright question, however; in 1842 he gave a long and prepared speech in the House of Lords when Mahon's copyright bill reached the committee stage.[48] Mahon had done his best to neutralise Brougham by sending him an early printed copy of the bill, but his efforts had failed.[49] Fortunately for the bill, Brougham's influence and persuasiveness were less effective than in previous times, and there were no significant alterations. Brougham must have known that he had no chance of overturning the hard-won compromise that the 1842 copyright bill represented, in spite of his high-minded protestations that he was party to no bargain. Of course the lord chancellor's irritation would not have troubled him in the least, and might even have given him a certain satisfaction, but this would seem an insufficient reason for action.[50]

It is only possible to speculate, but perhaps Brougham's outburst was provoked by the fact that the compromise bore Macaulay's stamp. Although Brougham had engineered Macaulay's entry into politics, they had later become enemies, largely due to Brougham's jealousy of his younger rival's success. Macaulay's intervention in the copyright debate had been hailed as masterly by senior parliamentary figures: he was regarded as an important statesman. The sidelined Brougham may have found the opportunity to take a swipe at Macaulay quite irresistible. Whatever Brougham's reasons, it is undeniable that Macaulay's solution formed the basis of the new Act, and that his contribution was therefore far more significant.

fortes': Charles Cavendish Fulke Greville, *The Greville memoirs, 1814–60*, 8 vols. (1938), eds. Lytton Strachey and Roger Fulford, II, pp. 421–2 (November 1833).

48 *Hansard, Parliamentary debates* (3rd series), lxiii, 787 – much to the annoyance of the lord chancellor, Lord Lyndhurst, who had introduced it.

49 Mahon to Brougham, 15 March 1842, University College London, Brougham papers, ms 6361, quoted by James J. Barnes, *Authors, publishers and politicians: the quest for an Anglo-American copyright agreement, 1815–54* (1974), p. 122.

50 Brougham and Lyndhurst were old friends, in fact, and on good terms: they had often been colleagues in intrigue.

MACAULAY

There are conflicting views of Macaulay's involvement in the copyright question. His own was that it was a triumphant success, as he explained to Macvey Napier, editor of the *Edinburgh Review*:

> We had a field-day in the House of Commons yesterday. The question was one of the very few on which we do not agree – the Copy right bill. I succeeded in modifying Mahon's plan to a great extent; and I really hope that you will be of opinion that what I proposed is a far greater boon to literature than his measure would have been. . .It is lucky that both Talfourd and Warburton are out of the way.[51]

Talfourd himself was less sure, as Trevelyan's account suggests: 'Talfourd, in the bitterness of his soul, exclaimed that Literature's own familiar friend, in whom she trusted, and who had eaten of her bread, had lifted up his heel against her.'[52] Wordsworth wrote to Talfourd asking if he should write 'in refutation of that trash advanced by Macauley [*sic*]'. Their reaction was understandable. Macaulay had been in India during the initial struggles with the bill. His intervention was unexpected and highly individual, following none of the previously adopted positions, yet it was effective. It is therefore important to consider the reasons which led Macaulay to adopt the stance he did.

As a popular writer, Macaulay had an obvious interest in the copyright question. He had, like all successful authors, been the subject of extensive plagiarism, mostly in America.[53] Macaulay was apparently particularly galled when works not his own were attributed to him, but his reaction seems in general to have been one of resignation. It seems unlikely that self-interest did much to shape his views.

Nor did he particularly favour the claims of the individual literary figures expected to benefit from the bill. Although he

[51] Macaulay, *The letters of Thomas Babington, Baron Macaulay*, ed. Thomas Pinney (Cambridge, 1974–81), IV, p. 25 (7 April 1842). It is commonly assumed that Talfourd was defeated in the 1841 election, but he did not fight it, fearing the expense. Warburton was returned for Bridport in 1841, but accepted the Chiltern Hundreds following his opponent's presentation of an election petition on grounds of bribery.

[52] Sir George O. Trevelyan, *The life and letters of Lord Macaulay*, 2 vols. (1876), II, p. 134.

[53] Trevelyan details various plagiarisms; ibid., II, pp. 110, 124. For an example of Macaulay's comparative nonchalance see ibid., II, pp. 34–5n.

admired Scott's work he was highly critical of his character, 'perpetually sacrificing the perfection of his compositions and the durability of his fame to his eagerness for money'.[54] He had similarly harsh words for Southey,[55] and is said to have been known as an 'inveterate enemy' of Wordsworth's.[56] Although he enjoyed some 'works of the imagination', even so partial a judge as Trevelyan felt obliged to note the 'wilfulness of his literary conservatism'.[57] However, he was concerned about the remuneration of writers, and had made exceptional efforts to support Leigh Hunt, for instance. As might have been expected, Macaulay was on friendly terms with several of the sponsors of the copyright bill: he corresponded with Spring Rice even during his time in India, and he knew Lord Mahon very well. Talfourd himself sent Macaulay a present of a book, probably a copy of *Ion*, in July 1838: the letter of thanks survives.[58] It is not inconceivable that they might have discussed the copyright issue, although there is nothing to indicate that they did.

Given the extraordinary impact that Macaulay's views were to have, all this seems rather circumstantial evidence of his likely position. Trevelyan's account of the reception of the 1842 speech suggests that a point of principle was decided:

When [Macaulay] resumed his seat, Sir Robert Peel walked across the floor, and assured him that the last twenty minutes had radically altered his own views on the law of copyright. One member after another confessed to an entire change of mind; and, on a question which had nothing to do with party, each change of mind brought a vote with it. The bill was remodelled on the principle of calculating the duration of

[54] Macaulay, *Letters*, III, p. 246 (June 1838).

[55] Trevelyan, *Macaulay*, II, p. 462, quoting from Macaulay's journal: '[Southey] was arrogant beyond any man in literary history; for his self-conceit was proof against the severest admonitions. The utter failure of one of his books only confirmed him in his opinion of its excellence . . . He says that Thalaba is equal or superior to the Orlando Furioso, and that it is the greatest poem that has appeared during ages; – and this over and over again, when nobody would read it, and when the copies were heaped up in the booksellers' garrets. His History of Brazil is to be immortal, – to be a mine of wealth to his family under an improved system of copyright. His Peninsular War, of which I never could get through the first volume, is to live for ever.'

[56] Clive states that Macaulay was 'hostile to W's attempt to erect a metaphysical system on the basis of natural objects and ordinary men and women' whereas Macaulay was 'self-consciously urban and common-sensical': John Clive, *Thomas Babington Macaulay: the shaping of the historian* (1973), p. 79.

[57] Trevelyan, *Macaulay*, II, p. 464.

[58] Macaulay, *Letters*, III, p. 249 (9 July 1838).

copyright from the date of publication, and the term of forty-two years was adopted by a large majority.[59]

This is not strictly true, since it was Peel's modification of Macaulay's proposal that was ultimately adopted, and this had a post-mortem element. Nevertheless, Macaulay's comments evidently had a startling effect.

Harriet Martineau, who had petitioned for Talfourd's bill, found the 1841 speech almost inexplicable:

As for the riddle how an able literary man could utter such a speech, and venture to offer it to the House, the answer given at the time was that there must be reasons behind – some cause which could not be alleged – for such a man exposing himself in a speech unsound in its whole argument, and for the House acting upon it. The reason most commonly supposed was that the bill before the House was badly drawn, and could not have been worked; if so, it might have been better to have pointed this out'.[60]

It does seem important to respond to this surprise: Macaulay's comments had transformed the copyright bill, although he had not been in the least involved in the years of debate. How could he have succeeded in uniting the House, when the best efforts of the greatest literary figures in the country had achieved so little?

Some clues can be found in the speeches themselves. Macaulay's analysis in his 1841 speech draws freely on the language of free trade, although the apparent orthodoxy is heavily overlaid with his own value judgments:

It is desirable that we have a supply of good books: we cannot have such a supply unless men of letters are liberally remunerated; and the least objectionable way of remunerating them is by copyright. You cannot depend for literary instruction and amusement on the leisure of men occupied in the pursuits of active life. Such men may occasionally produce works of great merit. But you must not look to such men for works which require deep meditation or long research. Works of that kind you can expect only from persons who make literature the business of their lives. Of these few will be found among the rich and noble. The rich and noble are not impelled to intellectual exertion by necessity. They are impelled to intellectual exertion by the desire of distinguishing themselves, or by the desire of benefiting the community. But it is generally within these walls that they seek to serve their fellow creatures . . . It is then on men whose profession is literature, and whose private means are

[59] Trevelyan, *Macaulay*, II, p. 135.
[60] Harriet Martineau, *A history of the thirty years' peace* (1878), p. 196.

not ample, that you must rely for a supply of valuable books. Such men must be remunerated for their literary labour.[61]

Much of this material is drawn straight from Macaulay's own experience. His father, Zachary, was one of the Clapham 'saints'. Although his ship-owning and trading business had prospered initially, poor management led to its decline. By the time Macaulay left Cambridge in 1823 he was already contributing to his father's business, and was well aware that he would have to provide for himself financially. He had some writing experience behind him, courtesy of two journals published by Charles Knight, the *Etonian* and *Knight's Quarterly*. Although a career as a lawyer was planned, his essay on Milton in the *Edinburgh Review* brought him instant literary success. However, it was Macaulay's Cambridge reputation as a public speaker which first brought him to Brougham's attention, and thus led indirectly to his entry into politics. Brougham had recommended Macaulay to Lord Lyndhurst, the Tory lord chancellor, but it was Lord Lansdowne, a moderate Whig, who was sufficiently impressed by Macaulay's *Edinburgh Review* articles on utilitarianism to offer him one of the pocket boroughs under his control. Brougham's jealousy seems to have been roused by this dual literary and political success: he never willingly acknowledged Macaulay again.

Macaulay became member for Calne in 1830, in the midst of the reform crisis. His own reputation as a Parliamentary orator stemmed from the part he took in the Reform Bill debates. His speeches were always carefully researched in advance (though not written), and were known for their oratorical splendour as well as their content. Macaulay was moderately pro-reform, regarding it as the way to safeguard the country against revolution and radicalism. When the Reform Bill finally passed, Macaulay found himself the subject of extraordinary social attentions. Gladstone's description is of 'adulation and idolatry, and as perhaps the high circles of London never before or since have lavished on a man whose claims lay only in himself, and not in his desert, rank or his possessions'.[62] By the end of 1832 he was the secretary of the Board of Control for India, and the following year he was offered

61 *Hansard, Parliamentary debates* (3rd series), lvi, 346 (5 February 1840).
62 William E. Gladstone, *Gleanings from past years* (1879), II, p. 268.

a place as 'law member' on the Supreme Council – the supreme executive authority in British India, and also a law-making body.

Just as Lord Lansdowne had been impressed by Macaulay's credentials, so too was James Mill, at this time assistant examiner to the East India Company; it was Mill who recommended that Macaulay should be given the Indian post, and who provided much of the vision of what needed to be done. The existing legal structure consisted of three sets of 'regulations' made by the governors-in-council of the three presidencies of Madras, Bombay and Bengal: the task was to replace this with a uniform legal code. Macaulay had no executive role on the council: his sole function was to assist in the preparation of laws by being the person thoroughly versed in the philosophy of man and government that Mill had considered so desirable. Through a combination of circumstances, Macaulay was left to discharge extensive parts of this task, such as the drafting of the Indian Penal Code, virtually single-handed. Other notable contributions included his support for the Press Act of 1835, which formally instituted freedom of the press in India, and his famous 'Education Minute'.[63] It is therefore unsurprising that, on his return to England, he felt himself well able to approach the copyright question with the eye of a practical and experienced legislator.

This approach is much in evidence in the 1841 speech. Macaulay took it as given that literary men 'must be remunerated', the two possible methods being patronage and copyright. Patronage was rejected, particularly if a formalised government system: 'I can conceive no system more fatal to the integrity and independence of literary men than one under which they should be taught to look for their daily bread to the favour of ministers and nobles.' Macaulay was known for his integrity and independence, but the feeling that patronage was an outmoded and undignified method of encouraging literature was becoming more generally accepted. In part this acknowledged the rise of the profession of authorship: the world of letters was no longer occupied exclusively by gentlemen, or at least by those writing for

[63] In 1834 there was considerable controversy concerning the future of Indian education, in particular the language(s) to be used. There were two factions, Anglicist and Orientalist. Macaulay's *Minute on Indian education* (2 February 1835) took an Anglicist position, and this prevailed. For more, see Clive, *Macaulay*, pp. 342–99.

gentlemen. But, in addition, the market itself had changed so dramatically that patronage, whether by individuals, publishers or government, was inevitably of much less significance than before. The huge growth in the reading public had resulted in a market driven by consumers, and Macaulay was attempting – in best Benthamite fashion – to apply those free-trade principles in a legislative environment.

In Macaulay's assessment of the 'inconvenience' of copyright, political economy doctrines were applied explicitly: 'I believe . . . that I may safely take it for granted that the effect of monopoly generally is to make articles scarce, to make them dear, and to make them bad.' Passing references to the notorious East India Company monopolies drove the point home. He saw no difference between copyright and other privileges, so that a monopoly of books would produce results equivalent to those produced by the East India Company's monopoly of tea. This terminology was important: Macaulay used 'copyright' and 'monopoly' as equivalents, whereas Talfourd and his supporters had made a consistent effort to talk about 'literary property'.[64] Monopolies of commodities were regarded with great disfavour by the public, and Peel admitted to Wordsworth that he was afraid of being charged with supporting a 'monopoly' if he favoured the copyright bill.

Macaulay believed that the evil effects of a monopoly were in direct proportion to its length, unlike its benefits. He asserted that any previous extension of the copyright term would have resulted in an astronomical selling price for contemporary readers: the additional 'taxation' on the public would, he argued, have amounted to £20,000 for Johnson's *Dictionary* alone. This was the language of a skilled debater who had warmed to his theme. Macaulay was similarly powerful when dealing with the danger that works might be suppressed, taking as his example the Wesleyan Methodists. If the copyright of their works were to fall

[64] Notably Disraeli, who addressed this confusion explicitly: 'there was no good evidence to show that authors themselves enjoyed anything like a monopoly. There was, however, a monopoly, not in favour of authors, but a monopoly in favour of the booksellers. It was a monopoly enjoyed by those who did not labour for it, and which has all the odious features of other monopolies. By the old system that monopoly was called into existence, and he asked the House now to convert that monopoly into a property for authors': *Hansard, Parliamentary debates* (3rd series), xlii, 555 (25 April 1838).

into the hands of one who found their message repugnant, public access to them might be denied:

such a grievance would be enough to shake the foundations of Government. Let Gentlemen who are attached to the Church reflect a moment what their feelings would be if the Book of Common Prayer were run up to five or ten guineas. And let them determine whether they will pass a law under which it is possible, under which it is probable, that so intolerable wrong may be done to some sect consisting perhaps of half a million people.

This is an extraordinary assertion, but would have touched many raw nerves. It also recalls the printing monopolies under Elizabeth and Mary. The scenario painted can scarcely be termed 'probable', although the rhetorical effect was devastating, setting up Macaulay's conclusion:

At present the holder of copyright has the public feeling on his side. Those who invade copyright are regarded as knaves who take the bread out of the mouths of deserving men. . .Pass this law: and that feeling is at an end. Men of a character very different from the present race of piratical booksellers will soon infringe this intolerable monopoly . . . the whole nation will be in the plot.[65]

Macaulay could not see any possibility of reaching a compromise which would satisfy both Talfourd and himself, and moved that the bill be deferred. Inglis and Talfourd protested in vain that all Macaulay's objections applied equally to the existing twenty-eight-year term, and even to all property: the damage was irreparable. In a very thin House, Talfourd narrowly lost the division by forty-five votes to thirty-eight.

The following year Macaulay spoke against Mahon's proposals, this time arguing that they gave too short a period of protection.[66] He also argued that emphasis on the life element gave too great a role to chance, favouring juvenilia with an excessively long term: he regarded it as axiomatic that an author's later works would be superior to earlier ones, and buttressed his argument with dozens of examples. He made the undeniable point that, under Mahon's plan of life plus twenty-five years, any works written in the last three years of an author's life would gain nothing over the existing twenty-eight-year term. He proposed a life term, with a minimum

[65] *Hansard, Parliamentary debates* (3rd series), lvi, 350–7.
[66] *Hansard, Parliamentary debates* (3rd series) lxi, 1363–97.

of forty-two years, which could be enforced by the author's family if the author were to die before this.

After a good deal of argument, Peel suggested that an author's family should always be provided for, by a seven-year term after the author's death. Macaulay resisted this strenuously, and was rebuked for his obduracy by Lord John Russell. Russell admitted to being less convinced of Macaulay's arguments than Macaulay himself, and was attracted by the simplicity and justice of the life-plus suggestion. Macaulay's forty-two-year amendment to Mahon's plan was carried 68:56; he insisted on dividing the House again on Peel's parallel life plus seven years term, which was adopted by a very significant majority.

Under such circumstances, Trevelyan's claim for Macaulay, that he had 'framed according to his mind a Statute which may fairly be described as the charter of his craft', does not survive detailed scrutiny.[67] However, Macaulay certainly bore the responsibility for the demise of the bill in 1841. Even after close examination, his contribution to the copyright question resists categorisation: it was a highly individual response, open to different appraisals.[68] Among authors, Wordsworth, for one, found Macaulay's stance hard to forgive. Nevertheless, Macaulay's model, regardless of the shallowness of its foundations, did form the basis of the 1842 Act.

Important and influential though these prominent parliamentary figures were, their visions of copyright were not backed by the kind of popular support which the radical model commanded. It is important to see this parliamentary foreground against the extraordinary background of popular protest which was generated first by the printing trades and later more generally.

[67] Trevelyan, *Macaulay*, II, p. 136.

[68] Birrell condemns Macaulay's position as 'highly irrational': 'in no possible event should copyright be made to depend on the date of first publication, since to do so is to make an author's intellectual output become common property in driblets, and to throw open to the printers the early and uncorrected editions at a time when the later and corrected ones are still protected': Augustine Birrell, *Seven lectures on the law and history of copyright in books* (1899), p. 146.

4

CRITICS IN THE BOOK TRADE I: PRINT WORKERS AND THEIR ALLIES

Early petitions against Talfourd's bill came almost entirely from members of the printing trades, indicating that modifications to copyright were regarded as a threat to trade interests. Yet most, although not all, were presented by radical MPs, suggesting a wider political framework. In order to position the copyright agitation in its correct context, it is necessary to understand the structures which governed these trades in the 1830s, and also the effect that these had on petitioning practice.

Printers were an important group. In relation to the specific issue of copyright, the volume and nature of their petitions was such as to make a real impact. However, it should be remembered that printers no longer enjoyed the state-supported power of the sixteenth and seventeenth centuries. They now worked as paid agents of the publishers, who had come to wield the real economic power in this period.[1] As will be seen in the next chapter, the once feared and revered booksellers of Paternoster Row and the Chapter Coffee House, who had been able to divide up the trade between them, found their gentlemen's agreements ignored by newcomers anxious to exploit the rapidly expanding market for books of all sorts: a new matrix of power was forming.

Nevertheless, the strength and coordination of print trade organisations ensured that they were able to exert considerable and noisy pressure on parliament during the years of copyright debate. They were, however, indebted to the radical MPs, at the very least for the actual presentation of their petitions. What has not been recognised previously is that a significant number of the

[1] Feather notes of this period that 'except for the two universities, no major publisher was his own printer': John Feather, *A history of British publishing* (1988), p. 132.

later petitions were generated and gathered by purely radical machinery, skilfully crafted during decades of agitation for mobilising protests of precisely this type. As the dispute continued, although many sections of the book trade were reconciled to Talfourd's modified plans, radical activists continued to show unrelenting hostility to copyright. In 1837, however, copyright was still a matter for the printing trades alone.

PRINTERS

Labour policy in the sixteenth- and seventeenth-century printing trades was governed by the Stationers' Company, which had the power to control the practices of both master printers and journeymen. Master printers had to have the freedom of the Company, which was not lightly granted. In addition, Star Chamber decrees had imposed legal limitations on the number of master printers, and their presses, reinforcing this tight control. Although these were not enforced after 1641, and the Licensing Act of 1662 finally lapsed in 1695, regulations in the City of London reserved most trading to freemen of the city. Foreigners, outsiders, and those from the provinces thus found trade difficult, although the rules were gradually relaxed, and then abolished in 1856. According to trade directories, the number of master printers rose from 35 in 1668 (under the Licensing Act), to 125 in 1785, 216 in 1808, and stabilised at around 300 in 1825–50.[2] These rises obviously reflect the easing of trading conditions, particularly as the demand for printing increased after Waterloo, although the period of relative stability which followed may have been in part a function of the instability of the economic climate.

Master printers

An association of master printers was active in 1816, managing to impose a reduction in wages on compositors and pressmen, justified on the ground of adverse trade conditions. This activity was not maintained, however. In 1836 another Association of Master Printers met at Stationers' Hall, and passed seventeen

[2] Ellic Howe (ed.), *The London compositor* (1947), pp. 30–43.

resolutions defining their activities.[3] By the end of 1837 the Masters' Association had nearly eighty members.[4] This figure is confirmed by the evidence of the petitions. The 'Master Printers of the Metropolis' submitted two petitions, in 1838 and 1840. The earlier has ninety-four signatures, suggesting strongly that it is the same organisation.[5]

The 1840 petition has sixty-eight signatures, and offered 'to produce before a committee of your honourable House, abundant evidence to show the fallacy of the arguments urged in support of the measure, and the evils that must inevitably result from an extension of the existing period of Copyright'.[6] The master printers put several arguments against the bill. They feared the effect on their trade and that of the 'numerous artificers whom [the petitioners'] capital calls into action'. Whilst the 1838 petitions come from printing trades and focus on these only, this new broadening of the dispute to include other traders is characteristic of the 1840 campaign. The wording is confident, almost aggressive in places: the bill as it stands could only benefit the booksellers, 'who, in all time, have been and ever must be almost the sole proprietors of Copyright'. Concern for the public was expressed, particularly the likely impediment to the circulation of cheap books, which would 'deprive the humbler classes of Her Majesty's subjects of the enjoyment of those intellectual treasures which the munificence of the higher classes daily calls into existence'. The lack of petitions in support of the measure received unfavourable comment, as did the petitioners who had supported the changes: few of the latter 'have produced any work of real utility and lasting benefit to the world, or for which the law does not afford a sufficient protection'. Both the tone of the petition and the request for a committee are unusual: they are more characteristic of letters to the press or parliamentary speeches.[7]

[3] Those present: George Woodfall (chairman); Walter M'Dowall (secretary); the committee – Spottiswoode, L. G. Hansard, J. B. Nichols, Clowes, Taylor, Tyler, Clay, Gilbert, Balne, M'Intosh, Baldwin, J. L. Cox.

[4] Fourth Annual Report of the LUC, for 1837, published 1838. Ellic Howe and Harold E. Waite, *The London Society of Compositors* (1948), p. 101.

[5] 4,814, presented 25 April 1838.

[6] 2,050, presented 24 February 24 1840, App. 154.

[7] One previous 1838 petition from compositors had called for a committee of inquiry: see below, p. 78 (petition 4,633). It is conceivable that the master printers' 1838 petition, which remained unprinted, also called for this.

Journeymen

The Stationers' Company, like most guilds, included masters, journeymen and apprentices – although power was concentrated in the hands of the few. This fact, combined with the attempt to restrict the number of master printers, resulted in an increasing gulf between the employers and the employed. A class of permanent journeymen began to emerge, who could not hope to progress further, but nevertheless were highly skilled workers. Musson describes them thus: 'Journeymen printers. . .were steeped in gild [*sic*] tradition, men as a rule of superior education and almost aristocratic exclusiveness, better trained and better paid than the mass of wage-earners.'[8]

It is therefore not surprising that these men were able organise themselves into groups, which were among the first to use their collective strength to further their particular interests: combination was natural for a guildsman. During the seventeenth century these organisations remained subordinate to the Stationers' Company, which looked to the interests of all of its members. The power of the Company waned in the eighteenth century, leaving the journeymen less restricted, but also less protected. Once left to fend for themselves outside the fold of the Stationers' Company, it is understandable that the objectives of the journeymen were often different from those of the employers: evidence of this can be found in the perennial disputes about the number of apprentices, or wages and conditions. And natural though combination may have been, it was regarded with deep hostility by the state.

Another aspect of the trade's organisation needs to be considered, namely the separation of the roles of compositors and pressmen. Until at least 1850 the printer's locality would determine whether his skills were broad or specialised: '[i]n the provinces . . . there was as yet no differentation between compositors and pressmen: an apprentice was taught to be a printer, to work at both case and press, whereas in the more highly developed metropolitan trade specialization developed and compositors, pressmen, and machinemen became distinct, each with their own trade society'.[9] The process of separation was hastened by the

[8] Albert E. Musson, *The Typographical Association* (1954), p. 1.
[9] Ibid., p. 18. Compositors set up the type, checked the proofs, and distributed the

unequal advances in the technologies of press and case work. Machines began to replace pressmen, whereas the technical difficulties inherent in mechanical typesetting were less easily overcome, leaving the compositor in a powerful position for longer.[10] Understandably, this distinction was reflected in the trade organisations, particularly in London.

The 1838 petitions against Talfourd's bills mirror this pattern of separation of the two roles. In London, petitions almost invariably come from 'compositors, pressmen and others'. Petitions from other towns are more likely to use the generic descriptions, 'letterpress printers' or 'printers', although in big towns the division between compositor and pressmen may be noted. However, looking ahead, there are striking changes in the pattern of petitioning. In 1838 the copyright bill was, for petitioning purposes, exclusively a printing trade matter.[11] By 1840 it had become a dispute of much more general concern, and was less closely tied to traditional printing trade organisations.

Compositors

An indication of the numbers of compositors in London is available in the Annual Reports of the London Union of Compositors. In 1834 about 1,700 names were on the union's books, rising to about 1,900 in 1839 (1,343 men, 534 boys).[12] Howe suggests that in 1839 the average office would have as compositors fourteen men and five boys. When pressmen, machine-room, warehouse and clerical staff were included, each office might employ from 30 to 100 people.[13] The statistics do not include Spottiswoode & Co., Her Majesty's Printers, which was regarded as an 'unfair' house and was thus closed to union members: Spottiswoode's had 121 compositors and fifty-five apprentices.

These numbers are broadly consistent with the evidence of the

type back into the cases at the end. Pressmen were concerned only with the printing process – the press itself.

10 As well as iron and steam presses, the paper-making machine was helping to provide cheap and plentiful supplies of paper for the presses.

11 Of the 114 petitions in 1838, there are only two exceptions to this: 4,787 from the British Medical Association and 5,953 from Dr Birkbeck. Both have links with the supporters of cheap print: see below, pp. 91–4.

12 The London census records 3,500 'printers' in 1831, 5,500 in 1841.

13 These figures are presumably based on information recorded in the LUC Annual Report for 1839: Musson, *Typographical Association*, p. 18, confirms them.

petitions. The numbers of signatures from an individual office varied enormously, from less than a dozen, to over 150 from Clowes' enormous steam-powered house, with about thirty as an average. The Census Abstract of 1831 gave the numbers of those employed in the printing trade (aged over twenty) as 9,000 in the United Kingdom, of which 4,000 were in London. Even allowing for the likely increase by 1838, the fact that opponents of the copyright bill could collect almost 8,000 signatures from the printing trade suggests both significant agreement and significant coordination.[14]

As has been indicated, some of the petitions came from individual offices, which would have formed a natural unit of organisation. There would perhaps have been about 325 firms in London at this time, possibly slightly more. Over fifty London houses sent petitions in 1838. This was a large number, given that many print workers would have had the opportunity to sign elsewhere, at public or trade meetings. The big houses were well represented: for instance, there are petitions from the houses of virtually all of the 1836 committee of master printers. There were eighty signatures on petitions from Spottiswoode & Co., so about half of even a non-union house was able to petition.

The only 1838 petition from a London house to be printed came from one of the larger offices, Bradbury and Evans.[15] It was probably selected because of this, and also because it was the very first petition to be presented against the copyright bill. It was quite short and did not attempt detailed argument, simply expressing the belief that the copyright bill would threaten the progress of literature and of trade. It foreshadowed the master printers' petition by calling for a committee of inquiry, although in much less trenchant tones than they were to use.

During 1838 petitions also arrived from most of the other centres of the book trade, often with large numbers of signatures: for instance, 95 from Carlisle, 117 from Cambridge, 120 from Manchester, 130 from Leeds, 146 from Oxford, 232 from Dublin, 242 from Liverpool, 309 from Glasgow and 727 from Edinburgh. The Carlisle petition was the only one of these to be printed.[16] It

[14] Although not all signatories would necessarily have been over twenty.
[15] 4495, presented 4 April 1838, App. 365.
[16] 4629, presented 9 April 1838, App. 389.

argued that authors were already amply rewarded, and that the payment of an equitable reward entitled the public to the property in the book, which should be widely circulated 'in order that society at large may be improved by the diffusion of that information which it contains'. There was particular concern that the proposed law would threaten compilations of extracts of copyright works.

Another group of petitions came from those working on newspapers, although not from any of the really significant London daily papers. Only a handful of papers were involved, from London and elsewhere, and there seems to be little pattern to their efforts.[17] This may well have been due to the fact that Talfourd's bill did not address newspaper copyright, but it may also reflect the division between newspaper and book work, at least in London, and a potential lack of solidarity. Newspaper compositors had separated from book hands by 1793, and negotiated different rates and terms – which became the News Scale in 1820. Shortly after this the News Society was formed, which remained independent until 1856, despite the invitation to amalgamate with the new London Union of Compositors in 1833, and the subsequent formation of a rival News Society.

In the petitions so far discussed, the journeyman printer was classified by printing office or by locality. An interesting exception was the petition from the 'Compositors, Pressmen and others engaged in the Printing Profession, agreed to at a public meeting held at the Mechanics' Institution, Southampton Buildings, Holborn'.[18] It was signed on behalf of the meeting by the chairman, James Darkin, so only his signature was counted.[19] There was no indication of the numbers present at the meeting, nor of their specific trades. The petition itself focused on the government's duty 'to provide for the extension of knowledge'. It argued that a longer copyright term would make books scarce and dear, thus 'shutting up the channels by which knowledge is conveyed to the great mass of people'. The potential threat to the

[17] *Stirling Observer* (4,630), *Morning Advertiser* (4,642), *Guardian*, Lancaster (4,751), *Weekly Dispatch* (4,755), *Morning Herald* (4,771), and 'the newspaper offices, Bristol' (4,779). None was printed.

[18] 4781, presented 25 April 1838, App. 405.

[19] Two days earlier Darkin had chaired a similar meeting of compositors, which resulted in petition 4,633 (discussed below).

printing trades was noted, although there was no perceived threat to a broader range of trades. Authors' deserts were weighed against those of printers and found wanting, for 'the profits derived from a book depend not on the art of writing, but on the art of printing'. It was therefore 'unjust' that authors should enjoy exclusive laws at the expense of a profession 'to which they are indebted for the rank they hold, and the wealth they possess'.

In the petitions as a whole, the distinctions between the different types of printing work were not made particularly sharply: a common designation for petitioners is 'compositors, pressmen and others connected with the profession'. There is one isolated instance of pressmen petitioning as such, perhaps reflecting the weakening of their role in the face of the new machinery. However, compositors did petition as a trade group, and in large numbers. Without the strength of the trade associations, the task of assembling these petitions based on categories of worker would have been much more difficult.

Most London compositors were paid for piecework according to the London scale of prices. An initial agreement in 1785 had been consolidated into a scale in 1805. Although it was revised and added to, it prevailed until the 1890s, including twenty-two of the original twenty-seven paragraphs. It should be noted that the Stationers' Company was not involved in these negotiations, and that the old guild machinery for settling disputes was no longer being used.[20] The new scale was strictly observed by both master printers and compositors, which made for good relations between them. Trade concerns included the cheap rates charged by country printers, and mechanical typesetting, although the latter was only used experimentally in London before the 1890s.[21] Beneficial changes included the 1836 reduction in the newspaper stamp, and the introduction of the penny post in 1840.

The compositors' first formal union, the Union Society, was founded in 1801 to protect the interests of journeymen – which were no longer effectively protected by the Stationers' Company. It negotiated very successfully with the employers' committee over the 1805 scale of prices. The pressmen did not come to terms

[20] Howe and Waite, *London Society of Compositors*, p. 27.

[21] *The Times* used a Kastenbein machine from 1872, but was not a union house, so this had little influence.

so easily. Following agreement on a new scale in 1810, the Union Society was dissolved. However, a reduction was imposed on both pressmen and compositors in 1816 because of 'state of Trade' following the Napoleonic Wars. This resulted in the formation of the London Trade Society of Compositors, although too late to resist the reductions. In 1826 the rival London General Trade Society of Compositors was founded.

In 1832 the two societies created a body called the Union Committee of the London Trade Societies of Compositors. Both societies had an equal number of representatives, and the Committee was stated to be one 'of final appeal and consultation, and not an executive body'. This high level of cooperation resulted in the 'Green Book' – the exegesis of the 1810 scale – which was published in 1836. The Union Committee also considered other matters, such as the problems of charging caused by unstamped periodicals, and plans for amalgamation of the two Unions and the News Society.[22] The London Union of Compositors (LUC) was the result, although the News Society could not agree terms and did not join. Provincial societies also began to emerge: the Northern Union was founded in 1830, from an amalgam of local associations in the midlands and the north, and a Western Union was formed in 1839.

Membership of the LUC was almost 1,600 at the end of its first quarter (July 1834), and reached a high of about 1,900 in 1836. Then the union began to face real difficulties in the poor economic conditions. By 1838 there was much unemployment, with men unable to pay their subscriptions:[23] receipts fell sharply, and in 1843 expenses exceeded subscriptions. In 1845 (with membership down to 600) the LUC was forced to recommend affiliation to the National Typographical Association (NTA), a new amalgamation of all the printing trade unions in the United Kingdom.

The NTA was concerned with the provincial printing industry, which was very different from the London trade. Offices were

[22] Howe indicates that the impetus for this was a fear of an employers' union: the first association of master printers had been inactive after 1816, but another was formed in 1836.

[23] Conditions were evidently very serious. Unemployment caused such distress that a Relief Committee was formed in the autumn of 1838, and again in 1839. This timing is very significant for the purposes of Talfourd's bill – perceived threats to the trade would have been particularly acutely resented.

smaller, rates were less tightly controlled and there was much less opportunity for cohesion or cooperation. It does seem remarkable that any union could be formed over such a wide area. The larger provincial towns did support organised unions, although it was an uphill battle to maintain wage rates and apprenticeship regulations.[24] By the beginning of the nineteenth century the Stationers' Company no longer provided adequate protection, nor were there any legal restrictions on the numbers of masters. It was therefore relatively easy for a journeyman to set up on his own account in a tiny country office, without concerning himself about undercutting or the use of many apprentices.

However, there were links between the existing societies, which were cemented by the tramp-relief system,[25] and which were called upon during serious disputes or times of hardship. This led to the establishment of the Northern Typographical Union in 1830, provoked by frustration at the ineffectiveness of individual local societies. It grew quickly, and by 1837 had 783 members.[26] The Scottish Typographical Association and the Irish Typographical Union were founded in 1836. It is at least possible that provincial petitioning against the copyright proposals was organised within the structure of the Northern Union: petitions came from many towns with union branches. Whatever the ambitions of the parent unions, local independence was high, and there was little central control. This makes the response to Talfourd's bill seem the more remarkable.[27]

The four big societies kept in touch by letter, and also at the meetings of the delegates of the northern unions, to which representatives from all independent societies were invited. Proposals for amalgamation were made as early as 1840, but came to nothing. The main problem facing the unions was the heavy cost of tramp relief, both financially and socially. The prolonged trade depression only

[24] The Manchester Society is probably the earliest (possibly 1797), but there were over forty branches of the Northern Union, established in 1830: Musson, *Typographical Association*, p. 25.

[25] A system of financial and other benefits given to unemployed or striking members of typographical societies who wished to leave town in search of employment. See ibid., pp. 26–7.

[26] Membership figures: 1837, 783; 1838, 893; 1839, 942; 1840, 984. This represented perhaps half of provincial compositors: ibid., p. 35.

[27] Equally, towns were obvious places to find presses, and the cooperation which resulted in petitioning by town may have come about some other way.

served to highlight its defects: in such hard times neither the tiny strike allowance nor the inequitable and demoralising tramp-relief system provided sufficient incentive to loyalty to the union. Several plans for reform were floated and rejected. Finally amalgamation was agreed upon, at the 'Printers' Parliament' at Derby, July 1844. The London, Scotland and Irish organisations were all in favour of amalgamation, and the National Typographical Association was born. The Association was not a lasting success. Although its foundation coincided with the end of the trade depression, the Association could not survive the further slump of 1846. After its collapse in 1848, the old local societies were gradually re-established.

With regard to the specific issue of copyright, it is possible to detect trade structures underlying the spread of petitions. At least in London, compositors' independence was often reflected by the separate identification of 'compositors' and 'pressmen' within firms. In addition, there are two petitions from compositors alone. The most important of these was one of the first petitions against the bill, resulting from a general meeting of the trade on 3 April 1838.[28] The familiar themes of trade hardship and public education were at the centre of the petition. Specific reference was made to the 'severe privations from the want of full employment' over 'many years'. The language was less restrained than many petitions; copyright was thought to protect authors enough already, and 'though their emoluments may not be as great as their desires, [they] are, nevertheless, in most cases equal to their deserts'. There were also dark hints that the public would turn to other activities: 'your Petitioners believe that the safety of our social system depends upon an enlarged system of national education and the widest diffusion of useful knowledge'. Like the master printers were to do in 1840, they called for a committee of inquiry.

The petition was signed on behalf of the meeting by the chairman (again James Darkin) so only one signature was counted, unfortunately thus obscuring the number of those in favour. An 1840 petition from London compositors recorded seventy-five signatures, although this is not stated to have been generated by a general trade meeting, at which attendance was likely to have been even higher.[29] Even with this limited material, some tentative

[28] 4,633, presented 11 April 1838, App. 391.
[29] 15,189, presented 20 May 1840.

conclusions about the compositors' trade can still be drawn. The fact that the 1838 trade meeting was called at all suggests an active trade organisation, although there is little evidence to indicate how representative of the profession this meeting was, either in terms of views or in terms of the numbers attending.

Nevertheless, the petitions as a whole show that the individual printing office was the unit of organisation which functioned most effectively in this dispute. It would probably have been easier to collect signatures at this very local level. Compositors may even have provided the main energy behind the campaign, coordinating and collecting the petitions from the various offices. Presumably this context would also have made it possible to include and recruit support from the clerical and unskilled workers in the office, and from those with less vigorous trade defences, such as the pressmen.

Pressmen

Although new printing technology was later to threaten the bargaining power of the pressmen, there is evidence that they were the first in the industry to organise a trade union.[30] The work was highly skilled, and much care was taken as to who was admitted. Pressmen tended to be closely associated with compositors. In 1834 the London Union of Compositors was founded, and this spurred the pressmen into parallel action: the London Union of Pressmen also dates from this time. Pressmen were traditionally organised in small groups known as 'gifts' or 'guilds'. A (much smaller) rival organisation was started for the non-gift men, called the 'Equitable Association of Pressmen'.

There were scales for presswork in 1787 and 1794, revised in 1800. New proposals in 1805 were rejected by the employers, at which the pressmen all gave warning. The master printers, supported by the booksellers, retaliated by stopping printing of all works, and then by taking on extra apprentices. Meetings of 'The Proprietors and Publishers of Reviews, Magazines, and other Periodical Publications', and 'The Booksellers of London and Westminster' expressed solidarity with the printers. The pressmen

[30] Clement J. Bundock, *The story of the National Union of Printing, Bookbinding and Paper Workers* (Oxford, 1959), p. 258.

finally returned to work without securing any concessions. A new scale was agreed in 1810, but revised downwards in 1816.

Presswork was more affected by new technology than composing work.[31] The iron press began to supersede the wooden press from about 1800, and steam-driven printing grew gradually in importance from 1814.[32] At the end of 1826 the pressmen began a campaign against the spread of steam-powered printing machines. Significantly, the compositors refused to help: they felt secure in the knowledge that their job had not been mechanised successfully, and they thus saw steam-printing as good for business. Other trades were less complacent, and a series of meetings followed: a petition was approved proposing a tax on machinery. However, the pressmen could not prevent the introduction of steam: their influence declined significantly. This, too, can be traced, at least tentatively, in the petitions. Where they are separately noted, pressmen are invariably listed after compositors in the categories of those petitioning. Although eighteen of Spottiswoode's (non-union) pressmen signed one petition, this is the only petition to come exclusively from pressmen.[33] There is no other indication of a separate response.

Machinemen

The resistance of the London pressmen to steam printing had little long-term impact on the advance of this technology, but it did incidentally help to create a new class of 'machinemen', 'machine minders', or 'machine managers'. These men were mechanics and others who had never served an apprenticeship to printing. They eventually established their own organisation, in 1839, the London Printing Machine Managers' Trade Society. Provincial printers were likewise opposed to machinery, but had to make provision for it in order to retain control of the press room. 'Machine-minding' or 'managing' tended to be regarded by

[31] 'The compositor of 1850 still had to set every *en* of type by hand and distribute used matter back into the cases as soon as they became empty': Musson, *Typographical Association*, p. 17.

[32] *The Times* used Koenig's steam-driven printing machine from 1814, although the capital expense deterred emulators. In 1835 Clowes assembled the largest plant then known to print the *Penny Magazine*.

[33] 4,770, presented 25 April 1838.

journeymen as beneath their dignity, and some of the largest employers had specialist apprentices for this.

Most machinemen were not within the union: the official policy was that of the Manchester Society, which excluded machinemen from the union unless they had been apprentices. It is therefore unsurprising that there is only one petition from machinemen throughout the copyright dispute.[34] It came from twenty-two machinists of a named London firm, and thus provides no supporting evidence for the existence of an active trade society.

THE DISPUTE SPREADS – JOURNEYMEN 1839–40

The pattern of printers' petitioning changed sharply in 1839 and 1840. 1839 was a year of comparative silence. Bradbury and Evans was one of only two London houses to petition in this year.[35] The other petition came from compositors at Messrs Balne: the likely hindrance to the diffusion of knowledge was stressed even more than the likely hindrance to trade.[36] In this later petition copyright was clearly regarded as an unjustifiable barrier to cheap editions of works, and was seen in the same light as taxes such as the newspaper stamp: 'your Petitioners consider it unjust to place beyond their reach, by severe restrictions, that information which your honourable House have recently agreed, by the reducing of taxes on knowledge, ought to be placed within their reach'. This is evidence that positions the extension of copyright at the heart of the radical agenda, which helps to explain its unexpectedly hostile treatment.

The stream of petitions from journeymen printers resumed in 1840, although they are no longer focused on the individual printing offices: some other method of collecting signatures must have been used. Although there are almost fifty petitions which are recorded as coming from printers, only a handful come from named offices.[37] Furthermore, only two of these offices use the

[34] 15,195, presented 20 May 1840.

[35] 9,085, presented 5 June 1839, 168 signatures, not printed.

[36] 2,567, presented 5 March 1839, App. 238.

[37] 2,048 (Bradbury and Evans), App. 152; 10,568 (Balne); 11,433 (Alfred Sweeting); 15,207 (Clowes); 15,208 (25 Rupert Street); 15,230 (51 Rupert Street); 17,941 (Bible Offices, Shacklewell).

standard 1838 formulation, 'compositors, pressmen, others': apart from these two cases, 'pressmen' are never mentioned. The most common designation is 'Printers of London' – on over a third of these petitions. Compositors, however, maintain their independent presence, at least in London. There are four petitions from 'compositors' (each with at least sixty signatures) and two from 'compositors, printers and others'.

Taking these petitions alone there is little to explain this change, as none has been printed: it might, conceivably, stem merely from a change in practice by the Committee on Public Petitions. However, in the context of the other 1840 petitions, particularly those from London, the printers' petitions seem to reflect the defocusing of the copyright dispute. The 1838 petitions indicate that the copyright bill was perceived as a threat to the printing trades, even if some of the arguments used were based on broader grounds. Objections to copyright came only from the printing trades, and could therefore be channelled along existing lines of trade organisation. By 1840 these wider arguments had begun to dominate the debate.

The themes of monopoly, the general threat to trade, and the diffusion of knowledge, expanded the copyright question until it encompassed issues which Talfourd had never envisaged. These issues were, specifically, issues at the heart of the radical political agenda. This naturally had implications for the organisation of protest. Once copyright was regarded as a tax on knowledge, the mechanisms of radical protest were made available, including that of the popular petition. Since careful use of petitions had allowed radical politicians to claim more parliamentary time than their numbers strictly merited, petitioning had become a common means of expressing the radical point of view. Signatures were collected in their tens of thousands, for all the important issues on the radical agenda.

The expansion of the debate was plainly orchestrated by radical activists both in and out of parliament. It is arguable that this process, the management of protest, is responsible for the changes in the patterns of copyright petitioning in 1840 – at least in London. There are two main indicators of this. Firstly, the blurring of the traditional categories of trade protest already noted: 1840 printers' petitions are not organised by printing offices, nor do they acknowledge the traditional division of specialisms. Secondly, the 1840 petitions are not limited to the printing trades, but cover a wide range of trades and specialisms: copyright had clearly become relevant to more people.

A comparison of the numbers of signatures on the 1838 and 1840 petitions confirms that there is a genuine change in petitioning practice, and not merely a change in the recording conventions of the Committee on Public Petitions. In 1838, approximately fifty printing houses petitioned individually. Often less than twenty signatures were collected, with only a handful exceeding fifty, and only two exceeding 100.[38] Most of the 1840 petitions from 'Printers of London' have over fifty signatures. Either the individual offices are combining, or there is some other mechanism of organisation, which appears to be based on something other than traditional trade divisions.

This phenomenon is apparently confined to London. Petitioning from the provinces in 1840 followed a very similar pattern to that of 1838. Petitioners continued to sign by town. Again, several towns collected over 100 signatures, although the list of towns changed. Some towns collected very similar numbers of signatures, perhaps suggesting a stable trade; Liverpool (242, 258), Dublin (232, 254), Glasgow (309, 278+45). But the massive 727 from Edinburgh is not repeated: in fact there are none from Edinburgh. Inverness, which delivered no petition before, now submitted 268 signatures. The substantial petitions from Cambridge, Manchester, Oxford and Leeds were not repeated, although they were replaced by similar petitions from York, Wigan and Belfast. It is a matter of speculation as to whether this was due to satisfaction or inertia, as none of these petitions was printed.

Nevertheless, within London at least, by 1840 the copyright dispute had overflowed the boundaries of a single-trade dispute, and had reached workers with little or no connection with printing. One petition perhaps provides a clue to the nature of this process: it comes from 'Printers and other Mechanics', and it is possible that signatures were collected via a Mechanics' Institution, or

[38] Bradbury and Evans, and Clowes are the two which exceed 100. Both are among the handful of firms who petitioned individually in 1840. Bradbury and Evans collected 141 signatures in 1838, and 140 in 1840. Clowes dropped from 281 in 1838, to 27+158 in 1840.

similar group.[39] The identification with 'Mechanics' as a group is suggestive of an issue governed not by narrow trade considerations, but by broadening social, and perhaps political, ambitions.

THE PROCESS OF DIFFUSION

The process of diffusion of the copyright question can be retraced in the petitions. Petitioners who were not printers can be divided into those whose trades were associated with printing, and others.

Associated trades

Those whose livelihoods depended heavily on printing were naturally concerned by any potential threat which the copyright bill posed. Some of these groups, such as the bookbinders, the typefounders and the papermakers, had a long history of trade organisation. The Stationers' Company itself included printers, bookbinders, booksellers, stationers, typefounders, mathematical instrument makers, as well as a small number of men carrying out miscellaneous callings. These groups were well represented in the 1838 petitions, which came almost entirely from the printing trades; and their efforts continued in later years. Again it is possible to see a relationship between the vitality of trade groups and petitions, particularly with regard to bookbinders.

Bookbinders

There are records of three lodges of London bookbinders combining in protest at long working hours as early as 1786. Severe prison sentences were imposed, but the hour requested was conceded. Further alterations to hours were negotiated in 1794 and 1806, by what became the United Friendly Society of Journeymen Bookbinders.

In 1833 the issue was not hours, but prices. The Society for the Promotion of Christian Knowledge (SPCK) had put pressure on bookbinders to reduce the price of bibles, and the Glasgow Society of Bookbinders wrote to the London Society to suggest cooperation, although this was refused. Bundock states that at this

[39] 13,905, presented 14 May 1840 (106 signatures).

time there were local organisations in most centres of bookbinding – Edinburgh, Glasgow, Manchester, Birmingham and Bristol, for instance.[40] In 1835 various delegates of local societies met in Manchester, and again in Birmingham, to form 'one consolidated and equitable combination'. Although the important London and Edinburgh groups refused to take part, the result was 'The Bookbinders' Consolidated Relief Fund'.

As far as the copyright issue was concerned, there was a tightly coordinated response from London bookbinders. However, there is no evidence of local groups of bookbinders outside London, at least not petitioning specifically on their own account. In 1838 only three petitions mention bookbinders at all, and one of these[41] merely included them in a list of printing workers from Leicester. The others are much more significant. One was signed by 114 'Master Bookbinders residing in London and Westminster'.[42]

These petitioners considered that the extension would limit their trade and give a monopoly to authors which would be unfairly longer than the expensive patent term. The recent decision to reduce paper duty, 'with a view to the greater consumption of that commodity by an increased circulation of cheap literature', was used as an argument against a longer term: the potential benefit of the reduction would be threatened. They also expressed anxiety about the effect on the public, in terms which mirror much of the material in the newspaper press: 'at a time when the greatest exertions are made to educate and enlighten the population by the diffusion of cheap literature, and to satisfy the thirst which it has excited, it would be most unjust and injurious to society to pass any law which is calculated to perpetuate ignorance and to check the progress of civilisation'. However, unlike the master printers and the compositors, there was no call for a committee of inquiry, and the tone of the petition was more measured.

The other significant petition from bookbinders in 1838 came from the 'Journeymen Bookbinders of London and Westminster'.[43] Unfortunately the Committee on Public Petitions did not think it necessary to record its contents in an appendix. Its

[40] Bundock, *National Union of Printing*, p. 9.
[41] 4,635, presented 11 April 1838.
[42] 4,637, presented 11 April 1838, App. 392.
[43] 7,780, presented 25 May 1838.

significance comes from the 1,761 signatures to it, which indicates the existence of a thriving trade body.[44]

There were no petitions at all from bookbinders in 1839, although this may perhaps be explained by the very serious internal dispute which occurred that year. The master bookbinders tried for thirty weeks to destroy the trade society by means of a lock-out, but failed: the evidence of the 1838 petition suggests that it was very robust.[45] In addition, the small 'unassociated masters', seem to have formed a friendly society and supported the men. The masters, facing the busy season of annuals, compromised: they were forced to recognise the journeymen's right to combine, and to agree to reductions in their numbers of apprentices.[46] This success led to further plans for consolidation of the whole trade, including the London lodges.[47] In fact, two bodies emerged in 1840: the Bookbinders' Consolidated Union (Provinces) and the London Consolidated Lodge of Journeymen Bookbinders.

Certainly bookbinders are much more in evidence in the 1840 petitions, nearly all of them from London. Some petitions come from named specialised bookbinders shops, others state simply 'Bookbinders of the City of London' or even 'Bookbinders of

[44] The London census of 1831 recorded 1,000 bookbinders. Unfortunately the categorisation changed in 1841, lumping together booksellers, bookbinders and publishers: the figure for these was 3,500. Against these figures, 1,761 signatures seems to represent a large proportion of those involved. Goodway states that the Trade Society of Journeymen Bookbinders of London and Westminster had 743 members in 1838: David Goodway, *London Chartism 1838–1848* (Cambridge, 1982), p. 208.

[45] For a bookbinder's account of this, see *The Book-Finishers' Friendly Circular* (1845–51), p. 28. For the other side of the story see *Proceedings at a meeting of the booksellers and publishers of London and Westminster held at the London Coffee-House, Friday, January 18* (1839). These were clearly well able to mount a concerted campaign of opposition: over twenty-five influential publishers were present, and agreed to a resolution already signed by nearly fifty of their number. The decision was made 'to wait the completion of our respective orders until the master bookbinders can get men able and willing to work without imposing upon their masters any illegal restrictions'.

[46] See the *Address of the Journeymen Bookbinders of London and Westminster to the Trade Societies of Great Britain and Ireland on the conclusion of their struggle*, dated 9 September 1839, but actually sent out 1 February 1840. This is the group name familiar from the 1838 petition (7,780).

[47] There had been five London lodges at one time, but by 1833 there were only three, each with approximately 200 members. The fact that 1,761 signatures could be collected in 1838 indicates rapid growth.

London'. The London petitions carry over 1,100 signatures. In contrast, there are no petitions exclusively from provincial bookbinders, although a handful of provincial petitions include bookbinders somewhere in their petitioning categories.

The text of three London petitions is available.[48] Again the main concerns were that the trade in cheap books would cease, with consequent ill effects for the public and the trade.[49] One petition listed those who (it was claimed) had enjoyed large increases in business as a result of the great demand for cheap publications: the list included papermakers, printers, machinists, bookbinders, tanners, cloth manufacturers, dyers, artists, engravers, copper-plate printers, toolcutters, brassfounders, pressmakers and goldbeaters. This perception of a dispute which affected more than the traditional printing trades is reflected in the 1840 petitioners, who (as will be demonstrated) came from a much wider range of trades than before.

Papermakers

In contrast, papermakers of this period did not share a common organisation, and the petitioning patterns seem to reflect this. Makers of hand-made paper were originally in guilds, and used strikes to defeat attempts to reduce their wages in 1784 and 1797, for instance.[50] However, in about 1800, as paper-making machines were being introduced, the guilds were replaced by the Original Society of Papermakers.[51] This body was very powerful in its early years, although divisions appeared as the Fourdrinier machine made headway.[52] In 1826 a dispute erupted over the making of ledger paper – the so-called 'Star and Deckle trouble', which eventually split the union in 1830, although they reunited

48 2,049, presented 24 February, App. 153; 3,261, presented 12 March, App. 251; 13,124, presented 7 May, App. 683.

49 In one of these (13,124) there is an interesting side-swipe from bookbinder to bookseller: 'the learned Serjeant has modified his old Bill, and made it the interest of the rich booksellers to join him, and they have done so'. This perhaps reflects lingering bitterness over the 1829 Booksellers' Regulations: the London Booksellers' Committee would not accept retail bookshops as 'trade' if their proprietor was also a bookbinder. See ch. 5, p. 104.

50 Bundock, *National Union of Printing*, p. 356.

51 Donald C. Coleman, *The British paper industry, 1495–1860* (Oxford, 1958), p. 262.

52 For the development of this technology see Richard L. Hills, *Papermaking in Britain 1844–1988: a short history* (1988), ch. 7.

under the original name in 1837. After this, the society's rules on apprentices caused several important mills to take themselves outside it, and this continued trend put severe pressure on union funds.

Employers also had an association, which in the 1790s described itself as the 'Committee of Master Paper-Makers'. In 1803 it became the 'United Society of Master Paper-Makers of Great Britain', although its coverage was not in fact truly national, in contrast to the range of the workers' society. There are records of a meeting of the Manufacturers of Paper and Pasteboard in England and Wales, held at the London Coffee House in 1831, to organise a campaign against paper duties.[53] However, once these were reduced in 1836, the organisation seems to have faded away. There is no evidence of concerted resistance to the copyright bills.

There are only three petitions which come exclusively from papermakers (presumably employers), amounting to roughly fifty signatures, but all in different years. The first is in 1838, from twelve paper manufacturers from Edinburgh.[54] A petition from paper manufacturers of High Wycombe and Woburn is one of the few petitions against the bill in 1839.[55] Neither merits an appendix. The 1840 petition has been printed, and comes from paper manufacturers in the counties of Berkshire, Buckinghamshire and Hertfordshire.[56] Again, the concern is the effect on trade, particularly the consumption of paper, 'by preventing the free publication of many useful works at a cheap rate'.

Other print-related specialisms

By 1840 the rapid expansion of the market for printed material and the increase in the scale of production had begun to result in an increased emphasis on specialisation, which was to be further developed later in the century. This is also reflected in the copyright petitions. For some of these groups, specialisation was not new. For instance, although typefounders had operated under the broad umbrella of the Stationers' Company, they were always regarded as a distinct group, and they were not members of the London printers' unions.[57]

[53] Coleman, *Paper industry*, pp. 273–83.

[54] 5,182, presented 30 April 1838.

[55] 7,256, presented 7 May 1839.

[56] 15,217, presented 21 May 1840, App. 778.

[57] Typefounding was generally considered a noxious and hazardous profession.

Notwithstanding, there is some evidence of collective organisation. In June 1837, typefounders struck against an Edinburgh firm which had a foundry in London paying wages below London rates.[58] They did not, however, petition separately in 1838 and 1839: the single exception was a large group of Edinburgh typefounders; their complaint does not survive.[59] In 1840 there were four petitions exclusively from typefounders, and another lists them separately before 'Printers and Others'.[60] Two of these came from named offices.

There is a single petition from 'Stereotypers of London', which is worthy of mention.[61] Stereotyping had been developed after about 1800, first by Lord Stanhope's plaster-of-Paris method, and then in the 1840s by Kronheim's 'flong' method.[62] However, Musson states that stereotyping was not in extensive use before 1800, so the existence in 1840 of thirty-four petitioning stereotypers is of interest. Perhaps this group of petitioners functioned as an embryonic trade society. Stereotypers were not included in the traditional typographic societies, and gradually developed their own organisations, although not until the end of the century.

Specialism in printing is again reflected in the separate petitions from lithographic and copper-plate printers.[63] Copper-plate engraving had been used for highly detailed and decorative illustration since the fifteenth century, in spite of the technical problems it presented. This sort of engraving was associated with the finest book work, so presumably copper-plate printers would have been welcome members of the typographical unions. The same was not true for lithographic printers.

Lithography was a comparatively new process, invented in 1798 by a Bavarian, Senefelder, who filed claims at the British patent office in 1800. Like stereotyping, Musson states that it was not

Type was cast from lead and antimony at very high temperatures, and the rubbing and dressing led to dust inhalation. No benefit society would admit typefounders as members: Goodway, *London Chartism*, p. 206.

58 Iorwerth J. Prothero, *Artisans and politics in early nineteenth-century London* (Folkestone, 1979), p. 317.

59 4,782, presented 25 April 1838.

60 13,907; 15,193; 15,209; 15,266. 16,055.

61 4,643, presented 11 April 1838.

62 Musson, *Typographical Association*, p. 18.

63 15,190 (copper-plate printers); 15,191 (lithographic printers): both presented 20 May 1840. The consecutive numbering may perhaps imply a very local insistence on the distinction.

widely used until about 1850, so it is significant that lithographic printers should be petitioning as such (even in small numbers) in 1840. The petition is perhaps also a badge of pride, as well as a sign of the hauteur of the typographical unions: like stereotypers, lithographic printers had to form their own societies.

Some of the petitioning printing specialisms are subdivisions of an older trade.[64] Several petitions came from 'Sewers and Folders', whose task had previously been done as part of the general work of the bookbinder. However, even during the eighteenth century, women had been employed in folding and sewing book and news sheets.[65] The skilled printing trade was almost exclusively confined to men, and women (as cheap unskilled labour) could not join any of the main unions.[66] However, at least in the large London offices, sewing and folding came to be regarded as 'women's work', requiring no heavy labour or responsibility and little skill. It was thus beneath the dignity of the male print workers, though it was commonly done by their wives.

Understandably, there was no formal organisation of women in the printing trades during this period.[67] Thus it was quite possible that the 300 names on four petitions from sewers and folders[68] include many women. One petition came explicitly from 'Females, Bookstitchers of London', and carried 100 signatures.[69]

[64] The printing trades had always contained specialists, but they had not previously appeared to form separate sub-groups for the purpose of agitation. This is in contrast to their association for prudential matters, as can be seen from the names of their mutual funds, such as the Book-Finishers' Friendly Association.

[65] J. Ramsay MacDonald (ed.), *Women in the printing trades: a sociological study* (1904), ch. 3.

[66] Nor would the typical local friendly society admit women to membership. Some societies run by patrons admitted women too, but excluded periods of pregnancy.

[67] Emily Faithfull's Victoria press opened in 1860, which employed and trained women compositors who worked an eight-hour day and received wages of £1 a week. Other early organisations include the Women's Printing Society (1876) and the Society of Women employed in Bookbinding (1874), although the latter was more a benefit club than an active union. In 1833 Benjamin Teasdale, a friend of Thomas Dunning (secretary of the powerful London Society of Bookbinders), suggested the formation of a women's society: the bookbinders failed to adopt the idea. Felicity Hunt, 'Opportunities lost and gained: mechanization and women's work in the London bookbinding and printing trades', in *Unequal opportunities: women's employment in England 1800–1918*, ed. Angela V. John (Oxford, 1986).

[68] 15,151; 15,206; 15,267; 16,071, all presented May 1840.

[69] 13,908, presented 14 May 1830.

Another came from 'Females employed in the manufacture of books', and had 194 signatures.[70]

Supporters of cheap print

Although many of the trade petitions raise a concern about the price of books and the availability of knowledge, and typographical unions were known for their interest in education, it is reasonable to regard at least some of these arguments as convenient cloaks for self-interest. However, a handful of petitions can be linked by their expression of a specific concern with education.

The two petitions from the original, London-based British Medical Assocation have already been mentioned.[71] They were presented by Wakley, and presumably masterminded by him. Obstinate and troublesome to Talfourd though Wakley was, there is every reason to accept the sincerity of his concern for the ready availability of (particularly medical) knowledge.[72] Similarly, opposition to a measure that would allegedly raise the price of books was predictable from a class of medical men whose own access to training literature might have been precarious. The first petition adopted the air of gravitas expected from the medical profession, expressing particular concern for scientific literature, and taking the view that general literature was sufficiently protected. The second petition was significantly longer, taking parts of the first petition verbatim, but expanding other points in Benthamite language: 'your Petitioners consider every unnecessary restriction on the liberty of the press and on literary productions to be a great national injury, as tending to prevent that diffusion of knowledge and general education so important in promoting habits of industry and morality, and thereby increasing happiness and preventing crime'.

Similar anxieties were expressed in the petition from 'Dr. George Birkbeck, and certain other persons interested in the general diffusion of literature and science, assembled in a public

[70] 17,972, presented 8 July 1840.

[71] 4,787, presented 25 April 1838, App. 406. 6,967, presented 1 May 1839, App. 661.

[72] For Wakley's interest in copyright see ch. 3, pp. 42–5.

meeting in the Freemasons' Hall'.[73] The petition stated that authors would gain no more from an extended copyright term, citing evidence given to select committees in 1813 and 1818 to support this assertion. Furthermore it was argued that, since copyrights were generally sold to publishers, the extended term would simply produce a monopoly for the publishers which would injure the public.[74] The petition was unusual in its references to numbered clauses of the bill. The first of these was, predictably, clause 5 – the retrospective clause. Clauses 19 and 27 also caused anxiety, one restricting the taking of extracts, and the other granting copyright in sermons: the specific worries were that compilations for schoolbooks would be threatened, and that 'the diffusion of much valuable religious instruction among the mass of the people' would be prevented.[75]

Birkbeck had a long and admirable history of associations with education. Professor of natural philosophy at the Andersonian University, Glasgow, in 1799, in 1800 he had established a series of cheap courses of lectures on science for working men: these later developed into the Glasgow Mechanics' Institution (1823). He was a founder and first president of Birkbeck's Mechanics' Institution in London (1824), and a founder and council member of University College London (1827). He had been closely involved in the struggle against the newspaper stamp, working with Place to orchestrate the repeal campaign. Birkbeck addressed several public meetings, led deputations to the chancellor of the exchequer, Spring Rice, and to the prime minister, Melbourne.[76] He argued always for total repeal of the stamp, rather than reduction.

Birkbeck's co-agitators in the stamp matter included Grote, Wakley, Hume and Brougham – all of whom were later to oppose Talfourd's bills. Birkbeck had met Brougham at Edinburgh

[73] 5,953, presented by Hume, 9 May 1838, App. 455. For an account of the meeting itself, see ch. 6, p. 140.

[74] 'Although there are instances of authors who retain the Copyright of their own works . . . such instances are notoriously the exception to the general rule.' This is a telling point, although this practice was gradually changing, as authors became aware of the value of their retained copyrights. See ch. 7, p. 149.

[75] Religious tracts and pamphlets were often distributed at very low cost, in a deliberate attempt to supplant other (less edifying) reading matter.

[76] Thomas Kelly, *George Birkbeck: pioneer of adult education* (Liverpool, 1957), p. 165.

University in 1793, and they remained good friends. Birkbeck's letters to Brougham reveal that his disapproval of Talfourd's measure dated from February 1838, or perhaps earlier. A letter from Birkbeck concerning Brougham's rival bill survives:

> In your Copyright Bill I hope that you will not – indeed I know that you cannot – forget the people. Mr Austin,[77] the barrister, said to Serjeant Talfourd, 'You have taken care of the authors and publishers in your Copyright Bill, but what have you done for the people?' 'Oh damn the people!' was his liberal and patriotic reply. You will not, I believe, legislate for Wordsworth, Southey and Scott.[78]

The following year Birkbeck was party to a second petition.[79] The points made were similar to those taken in the 1838 petition; that authors generally sold their copyrights so only publishers would benefit, and that the diffusion of literature would be restricted, harming both authors and the public. One phrase strongly foreshadows Macaulay's speech in 1841:[80] 'Copyright is a monopoly, and all monopolies do and must restrict the general and cheap diffusion of the commodity.' However, the petitioners were not opposed to a power in the Privy Council to extend copyright in cases where the author was not sufficiently remunerated under the existing law. The entirety of this petition was used unchanged in a petition from Glasgow in 1840.[81]

Birkbeck's willingness to associate himself with the public campaign against copyright extension suggests that he considered it a matter of educational principle. The parallels with the campaign against the newspaper stamp are striking: principles,

[77] John Austin, the jurist, who had abandoned practice in 1825, and was first professor of jurisprudence at London University (1826–35).

[78] Birkbeck to Brougham, 7 August 1838 (Brougham MSS, University of London).

[79] 7,254, from 'Authors, and other persons interested in the general diffusion of literature and science', presented 7 May 1839 by the solicitor-general, App. 688. Birkbeck signed after Marshall Hall, the eminent physiologist, and before James Stephens FLS (the entomologist): only these three names are printed.

[80] 'I believe . . . that I may safely take it for granted that the effect of monopoly generally is to make articles scarce, to make them dear, and to make them bad': *Hansard, Parliamentary debates* (3rd series), lvi, 348. Of course, both phrases owe a good deal to Adam Smith.

[81] 1,756, from 'Certain Authors and other persons interested in the general diffusion of Literature and Science, Glasgow', presented 19 February 1840, App. 132. Only three of the twenty-four signatories are listed, one of whom was Edward Knull, printer to the University.

personnel and methods were all to some extent shared. Nevertheless, Birkbeck's importance here was as an individual, a respected and independent figurehead to represent the voice of popular education in the copyright debate. His opposition, though strong, was more characteristic of the moderate, middle-class view than the radical. This distinction had been of great importance in the struggle to repeal the taxes on knowledge, where the splits between the various groups eventually left the extreme radicals bitter and the liberal campaigners alienated. With regard to Talfourd's proposals, the strands of popular protest generally ran separate from the rest, perhaps because of the more distinct interest groups, but perhaps also because of the residual mistrust engendered by the stamp wars.

The remaining petitions that claim a primary interest in education are harder to classify, as they were not printed: only their dates and designations provide clues. One was 'signed on behalf of the Lambeth Mutual Instruction Society', two others come from 'friends of popular education': they bear only a few signatures.[82] Two others belong more properly in the next section, because of their probable links with radical political activism: from the vendors of cheap publications, they nevertheless merit mention in an educational context,[83] as does the petition from 'Inhabitants of Wick', 'desirous of seeing no impediment thrown in the way of knowledge'.[84]

Camp followers

The remaining trades represented in the 1840 petitions do not show any close connection with the world of print. Possible exceptions are the 'Piano Forte Makers', who may have been anxious for printed music, and the 'Working Goldsmiths and Jewellers', who might have claimed connections with bookbinding and engraving.[85] The list of other specific trades includes tailors, hatters, pencilmakers, coal meters, watermen and lightermen, coachmakers and machinists. Many of these were well known for their trade organisation, and the existing trade and/or union

[82] 13,120, 15,149 and 15,268, all presented May 1840.
[83] 15,243 and 15,245, both presented 22 May 1840.
[84] 17,949, presented 7 July 1840.
[85] 15,192 and 15,229, both presented 21 May 1840.

structures would have enabled these petitions to be produced quite readily.[86] Three petitions mention engineers, a professional title.[87] One of these came from 'Mechanics and others, especially Engineers', perhaps suggesting that it was collected through a Mechanics' Institute or reading-room. The petition from 'teetotallers' presumably resulted from a similarly organised, self-selecting group.[88]

Other petitions claim no alliances, such as the one from 'workmen'.[89] The vast majority of the 1840 petitions fall into this general category. About 220 petitions come simply from 'Inhabitants' of a named place. These amount to almost 13,000 signatures, and bear clear hallmarks of orchestration: the huge increase in numbers is itself indicative.[90] They are presented by a very limited range of MPs, mostly radicals: Wakley, Warburton, Hume, Strutt, Thornley and Finch are the main protagonists. Geographically, London and the surrounding areas are heavily represented, with about 190 petitions, amounting to approximately 10,500 signatures. Over 2,000 signatures were collected from the provinces though, and some large provincial towns gathered over 100 signatures. The provincial petitions were largely presented by Warburton, an old hand at these campaigns.

The texts of two petitions survive. The first was one of the earliest petitions to be presented in 1840.[91] It is brief enough to quote in its entirety:

The petition of the undersigned inhabitants of Shoreditch, Sheweth, That coffee-houses, cheap publications, knowledge and temperance are

[86] See, for instance, the petition from 'Tailors, Place & Carbery, 16, Charing Cross, the journeymen in their employ, and the journeymen of the House of Call, Windmill Street, at a general meeting', 13,913, presented 14 May 1840, 102 signatures. Houses of call were public houses where members of a certain trade who were looking for work could register their names. When masters needed men they would apply there and men would be sent, in the order in which their names stood in the book.

[87] 13,128, 15,152 and 17,699. The rapid development of machine-making from c. 1800 transformed industry. Jefferys notes a crop of new friendly societies in the 1820s, 'sectional in outlook and policy', based on the new specialisms. Trade union formation followed, especially 1833–8: James B. Jefferys, *Story of the engineers, 1800–1945* (1946), pp. 15–18.

[88] 13,909, presented 14 May 1840.

[89] 16,075, presented 29 May 1840.

[90] Those opposing the bill: 1838, 114 petitions, 7,979 signatures; 1839, 8 petitions, 303 signatures; 1840, 345 petitions, 22,547 signatures.

[91] 2,188, presented by Hume, 27 February 1840, App. 176, thirty-seven signatures.

far better for the public than gin-shops, dear publications, ignorance and drunkenness. Your Petitioners therefore pray your honourable House to reject Serjeant Talfourd's Copyright Bill, which would sacrifice the best interest of the public to the profit of a few rich men.

The other surviving petition contrasted the free availability of copyright with the prohibitive fee for a patent lasting only a short time, and concluded that 'the sentimental absurdity of authors' extraordinary rights is but the guise of a scheme to give a certain monopoly to a few rich publishers'.[92]

It is impossible to tell whether either of these petitions was characteristic of the mass of petitions which flooded in during 1840: the Committee on Public Petitions tended to print both petitions that represented a body of opinion, and those that expressed an unusual point of view. In any event, there was a quite extraordinary volume of protest in response to a rather technical copyright bill, and it is clear that already existing mechanisms of protest were being employed. Printing-trade structures had been very important, especially in 1838. However, by 1840, a much wider range of people had been brought into the protest, using different routes of communication.

The trade-centred response is relatively easy to understand: there was a history of strong links between the societies. London was obviously a centre for such cooperation, but the tramping federations provided another natural opportunity to develop networks. It was common to offer financial assistance (often loans) to help a trade group through a specific dispute. For example, between 1807 and 1811 bookbinders provided assistance to a whole list of trades; wireworkers, lockfounders, cutlers, papermakers, goldbeaters, pipemakers, corkcutters and brushmakers.[93]

The system of cooperation could also be mobilised against more general threats. When Thomas Peregrine Courtenay introduced a bill to tighten controls over benefit societies in 1828, the resulting campaign was astonishing. 108 London societies subscribed to the metropolitan delegate committee which, with the help of the *Trades' Free Press*, coordinated agitation on a national scale. Hundreds of petitions arrived from all over the country, and the

[92] 15,261, presented by William Williams, 21 May 1840, App. 779, forty-four signatures.

[93] Prothero, *Artisans and politics*, p. 42. Musson quotes an even longer list for the typographical unions taken together: Musson, *Typographical Association*, p. 72.

House of Commons responded by dropping Courtenay's bill at the committee stage.[94] This level of support had continued during the 1830s. The Dorchester Labourers' Committee, and the agitation provoked by the newspaper stamp, 'provided the foci for the multitudes of groups, trades, booksellers and newsagents, coffee and public houses, discussion and educational groups that flourished in London'.[95] As has been mentioned, the government 'compromise' reduction was seen as a betrayal, and those parliamentary radicals who accepted it had to face a bitter reaction. Spring Rice's proposal provoked a final burst of protest, which was coordinated by the Marylebone Radical Association.

Although these campaigns were over, the mechanisms remained. In spite of the depression, between 1836 and 1839 Prothero lists separate trade strikes by goldbeaters, potters, ropemakers, engineers and carpenters, and notes that in every case support came from other trades.[96] The recently formed Working-Men's Association also had a role, with its programme of addresses, petitions and public meetings. Both organisations helped during the typefounders' strike against an Edinburgh-based firm which was paying its London workers below the agreed rate.

During the copyright dispute, the familiar methods were evidently used again. A petition was received from 'Inhabitants of Spitalfields resorting to the Globe Coffee House', showing that the groups in coffee houses were still active.[97] Even more striking is the petition sent from 'Inhabitants of the Metropolis, signing at the shop of Mr Strange, publisher', because it provides a clear link with the war against the unstamped press.[98] William Strange was a bookseller and publisher who had been heavily involved in the sale of cheap, unstamped publications. He had been a founder member of the Society for the Protection of Booksellers, formed in April 1834 to provide legal and pecuniary aid for those prosecuted for infringement of the stamp laws.[99]

Given the availability of such personnel and such support, the question becomes why the copyright debate was confined to the printing trades for so long, rather than why the dispute took

[94] Prothero, *Artisans and politics*, p. 232. [95] Ibid., p. 307.
[96] Ibid., pp. 307, 310. [97] 15,218, presented 21 May 1840.
[98] 16,072, presented 29 May 1840.
[99] Patricia Hollis, *The pauper press: a study in working-class radicalism of the 1830s* (Oxford, 1970), p. 314.

several years to diffuse. One possible reason was the depression: men were generally not winning the disputes mentioned earlier. Also, the printing industry unions were not known for their radicalism or their belligerence: they valued their independence and status, and seem to have been slow to invoke the involvement of outsiders.[100] Musson states that the typographical unions 'maintained a definite non-political attitude' during this period, although the individual men may well have taken a different view.[101] Another reason for the initially limited impact of the copyright dispute might have been that it involved legislation, and was not a dispute with employers that could be approached with the weapon of a strike. Throughout 1838 the entire profession was united, and backed by vocal parliamentary support: this was probably thought to be sufficient defence. By 1840 some publishers were actually in favour of the measures, however, and the trade was beginning to divide – along the stress lines between masters and men.

It seems to have been at this stage that the radical protest mechanisms were activated. Their existence is obvious from the petitioning patterns earlier in the 1830s, although it is less clear exactly how this was achieved. One example is provided by a campaign whose aims and arguments significantly influenced the copyright debate – the war against taxes on knowledge. In 1836 the Society for the Promotion of the Repeal of Stamp Duties, directed by Place, attempted to mobilise provincial public opinion in its support.[102] Hollis has described how they set about the task:

> they sent out from their office in Leicester Square 1,600 letters, 4,000 copies of printed petition forms, 10,000 copies of Brougham's Evidence, 1,000 printed extracts from London papers, 124 written petitions ready for signing (with instructions that they should each be signed by 200 to 300 people), procured upwards of 300 petitions to Parliament and 32 known public meetings, listed some 2,000 individuals as provincial correspondents, and in all sent out some 20,000 circulars. As their letters

[100] Goodway has observed that 'despite the huge numbers of operatives, their economic vicissitudes in the period and general intellectualism (or maybe on account of this factor), the [printing and book] trades remained comparatively remote from radical political or industrial action': Goodway, *London Chartism*, p. 204.

[101] Musson, *Typographical Association*, p. 74.

[102] Its committee members included Birkbeck, Place, Falconer, Chapman, Hickson and Black. Birkbeck was directly involved in the opposition to Talfourd, and Place indirectly, through Brougham and Warburton.

were franked free by members of Parliament, and the clerical work was voluntary, Place claimed that all this was done at a total cost of under £40.[103]

The evidence of the copyright petitions indicates that very similar techniques were tried in this dispute. There was an enormous leap in the numbers petitioning, and the petitions were presented in batches by a handful of radical MPs. The designation 'Inhabitants', used by the Committee on Public Petitions, suggests that these petitions may have been identical: this would also explain the decision to print very few of them. Several were collected at trade or public meetings, and others in coffee houses or shops: these now seemed to be well-recognised modes of generating support. The volume of provincial petitions also indicates that known local contacts may have been used. There is, however, no evidence to indicate whether any letters or extracts were circulated.

Although the techniques of protest used were familiar, the question remains as to who activated these mechanisms. The print trade groups were known for their internal cohesion, and on matters which they regarded as affecting vital trade interests they had always felt entitled to speak out. However, they were generally hostile to a militant, political agenda: it seems unlikely that in 1840 the matter could have been thought sufficiently serious to merit a change in attitude which would have embraced expansion. The activism is more likely to have been a reflection of the political alignment of individual print workers, who were necessarily intelligent and well informed, and who moved in contexts other than their own trades.

[103] Hollis, *Pauper press*, p. 78. She notes that meetings and petitions were organised in places where the unstamped press was already strong: many of the copyright petitions come from these towns.

5

CRITICS IN THE BOOK TRADE II: PUBLISHING AND PUBLISHERS

The book trade's reaction to Talfourd's plans was to mount a well-coordinated and effective campaign of opposition. However, different parts of the trade responded in different ways. As has been demonstrated, workers in the printing trades were accustomed to resist threats posed by technology and other changes in practice: their trade organisations were well suited to this task. Their protests against Talfourd's bills were focused on the presentation of large numbers of petitions, as the only feasible way of making their views heard.

The employers in the world of print had more scope for action. Their modes of protest were therefore noticeably more diffuse: letters, articles, pamphlets and private lobbying were all used, in addition to the few carefully judged petitions: volume was of less importance than influence and profile. Nevertheless, the entrepreneurs in the book trade were also under pressure. The rapid expansion in the reading public had disrupted the market, transforming relationships within the trade. Nor had the transition from bookseller to publisher yet been entirely achieved, adding other tensions to economic anxieties. Another aspect of the changing market was the gradual emergence of the profession of authorship, an issue which was never far from the surface in authors' conceptions of copyright, as will be seen in chapter 7. These pressures gradually transformed the book trade's relationship with authors, and provoked new consideration of the worth of literature and of authorship. The reform of copyright law was not therefore a simple matter, cutting as it did across all of these sensitivities.

The arguments put forward by the book trade against copyright extension are in themselves interesting, and will be considered in detail. But the actual mechanism of the campaign in some ways reveals a great deal more about the trade, in particular its organisational structure and its responsiveness to perceived threats. These factors can in turn help to explain the positions adopted on the particular issue in hand – copyright – and the methods used to promote them.

THE BOOK TRADE AND AUTHORS

The relationship between the author and the book trade in the nineteenth century reflected the changes which resulted from a hugely increased reading public.[1] Authors in the sixteenth and seventeenth centuries had been largely dependent on court and aristocratic patronage, particularly if they wished to make a living from writing. Print became increasingly available after the Civil War, as public interest in political and religious matters increased. There were more magazines and journals to cater for this, and more and more fiction. By the eighteenth century the profession of letters was well established.

However, under Walpole there was neither money nor inclination for political patronage of authors, and the reading public was still relatively limited. This gave the booksellers great power, which was reinforced by trade practices. Particularly in London there were few booksellers, who cooperated to exclude competition: these combinations, or 'Congers', included the Printing Conger (1719), followed by the New Conger (1736), both replaced by the famous Chapter.[2] The most important aspect of this

[1] This account draws on the following texts: Terry Belanger, 'From bookseller to publisher: changes in the London book trade, 1750–1850', in *Book selling and book buying: aspects of the nineteenth-century British and North American book trade*, ed. Richard G. Landon (Chicago, 1978); A. S. Collins, *Authorship in the days of Johnson* (1927); James Hepburn, *The author's empty purse and the rise of the literary agent* (1968); John Whiteside Saunders, *The profession of English letters* (1964).

[2] From the Chapter Coffee House, Paternoster Row: Collins, *Authorship*, p. 19. Belanger refers to 'The Wholesaling Conger', c. 1715, although Septimus Rivington regarded the 1719 Conger as the first regular association of booksellers. Hodgson and Blagden distinguish between wholesaling congers (and allied practices) which dated from c. 1717–20, and copyright-owning congers: Norma Hodgson and Cyprian Blagden, *The notebook of some aspects of book trade practice* (1953), p. 67. Curwen records the existence of another group at the end of the eighteenth century; the Associated Booksellers who met at the sign of the bee

cooperation was the control over copyrights which resulted. William Jerdan, remembering the London publishers before 1815, commented on their power: 'in those days [they] acted in concert with regard to important new productions, and the joint purchase of established publications. This was "The Trade;" a name of wealth and might.'[3]

This power persisted into the nineteenth century. William Chambers's description of conditions in about 1815 confirms Jerdan's account:

> editions of the works of Johnson, Gibbon, Robertson, Blair, Hume and Smollett, Burns, and other standard writers, had been a monopoly of certain publishers, who united to publish them, and gave them the imposing name of 'Trade Editions'. Long out of copyright, these works were public property, and could legally be printed and issued by anyone, but not until now had any one had the audacity and enterprise to disregard the assumed etiquette of the profession, and print and sell editions on his own account.[4]

The original intention was to share both risk and expense by dividing copyrights. Copyrights were sold only at trade sales, and admittance to these was strictly controlled.[5] It was the exclusion of the Scottish bookseller, Donaldson, from the sale of the rights of Thomson's *The Seasons* that led to the great case of *Donaldson* v. *Beckett*,[6] and ultimately to the weakening of the system.

An author attempting to publish a work would find that the bookseller invariably took the copyright.[7] Authors who kept their

hive, and were thus known as the Associated Busy Bees: Henry Curwen, *A history of booksellers* (1874), p. 69.

[3] William Jerdan, *Autobiography* (1852–3), p. 142. Jerdan was himself a publisher, notably of the *Literary Gazette*.

[4] William Chambers, *Memoir of William and Robert Chambers*, 13th edn (Edinburgh, 1884), p. 143. The audacious rival was Thomas Tegg, who will feature again below. Tegg's great commercial success in the cheap publications market did not win him the approbation of the Trade, although it did generate a certain grudging respect.

[5] Cyprian Blagden, 'Booksellers' Trade Sales, 1718–1768', *The Library*, 5th ser., 5 (1951), 243–57.

[6] (1774) 2 Bro P C 129. See ch. 1.

[7] Although sometimes only the copyright of the first edition would be sold outright, with half profits on further editions. The true half-profits system, which allowed the author no pre-sale payment and also required of him a half share of potential losses, was not popular: even if profits were forthcoming it was generally thought that these were under-represented in the bookseller's account. A revised edition would result in a further payment usually, but payment on the basis of the number of editions sold was more common in France than in

copyrights would find that their works were unaccountably unsaleable. Patronage was a less common and rather unfashionable alternative, and anyway the prices given for copyrights were generally good.[8] However, booksellers behaved as if the acquisition of copyright gave them exclusive and perpetual rights, and the practice of buying what was termed 'perpetual copyright' appears to have continued after the lapse of the Licensing Act, and into the early eighteenth century. Even though trade practice provided a strong measure of protection, copyright was clearly a matter of concern, and there were several attempts to secure protection from Irish piracies.[9]

The de facto monopoly could not be maintained for ever, and in the 1760s Donaldson began selling in the Strand at prices which undercut the London booksellers. *Millar* v. *Taylor*[10] was the immediate consequence, which found in favour of perpetual copyright. On Millar's death the copyright of Thomson's *The Seasons* came up for sale, and though Donaldson had been excluded from the sale he still sold thousands of copies. The copyright had been bought by Beckett and fourteen others, who brought an action for an injunction and an account of profits. When this was granted, the famous appeal to the House of Lords followed.

In spite of the unfavourable result, the London shareholders still managed to maintain their position for a time, issuing jointly published editions of popular share books, relying on their extensive trade relationships for sales. Since their power was based only on custom, there is only anecdotal evidence of their ability to do this; yet those who report do so with a casualness that suggests that the habitual power was still accepted, at least by some. For instance, John Nichols, a well-educated printer who became master of the Company of Stationers, wished to print an edition of Swift, whom he admired. A version edited by Thomas Sheridan had been produced in 1784 with the sanction of all the booksellers who held part of the copyright. However, it was not until 1801

England. Subscription publishing was common in the eighteenth century, but grew tarnished with the demise of patronage. Publishing on commission was almost exclusively reserved for vanity publishing. Louis James (ed.), *Print and the people 1819–1851* (1976), pp. 7–12.

8 Collins, *Authorship*, p. 221.

9 Culminating in an Act in 1739: 12 Geo. 2 c. 47.

10 (1769) 4 Burr 2303.

that Nichols was permitted to produce a new version of Sheridan's edition, the printing of which he shared with three other firms.[11]

Nichols's case may not have been entirely typical, because of his strong links with the Stationers' Company. The monopoly was significantly weakened, and it was now in theory possible to publish old books in cheap editions without fear of legal action from the London booksellers.[12] However, since a cheap price meant a small profit, large numbers of copies had to be sold. The traditional publishers continued to prefer large profits on small editions, and the price of new books rose. This attitude did not acknowledge the huge growth in the reading public, who were catered for by others at first. James Lackington grew rich and famous selling second-hand books and remainders at half-price (for cash), having been appalled to find that booksellers would systematically destroy unsold books. He was extremely unpopular, and was excluded from trade sales, but the book trade lacked the cohesion necessary to stop him. Thomas Tegg was to follow in his footsteps, with perhaps even more ruthlessness.[13]

By 1829 there was a great anxiety about a related problem – certain booksellers were 'underselling' (i.e. selling below the agreed retail price). In December a committee of London booksellers and publishers met at the Chapter Coffee House to agree on a system to fix the retail price of books.[14] The resulting Booksellers' Regulations came into effect in January 1830, and 650 members of the trade agreed to abide by them. The committee which drafted the Regulations was known only to the trade until a disgruntled bookseller disclosed them in a pamphlet in 1832:[15] the

[11] John Nichols, *Literary anecdotes of the eighteenth century*, selected and ed. Colin Clair (1967).

[12] Although the concerted practices continued. For instance, in 1828 Principal Shareholders of Books met at the Chapter Coffee House. A note of the meeting records clear, specific and detailed rules about the management of these shares. Longmans Archive, Reel 63, 22 July 1828.

[13] Tegg was quite shameless about his imitations of Goodrich's popular (American) 'Peter Parley' books, telling their author, 'Sir, I do not owe you a farthing – neither justice nor law require me to pay you anything': Samuel Griswald Goodrich, *Recollections of a lifetime* (New York, 1857). Ironically, given Dickens's later stance on international copyright, in August 1836 he agreed to write a Peter Parley tale for Tegg, 'to be called *Solomon Bell the Raree Showman*'. The fee would have been £100, but it was never written. *The letters of Charles Dickens*, eds. Madeleine House and Graham Storey (Oxford, 1965–), I, pp. 161–3.

[14] James J. Barnes, *Free trade in books* (Oxford, 1964), pp. 1–18.

names form a predictable roll call of the largest and most powerful firms. The Regulations also controlled trade discounts and decided which premises counted as retail bookshops.

The harshness and apparent unfairness with which the Regulations were applied resulted in resistance and resentment, and the practice of underselling spread. Other changes resulted from the growing capital base of the major London booksellers; figures such as Longman, Blackwood and Murray could now afford to take risks and reap rewards solely on their own account. This led to a clearer distinction being made between retail booksellers, publishers and wholesalers.

CHEAP PUBLICATIONS – THE SOCIETY FOR THE DIFFUSION OF USEFUL KNOWLEDGE

Although the trade was at first slow to respond to the market for cheap literature, there were others interested in providing for it, for their own reasons. A flood of cheap literature had resulted from the activities of the unstamped press, but its moral and (radical) political content provoked concern in some quarters. Religious Societies, such as the Religious Tract Society and the Society for the Promotion of Christian Knowledge, attempted to counteract the trend by providing cheap religious material. There was also one completely new group working to improve the reading material available: the Society for the Diffusion of Useful Knowledge (SDUK). This organisation reached its commercial peak in about 1830, but its ideals and goals came to be so widely acknowledged that the society's effects lasted long after its formal demise. In particular, the influence of the SDUK is easily detected in the copyright debate, both in the ideas and assumptions which permeate the discussion, and in many of the petitions.

The SDUK has been described as 'first and foremost a society of idealists'.[16] There was certainly an element of concern that a working class provided only with radical material would prove unstable and rebellious, but this was not the driving force behind the society. Rather, the society was driven by its belief in the power of education to transform and improve, a benefit which

[16] David Vincent, *Bread, knowledge and freedom* (1981), p. 138.

should be available to the working class also. Knowledge was considered valuable for its own sake, although if it led to the political stability of the working class this was a welcome result. The intention was to channel the energies of the intelligent and articulate working man into something positive – the pursuit of useful knowledge. The society's idealism is particularly revealed in its concept of 'useful' knowledge: the goals were general ones, not targeted at individual economic success, or even at success within the individual's trade. The pursuit of reason and moral improvement was seen as a sufficient motive for study.

Politically, the SDUK was closely identified with the Whig party, which had been called 'education mad':[17] a significant number of Whig MPs were active members.[18] Founded in 1826 as a result of the enthusiastic reception of Brougham's *Practical Observations*, its central plank was always publications.[19] Within a complicated committee structure, the Publications Committee was powerful and paternal. The SDUK's aim was to provide cheap

[17] It should, however, be noted that the Whig position on general education during the period of Talfourd's bills differed in significant ways from the SDUK's stance in the decade following its founding. Although the Whig government under Melbourne came to pay a great deal of attention to public education, literacy per se was often regarded as subordinate in importance to moral instruction and the formation of character. An elementary education was intended to instil a sense of duty and responsibility which would benefit the general peace – not least by defeating the 'armed political monster' of Chartism. Lord John Russell, as home secretary, made this point in *Explanations of the intentions of Her Majesty's Government* in 1839, the year when the state began to inspect the work of the denominational schools receiving government grants: 'The sole effectual means of preventing the tremendous evils with which the anarchical spirit of the manufacturing population threatens the country is, by giving the people a good secular education, to enable them to understand the true circumstances which determine their physical condition and regulate the distribution of wealth among the several classes of society': James Kay-Shuttleworth, *Four periods of public education* (1862), pp. 230–1. Lord John Russell was also the vice-president of the SDUK, supporting its early decision to exclude politics and religion from its catalogue. The apparent inconsistencies reflect different objectives, but also the change in climate under a reformed parliament.

[18] For instance, there were twenty-four Whig MPs on the 1829 committee – over half. Meetings were set for Wednesday for the convenience of Members of the House. Monica C. Grobel, 'The Society for the Diffusion of Useful Knowledge 1826–1846' (unpublished M.A. thesis, London, University College, 1933), p. 69.

[19] For a sidelight on the SDUK's founding see W. F. Kennedy, 'Lord Brougham, Charles Knight, and *The rights of industry*', *Economica* 29 (1962), 58–71.

reading matter, but the choices were heavily directed: there was no fiction, no politics and no theology.

The first series to appear was the Library of Useful Knowledge, intended as elementary treatises for self-study, but sometimes too difficult and abstruse. A wide range of other publications followed, the most successful of which, the *Penny Magazine*, caused the book trade to take defensive action. Knight reported that several of the large wholesale booksellers were hostile, and that Longman & Co. had 'written to all their correspondents begging them to discourage the Sale of the Penny *numbers*, and cultivate that of the *Parts*'.[20]

Brougham would presumably have predicted such a reaction. John Taylor had been one of the more enlightened publishers, encouraging new poets such as Keats and John Clare even if sales were poor, and balancing his list with popular novels to minimise financial pressure. However, the economic problems of 1826 forced even Taylor to recognise the demands of the reading public, and it was at the end of 1826 that Brougham consulted him about the embryonic society. Taylor thought that an Association for the Promotion of Useful Knowledge might succeed, whereas a publisher would have to look to better-paying low-risk schemes, preferring the 'Prudent' to the 'Patriotic'. Even if a publisher ignored these risks,

> he cannot produce *any* of these works without some injury to that Honorary Copyright which forms perhaps a considerable part of his property; and while there is still a chance of these or of other Speculations undermining the Sources of his Income and carrying off his private supplies to benefit the Public, he will not be the active Promoter and he cannot be the wellwisher of such plans.[21]

Taylor was right in his belief that no publisher would provide for the public out of his own pocket, so the money and energy came from the SDUK committee and members. Those who wrote

[20] Grobel, 'SDUK 1826–1846', p. 116. This tactic would have reduced sales to the SDUK's target audience, who could not have afforded the outlay on parts. Longmans had tendered for the printing contract for the Library of Useful Knowledge, and were accepted. They were to have managed the stocks of publications, for a 10 per cent commission and half the 'speculation' after expense were paid. However, subsequently, they asked to be released from these terms. Baldwin and Craddock replaced them.

[21] Taylor to Brougham, 8 December 1826: quoted in Grobel, 'SDUK 1826–1846', p. 688.

for the SDUK also had to submit to stringent conditions. Brougham's early 'self-denying ordinance' that no member could write for money was later altered, to lessen the wrath of booksellers and other authors; but authors still had to permit circulation of their work among the committee, and had to promise that it would be fairly written. The committee had the right to make alterations or to reject the work entirely, even without payment.[22] Difficulties were presumably overcome by a combination of the influence of the committee members, and considerations of the prestige of the venture.

The copyrights in the works were a recurrent problem. These were usually assigned outright to the SDUK, with the obvious intention of ensuring that control was retained. The printer, Baldwin, had an interest in the copyright, which was vested in and preserved for him by the treasurer of the society. Either party could reprint if sales of a work exceeded 20,000, although Baldwin had to pay 'rent' if the work was still in its original form. The SDUK retained a controlling interest, however, and could repurchase Baldwin's share on his death or bankruptcy.[23] It was also claimed that an author could not use a piece again, even in a fuller work on the subject. The indignant protests of Peter M. Roget, who refused to write again on these terms, persuaded the society to consider each case on its merits:

> The doctrine laid down by Baldwin is that when an author of a treatise on any particular science surrenders the copy-right of it to the Society, he thereby binds himself never, at any future time, during his whole life, to write anything on that science in any other work, or for 'the benefit of any other party, not even of himself.' I am quite sure that no unbiased person, far less a Society professing liberal views, would even think of exacting such a pledge; nor would any author, not driven by necessity to write, submit to such a condition . . . It forms an . . . editorial prerogative, tending rather to the *monopoly* than the *diffusion* of knowledge.[24]

The SDUK enjoyed a period of great success, particularly with

[22] Grobel, 'SDUK 1826–1846', p. 141.

[23] Ibid., p. 621. Baldwin & Co. did in fact fail in 1837, with stocks and plates (especially of maps) on hand. The SDUK and Baldwin's trustees did not agree on a price for these until 1841.

[24] Peter M. Roget to Thomas Coates, 10 April 1830, quoted by Grobel, 'SDUK 1826–1846', p. 622. English physician and scholar, secretary of the Royal Society, 1827–47, and an original member of the Senate of London University, Roget is now best known for his *Thesaurus of English words and phrases* (1852).

the *Penny Magazine*. It rather overreached itself with the ambitious plans for the *Penny Cyclopaedia* and the *Biographical Dictionary*, but it did show that there was a demand for cheap and useful books which could be satisfied as a commercial proposition. Grobel suggests that 'the greatest benefit to the Trade was the creation and revelation of a large public prepared and eager to buy reputable publications'. This emphasis on the *creation* of a reading public is perhaps to put the case too strongly. Nevertheless, it is certainly true that by 1845 (the end of the SDUK's effective life) other publishers had come to appreciate the demand for cheap and popular books, and were responding to it. The educational potential was obvious, but one reason for early trade reticence was financial anxiety.

CHEAP PUBLICATIONS – THE BOOK TRADE

Economic conditions had fluctuated during the first part of the nineteenth century: the end of the Napoleonic Wars had been good for business, but there had been regular depressions. Barnes notes 'major panics' in 1819, 1825–6, 1829–32, and also from 1837–42, the exact period during which the copyright legislation was being planned.[25] These dates are confirmed by anecdotal evidence such as the notorious bankruptcy of Constable in 1826, which brought down Ballantyne with it, and hence Sir Walter Scott also. The position of Scott's heirs was fiercely debated as part of the copyright discussions, some having great sympathy with them, and others regarding the bill as legislation for individuals in the form of a general measure, and thus tainted by this perceived favouritism.

The book trade had also had to contend with government policies which served to increase the price of books, namely the taxes on paper and advertisements, and the newspaper stamp. Wages of print workers were high, particularly those of compositors, who were among the highest-paid skilled workers in

[25] James J. Barnes, 'Depression and innovation in the British and American booktrade, 1819–1839', in *Economics of the British booktrade 1605–1939*, eds. Robin Myers and Michael Harris (Cambridge, 1985), p. 211.

London.[26] Books were of high quality, produced in small editions, and prices were set to reflect this. This explains why early in the century books were generally regarded as a luxury, and cheap books gained ground only gradually. Altick suggests conservatism of the publishing trade and deliberate conspiracy among leading London houses as additional reasons for high prices.[27]

The unlucky Constable had been one of the first to experiment with lower prices, followed by Murray, Longman and others, all hoping to reap great rewards by reaching a huge new middle-class audience. Yet even a 5s or 6s price was really too much for this market, and would be far beyond the means of working-class readers. The increased popularity of both the circulating library and the part-work indicate responses to these pressures.[28] Some managed to benefit directly from the problems of others: Thomas Tegg, who was to become an important character in the copyright debate, made his firm famous for its domination of the reprint and remainder trade. His method was to buy up stock and copyrights which were not selling well or which were owned by bankrupt firms, and to sell the acquired titles at vastly reduced prices. Gradually the trade began to cater for the mass market, with penny periodicals and cheap reprints.

Although these responses to prevailing conditions were successful, the book trade also reacted by opposing policies and practices which made things difficult. Its ability to do this dated from the sixteenth century, when the Stationers' Company had exercised very tight control over printing, reinforced by restrictive state measures. The influence of both the government and the Stationers' Company declined in the eighteenth century, although many of the old rules were adopted as trade practices.[29] As has been seen, labour organisation in the printing trades was relatively sophisticated, particularly in London. However, during the eighteenth century, the printing and publishing functions had become separated. With the all-important copyrights in the hands of the

[26] Albert E. Musson, *The Typographical Association: origins and history up to 1949* (1954), p. 21.

[27] Richard D. Altick, *The English common reader* (Chicago, 1957), p. 260.

[28] Ironically, the circulating libraries became the publishers' best customers: the customary small editions at high prices were affordable if they could be lent out to many readers.

[29] For instance, there were continuing attempts to regulate the number of apprentices in the trade, and to control wages, hours and working conditions.

London publishers, printers became 'paid agents'.[30] Understandably, therefore, printers' views on the copyright question were shaped by different considerations from those which guided the publishers. To publicise their views, the print trades used the channels familiar to them from their existing trade organisations.

COOPERATION AND ORGANISATION

Concerted action in defence of the book trade was almost a reflex action. Barnes has commented that 'booksellers had long become accustomed to combine forces when petitioning parliament, and such petitions increased in number during the first quarter of the nineteenth century':[31] in 1802, 200 booksellers and publishers signed a petition to remove the excessive duty on paper; in 1808, forty-six firms supported a bill to reduce the number of libraries entitled to a copy of every new book; from 1812–14 the copyright question brought petitions from booksellers and publishers in London and Edinburgh, and again in 1818 when Edward Christian sought an alteration of the 1814 Act.[32] In 1829, the London booksellers and publishers had made their very controversial attempt to impose a minimum retail price for books, formalised in a set of Regulations.[33] This attempt to prevent underselling was enforced by a committee, whose members included Baldwin, Longman and Murray – all firms later prominent in the protests against the copyright bills. Several of those who did not satisfy the committee aired their grievances in pamphlets and in the newspapers, attacking what was termed the 'Booksellers' Monopoly'. This issue was still creating publicity in 1834, only a short time before Talfourd's proposals. The parallel Glasgow Booksellers' Association, which was formed in 1836, was also criticised: in 1844 a legal challenge that it was conspiratorial and monopolistic

[30] John Feather, *A history of British publishing* (1988), p. 105.

[31] Barnes, *Free trade in books*, p. 1.

[32] In 1813 the Stationers' Company appointed a committee to watch over its interest as the copyright bill passed through the House of Commons. There is no evidence that they did the same with Talfourd's bills, although the Stationers' Company did continue to enjoy the benefits of the copyright registration system, especially the 1s fee for each entry examined. Cyprian Blagden, *The Stationers' Company: a history, 1403–1959* (1966), pp. 272–4.

[33] Barnes, *Free trade in books*, Appendix 2.

led to its being disbanded.[34] This further undermined the London group.

A more visible example of the level of organisation achieved by publishers was the *Publishers' Circular*, which began in September 1837 and appeared fortnightly at the (stamped) price of 2d. An 'address' at the end of volume I explained that it was planned by 'the principal publishers of London' to serve as an 'authorised medium' for the publication of their advertisements for newly published books: there was evidently some significant cohesion of interests here. The *Circular* is interesting not only because of its range of advertisements – from the outset it carried notices of meetings relevant to the trade, but more editorial material appeared as it became more established. The aim was not to make money out of the magazine itself, the rates for advertising were set to cover only 'a fair remuneration to the Editor for his trouble' (and costs, presumably). A committee of fourteen was appointed to oversee the management of the enterprise: their numbers included many of the most influential London publishers. Longman, Murray, Rivington and Pickering had been on the committee enforcing the regulations on minimum prices. There are also new names: Tegg and Tilt, for instance, who were known for their cheap editions and remainders, and could never have been persuaded to enforce rules against underselling. Evidently it was possible to unite on some issues even if not on others.

Many other organisations were formed during this period. The Booksellers' Provident Association was founded in June 1838, and advertised a dinner planned to celebrate its founding: Tegg is amongst those listed as 'stewards'. The second annual dinner is likewise advertised and the *Publishers' Circular* published the treasurer's report that the Association had over £8,000 in cash and securities.[35] The list of sums received on the evening included ten guineas from Andrew Spottiswoode, and ten pounds from the ubiquitous Thomas Tegg. The report of the third annual dinner noted that nearly £10,000 had been raised, and also publicised several other similar groups:

> It is pleasing also to observe the support given to other institutions of a kindred spirit closely connected with ourselves – such as 'The Printers' Pension Society,' and 'The Newspaper Press Benevolent Association,' the

[34] Ibid., ch. 1 gives a fuller account. [35] 1 June 1839.

Third Anniversary of which was celebrated at the London Tavern, on Saturday, June 20th, when the Marquis of Normanby presided, and the list of Donations announced by the Treasurer was most cheering – 'The Stationers' and Paper Manufacturer's Provident Society' likewise had a Dinner at the West India Dock Tavern, Blackwall, on the 23rd, to celebrate its establishment: the chair was taken by the president, Sir James Williams. The honorary secretary, Mr J. E. Cooper, announced the amount of Donations and Subscriptions, already received £2027.17s., and the sum of £626.10s.10d. was afterwards collected in the room.[36]

These were mutual funds rather than trade unions in the narrow sense, but they provide evidence of a high level of organisation and trade cohesion, backed by significant financial reserves. Although their main purpose was to provide sickness benefits and life insurance, friendly societies also offered sociable and convivial fellowship. Most local societies had a monthly club night, and a yearly feast such as these ones.[37] The monthly premium was paid at a meeting, often held in a public house. Also, many friendly societies came to be associated with mutual improvement societies and institutes.[38] The book trade was evidently well supplied with mutual societies. The monthly meeting might well have provided a natural focus for the coordination of a response to perceived threats to the trade. Although there is no specific evidence of this during the copyright campaign, there is a clear indication that this mechanism was previously used by book-finishers to agitate for better working conditions.[39] The *Circular* was a loyal promoter of these organisations, consistently advertising and reporting their proceedings.

The *Circular* was also used as a means of general communication with the trade: there are advertisements for positions vacant and wanted, and news of libraries or businesses being disposed of. An increasing number of notices concerning copyright infringement began to appear. Some of these warned simply that a

[36] 1 July 1840.

[37] Peter H. J. H. Gosden, *Self-help: voluntary associations in the 19th century* (1973), p. 22.

[38] Trygve R. Tholfsen, *Working class radicalism in mid-Victorian England* (1976), pp. 288–91.

[39] A circular issued by the Committee of the Finishers' Friendly Assocation names three societies, The Friends, The Brothers and the City Brothers, founded between 1779 and 1785. It is careful to list the public house where each society met, and describes how they collected for a strike fund: *The Book-Finishers' Friendly Circular, conducted by a Committee of the Finishers' Friendly Association* (1845–51), p. 11.

particular book was a pirated version, and announced an intention to take legal proceedings against any bookseller offering it for sale. Others, who had managed to obtain an injunction, trumpeted the fact.[40] Copyright was obviously a matter of interest and concern: one of the early numbers contained a prominently positioned advertisement for a pamphlet which was heavily critical of Talfourd's bill.[41]

By 1841 many issues of the *Publishers' Circular* began with a section of 'Literary News'. This might contain simply notices of forthcoming books, but increasingly contained news relevant to the trade. In May, a piece on copyright appeared. There is evident satisfaction at the French Chamber of Deputies' refusal to extend the term, as it 'seems as little inclined as our House of Commons to extend the right of literary property, although the former appears to include a greater number of authors than our popular representation'. In contrast, M. de la Martine's condemnation of international piracy[42] as 'a disgrace to civilization', was quoted with evident approval. This public support for an international copyright law seemed to represent a new enthusiasm. The ten-year extension of the German copyright term (to life plus forty years) was noted briefly: there was a question as to whether it was retrospective – an issue very familar from domestic discussions. Details of the recent changes to Austrian stamp and other duties were also given: these must have been of direct concern.

On 1 April 1842 the *Circular* returned to the issue of domestic

40 One notice was headed 'Literary piracy – Mr Cooper's novels': it stated that Bentley had purchased the copyright of 'The Headsman' in Great Britain and Ireland, and that Foster & Hextall had been intending to publish it under the erroneous impression that they were at liberty to do so because it had been published in America. It was claimed that the injunction posed a considerable general threat: '[n]ot merely the Publishers, but all Vendors, as well as Purchasers even, will bear very serious risk by aiding in the circulation of Pirated Copies, against the authority of the Court of Chancery' (15 October 1839).

41 *Observations on the Law of Copyright; in reference to the bill introduced into the House of Commons by Mr. Serjeant Talfourd: in which it is attempted to prove that the provisions of that Bill are opposed to the Principles of English Law; that Authors require no additional protection, and that such a Bill would inflict a heavy blow on Literature, and prove a great discouragement to its diffusion in this country* (1838): *The Publishers' Circular*, February 1838, p. 132.

42 This appeared in a report to the Chamber of Deputies, quoted in the *Publishers' Circular*, 15 May 1841. Talfourd's bill had been thrown out in February, following Macaulay's intervention.

copyright: this was a topical matter, with the committee stage of Mahon's bill imminent. A brief account of the principal provisions of Mahon's bill was provided, without comment. However, there was another strong plea for a satisfactory international copyright law: 'It is to be hoped that while the New Copyright Bill is under consideration, the crying evil of Foreign Piracies of English Works will not be lost sight of . . . The clandestine importation exceeds the belief of those who may not hitherto have paid that attention to the subject which the interests of authors as well as booksellers imperiously demand.' The alleged community of interests – between authors and booksellers – was often remarked on by publishers.[43] Duration of copyright term no longer seemed to be of much concern: the amendments to the term which resulted from the bill's committee stage were recorded in a later number, without further comment.[44] However, the campaign for international copyright continued.

THE CAMPAIGN AGAINST THE BILLS

As a campaigning device, the *Circular* could only have been of limited use. Although its position on copyright was presumably a reflection of the general publishing opinion, its audience was limited to those already likely to hold similar views. Lobbying was an obvious alternative method. The established London publishers would have been well placed to discuss such matters with influential people in and out of parliament, as they would meet them quite naturally in a social context. Some evidence of this survives in letters and journals, as will be seen: it is necessarily incomplete and partial, but can provide some factual information, as well as insights into issues and personalities.

[43] Thomas Moore viewed this claim with some detachment, as he noted in his journal: 'Was much amused with a very chacteristic trait of the *ROW* which came out in Tom Longman's great anxiety from his great zeal for the bill – that publishers at least were well taken care of by it. I laughingly asked him "is there any good to come to *me* from it?" "Oh yes, there is," he eagerly replied. After a few more words between us I subscribed my signature to the List, when having gained his object, he with much composure said "The *good* is very *remote*".' Thomas Moore, *The journal of Thomas Moore*, ed. Wilfred S. Dowden (Newark and London, 1983–91), p. 2235 (March 1842).

[44] 15 April 1842.

A more public airing of the issues could be achieved in several ways. One very respectable way was to write to a newspaper. The quality London papers gave Parliamentary matters a central place, and were happy to print letters and write leaders on topical or controversial subjects. Newspapers were carefully read by those in power, and were known to be influential: they merit discussion in their own right.[45] Articles in periodicals were likewise important, although these were overwhelmingly in favour of an extension, as will be shown.[46] Pamphlets were another possibility, although there is little evidence that this device was much used: Tegg was a notable exception. Finally, there were petitions.

Publishers' petitions

The publishers' efforts at petitioning are very meagre when compared to the number of signatures which arrived on petitions from print workers. Only two petitions mentioning publishers came from the London area in 1838, although they contained almost 300 signatures.[47] One of these came exclusively from booksellers and publishers of London and Westminster, and was thought important enough to print in an appendix.[48]

It is significant that the London publishers petitioned jointly with booksellers. This conceals the growing divisions between these functions, as publishers abandoned this part of the trade. During the eighteenth century and before, London publishing

[45] See ch. 6. [46] See ch. 8.

[47] 4,816 presented 25 April 1838, from 'Certain Authors, Publishers, and Booksellers of London, and others' (199 signatures) and 4,821, also presented 25 April 1838, from 'Booksellers and Publishers of London & Westminster', App. 407 (98 signatures).

[48] The other, 4,816, mentions 'authors'. No really prestigious author petitioned against Talfourd's bill, although this may have been explained by the general reluctance of literary figures to become involved on either side. Authors were mentioned in a general way in a few petitions, although individuals cannot usually be identified. One exception is Peter Austin Nutall, who is styled 'Printer and Doctor of Laws'. His first petition asked that the retrospective clause should not be made law. Nutall's personal interest was in the production of his *Classical and archaeological dictionary* (published 1840) 'on a cheap, though extensive and original plan'. He appears to have emulated his publisher, Thomas Tegg, and borrowed liberally from copyright works which he had hoped would be out of copyright before the publication of his work: the merits of his actions are unclear. The text of another petition does not survive. 6,427 presented 24 April 1839, App. 593. 13,121 presented 6 May 1840.

houses had habitually maintained a retail business. The demise of joint-wholesaling and of the share-book system, coupled with the influence of competition, had meant that this was now almost impossible to justify. Most chose to specialise in publishing, particularly as the City lost its customers to the fashionable West End.[49] Conflicts of interest then arose between publishers and the retail booksellers whose profit margins were continually squeezed. Although the 1829 booksellers' regulations sought to guarantee both trade and retail prices, they proved unenforceable, and resulted in a great deal of bad publicity.[50] Certain retail booksellers, particularly in the provinces, were increasingly hostile to the rich London trade. This petition concealed these rifts, taking the retrospective clause as its main target. It began with a careful analysis of previous legislative interventions, all of which preserved assignees' existing rights by granting extensions only for works yet to be published. Significantly, the petitioners stated that they would welcome improved international copyright.

There were only three other publishers' petitions in 1838. One was from Scott, Webster, Geary, the publishers of the English Classic library: with only these three signatures, and presented by Lord Ossulton, it is not typical.[51] These publishers were unusual in their willingness to petition publicly:[52] most of the big publishers preferred to campaign in more discreet ways. Another petition was signed by twelve booksellers and publishers of Dublin – who were scarcely known for their respect for English copyright.[53] More importantly, there was a petition from the members of the Glasgow Stationers' Company.[54] This rehearsed the familiar objections of the book trade – they opposed any extension to the copyright term, and the retrospective clause. In particular, the provisions involving part-works, extracts and

49 Feather, *History of British publishing*, p. 123.

50 See ch. 4, p. 87.

51 4,783, presented 25 April 1838.

52 Perhaps they were used to this kind of publicity. In February 1842 Thomas Campbell was granted an injunction to prevent Scott & Geary from selling a compilation of copyright works, *The book of the poets*. Scott & Geary argued that their 'general design' was intended to illustrate the progress of poetry, such that the selections would promote the sale of Campbell's work, and also that 'it was the custom of the trade'.

53 4,817, presented 25 April 1838.

54 4,631, presented 11 April 1838, App. 390. This organisation seems rather elusive.

abridgements were styled as a threat to the general diffusion of literature and science, 'by destroying the kind of books which alone the common people have the means to purchase or the leisure to read'. A catastrophic effect on the book trade was predicted: 'Many thousands of workmen, who are now employed in the trades that pertain to the manufacture of cheap books, will infallibly be thrown out of employment.'[55]

The main publishers' opposition to Talfourd's plans is thus represented by five petitions, amounting to 350 signatures in total. The only publisher's petition in 1839 came from Thomas Tegg:[56] he is not characteristic of the recognised publishers, who had fallen silent.[57] In 1840 at least some of the booksellers and publishers of London and Westminster had changed their minds and were petitioning *in favour* of the redrafted measure, deploring the unsettled state of copyright law.[58] By 1842 Longman and Murray were actively campaigning for the bill, collecting signatures for the petitions in favour.[59] Presumably others were doing likewise.

The publishers' response to the copyright question altered significantly during Talfourd's campaign. Their initial reaction was characterised by a marked hostility, particularly to the 'retrospective' clause. This hostility was sufficiently influential to ensure significant changes to Talfourd's original scheme. Once

55 This worry was evidently shared by the workmen. Glasgow sent the largest provincial petition in 1838 – 6,380, presented 16 May 1838, 309 signatures (see ch. 4, p. 83).

56 Tegg petitioned in 1839 (2,324) and again in 1840 (13,122). His petitions will be considered separately, in the context of his overall role in the campaign: see below, pp. 123–5.

57 A few other petitions have peripheral links with these groups. One London publisher, Mr Strange, allowed his shop to be used as a collection point for the signatures, but these are recorded as being from fifty-six 'inhabitants of the Metropolis', and not publishers specifically: 16,072 presented 29 May 1840. Strange had been associated with the fight against the newspaper stamp: see above. Similarly, petitions from 'booksellers and others, Yarmouth', and 'news-vendors and others' are submitted in 1840; 17,948 presented 7 July 1840; 16,455 presented 5 June 1840. Again it is impossible to tell how many of the signatories fell into the named category. The petition of twenty London Law Stationers should also be noted in the publishing/bookselling context: 16,454 presented 5 June 1840.

58 1,755, presented 19 February 1840, App. 131.

59 For instance Thomas Moore's: see footnote 4, above, and petitions 6,252–5, 16 March 1842 (all presented by Mahon, see below, ch. 7, p. 173). Another influential publisher, Francis Rivington, also signed.

these changes had been secured, however, a period of relative indifference followed: if domestic copyright was to be extended, publishers were happy to take any benefits which might accrue, although they were not minded to work actively to secure this. In contrast, interest in the question of international copyright was growing throughout this period, and it was increasingly regarded as an issue of great importance. It is, however, essential to realise that their campaign was certainly not grounded solely in parliamentary petitions. Other methods of lobbying were used, with great effectiveness, to convey the publishers' position to those with influence.

Other means of protest

Important though the publishers' petitions were, they would not have been sufficient to defeat Talfourd's bills. Another important factor was the publishers' unity: the close-knit relations between members of the trade, and the concentration of power in a limited number of firms, ensured a relatively homogenous response, at least from the more traditional London houses. The trade's simple message could be easily conveyed: they disapproved of Talfourd's proposals – unanimously. However, all possible means of exerting influence were used in addition to petitions. Personal persuasion of those in power was of decisive importance, but public letters and pamphlets also had their place.

Evidence of this more subtle sort of lobbying is not conveniently assembled, but may be drawn out of contemporary sources. The story told by newspapers, letters, anecdotes and diaries is necessarily incomplete and partial. Nevertheless, since this sort of pressure was probably the publishers' most effective weapon, it is important to attempt to assess its extent. Looking at the activities of a range of firms, it is clear that their interest and influence varied considerably. Yet there are indications that some of the leading London publishers could wield a good deal of power.

One of these prominent figures was John Murray. Murray inherited his bookselling business from his father. The customary network of agencies with other booksellers, particularly in Scotland, was maintained, and Murray began to publish more on his own account. He was wise enough to break with both Constable and Ballantyne following differences over money matters: it was therefore Blackwood's who acted as his agent for the new *Quarterly Review*.

The *Quarterly* was started by Murray, with Canning's approval, as a Tory counter to the *Edinburgh Review*. It proved a great success, and Murray's drawing-room functioned more than ever as an important literary meeting-place, for figures such as Isaac D'Israeli, Gifford, Moore, Campbell, Croker, Byron, Scott and others. It would therefore have been hard for the *Quarterly* to ignore Talfourd's bill, particularly as Southey had already addressed the question of copyright in 1818.[60] However, the subject was not revisited until 1841, following Wordsworth's letters to Lockhart, the editor of the *Quarterly*, urging him to consider producing an article.

Although an important literary figure in his own right, Lockhart was also Scott's son-in-law. Wordsworth was clearly aware that Lockhart's scruples and sensitivity to public opinion might lead him to decline the subject, for fear of being seen to espouse a cause which would bring his own enrichment: 'The Copyright Bill is to come on again on the 28th. Has your relation to Sir W. Scott prevented your noticing this important subject in the *Quarterly*? I cannot but think an able Article upon it in that journal would do more towards putting the question in the way of being carried than anything else.'[61] Lockhart did not agree for over a year. In July 1841 Wordsworth was in London, where he lobbied Peel on the copyright question. Wordsworth's account of this unsuccessful interview seems to have persuaded Lockhart that he should act.[62]

The resulting article was sent to Murray, evidently for approval, although Lockhart's covering letter was both truculent and defensive:

> As to my own article, you can, if you please, reject it in toto; but if so, I am pledged to Mr Wordsworth and it must go to Blackwood's. I don't at present feel at all disposed to take thought about Peel's or any other politican's opinion. I have studied the subject, and so has Wordsworth, who is at least as likely to study any question to advantage as Sir Robert Peel. I propose no plan for an Act of Parliament. But I think I have shown that unless more protection be given to authors and publishers –

[60] Robert S. Southey, 'An inquiry into the Copyright Act', *Quarterly Review* 21 (1818), 196–213.

[61] Wordsworth, *The letters of William and Dorothy Wordsworth*, 2nd edn, ed. Alan G. Hill (Oxford, 1969–88), VII, p. 65 (April 1840).

[62] Ibid., VII, p. 214 (10 July 1841).

whose interests I have treated as identical, which they are – our literature must expire in a muddled heap of fraudulent and worthless compilations and base appeals to the lower passions. After all, just ask yourself whether the Editor of the *Quarterly Review* has not a right to express his own deliberate opinion on a subject of this sort whenever he pleases? It seems to me that if he has not that right, he has none.[63]

The content of Lockhart's argument, which is broadly in favour of greater copyright protection, will be examined with the other periodical articles, but his letter to Murray is noteworthy in itself, for several reasons. First, Lockhart's studied refusal to advocate any particular legislative measure suggests that Wordsworth's guess as to the sensitivities involved may well have been correct. Also, the barbed tone would not have been necessary unless Lockhart had reason to believe that Murray would disapprove: Henry Crabb Robinson reported Lockhart's complaint to Wordsworth that Murray was 'on the other side, and insisted on certain things being left out',[64] and this is confirmed by a comment from Wordsworth.[65] It is interesting that Murray seems to have felt it necessary and appropriate to consult Peel, and even more important is Lockhart's offhand dismissal of Peel's opinion: it would have required a certain amount of bravery for the editor of a Tory review to express such casual contempt for a Conservative prime minister. Perhaps more care should have been taken, for Peel's lack of support in fact proved to be very detrimental.

There is, then, direct evidence of Murray's caution with regard to Talfourd's bill. It is not clear whether this is motivated by political tact, or whether it stems from the subject of copyright itself. Murray was in fact well known for the high prices he offered for copyrights. Other letters to Murray indicate that foreign piracies were of repeated and growing concern.[66] Yet, paradoxically, international copyright was a much less controversial subject, in that everybody could agree that it was necessary. In this way, then, Murray's house seems to have taken a fairly typical

[63] Samuel Smiles, *A publisher and his friends: memoir and correspondence of the late John Murray* (1891), p. 499. Lockhart's article, 'The copyright question', appears in *Quarterly Review* 69 (December 1841), 186–227.

[64] Henry Crabb Robinson, *On books and their writers*, ed. Edith Morley (1938), II, p. 607.

[65] Wordsworth said of the article, 'if you had not been interfered with some deficiencies might have been supplied': Wordsworth, *Letters*, VII, p. 283 (January 1842).

[66] e.g. Smiles, *Publisher and his friends*, pp. 500, 501.

stance. However, whatever his reasoning, Murray's attitude served to deny Lockhart free access to the highly influential *Quarterly*. Mahon took care to consult Murray about the revised 1842 bill.

Longman & Co., one of the most prestigious and influential firms, was very much against aspects of the bill, particularly the retrospective clause: the Longmans wrote a public letter of protest to *The Times*.[67] They also engaged actively in private lobbying:[68] confirmation of this can be found in Thomas Moore's journals, which are a particularly interesting source of evidence, since Moore himself had protested at the existing state of copyright. Moore had explained the retrospective clause to his wife, 'which I had but just come to understand, myself, not having troubled my head much with the question'. Her reaction, 'Why, that's not honest,' Moore put in a letter to the Longmans – his publishers. Tom Longman, who happened to be calling on Lord John Russell to discuss the copyright question, seized on this opportunity and showed him the letter.[69] Longman was to become one of those lobbying most actively *for* the revised 1842 bill – without the retrospective clause.

Some of the smaller publishing houses did not toe the party line. Moxon, who published mostly poetry, including Wordsworth's, was apparently closely involved in the campaign: he was an old friend of Talfourd. Moxon's biographer quotes an extraordinary letter from Talfourd to Moxon, in which Talfourd suggested that a term of life plus sixty years would be too long: 'If we are to have a copyright of threescore years, the term had better be calculated from the birth of each of his offspring, rather than from the parent's death; for when a child, even in the shape of a book, has reached that stage, it is surely time for it to be settled in the world.'[70]

67 *The Times*, 16 May 1838, p. 3f. A very similar letter appeared in the *Morning Chronicle*, 17 May 1838.

68 They had often led from the front in this: compare their attempt to block sales of the *Penny Magazine*, their role in the share-book system, and in the Booksellers' Regulations.

69 Moore, *Journal*, ed. Dowden, pp. 1966–8 (May 1838). Russell's objections emerged without warning during the committee stage on 6 June: the coincidence is striking. He made oblique (but identifiable) reference to Moore's case in his speech: *Hansard, Parliamentary debates* (3rd series), xlii, 556–8.

70 Harold G. Merriam, *Edward Moxon, publisher of poets* (New York, 1939), p. 153.

Talfourd is also quoted as fearing that valuable books might be neglected in an author's lifetime, and then lost to the world: this anxiety seems to have generated his proposal that both past and future works of living authors be included in any new term of copyright – the retrospective clause. Although no date is given for these letters, Talfourd's thinking was evidently not firm when he wrote them: he also sketched a flexible (and quite unworkable) plan, whereby copyright would exist as long as public demand for a book was maintained, as shown by the amount of stock kept by booksellers. Presumably this places them before 1837.

Others who might have been expected to take a great interest in the matter are strangely silent. Charles Knight, who was heavily involved with the battle against the newspaper stamp, and the SDUK campaign for cheap good books, scarcely mentions national copyright in his autobiography. Perhaps Knight was too closely associated with Brougham to wish to remember Talfourd's contribution. He was eloquent on the subject of foreign piracies, however: 'the Belgian books were lowered in every quality of typographical excellence by the ruinous competition of the publishers to produce non-copy-right works . . . The literary labour having been common to every plunderer, the outward quality of the book was degraded to the lowest standard of unnatural cheapness.'[71] Again, international copyright was seen as an uncontroversial requirement.

Of all the publishers, Thomas Tegg (1776–1845) was the most hostile: he became almost an emblem of the extreme anti-copyright feeling in the book trade. His background, and his subsequent role in the publishing world, help to explain his position.[72] Aged only nine, the orphaned Tegg was apprenticed to a bookseller in Scotland, who treated him so badly that he ran away. He travelled all over the British Isles before settling in London in 1796, where he worked for various booksellers. Tegg opened his own shop in 1800, but the venture failed following the treachery of a friend. He then returned to the provinces, where he would buy the duplicates from gentlemen's libraries, or pick up

Merriam paraphrases Talfourd's letter(s?) to Moxon, giving neither date nor source.

[71] Charles Knight, *Passages of a working life during half a century* (1864), III, p. 136.

[72] Curwen, *History of booksellers*, pp. 379–98.

stock at trade sales. These could be sold at book auctions, where the seller would himself stand on the rostrum and give his patter. He quickly paid off his debts and returned to London where he opened another shop, and began printing cheap reprints and abridgements of popular works, which were enormously popular and lucrative. He also bought up large quantities of remaindered works, which he would sell very cheaply.[73] His commercial sense was reinforced by his enterprise: after Trafalgar, Tegg sold 50,000 copies of *The whole life of Nelson*, which he rushed through the press at a few hours' notice.[74]

Tegg was one of the first publishers to aim exclusively at the market for cheap and popular reading material. The comparatively large scale of his operation brought him significant commercial success, but made him unpopular with his colleagues. His reprints and abridgements were usually well-tried and popular standards.[75] However, the trade liked to regard these as their exclusive property, even though the copyright had long expired. William Chambers, who was to follow in Tegg's bookselling footsteps, describes what happened:

> In daring to break down this monopoly, [Tegg] encountered some abuse, which, however, did not deter him in his operations. His editions, as a rule, were not so highly finished as those issued under the auspices of the trade; but as they were sold at about half the price they were correspondingly appreciated by that portion of the book-buying world who are not scrupulously nice as to typographical elegance.[76]

Talfourd's scheme would have made abridgements much more difficult, and would probably have increased the delay before at least certain books were remaindered. Tegg's opposition was

[73] Some of his best remainder bargains came as a result of the 1826 panic, of which Tegg is reputed to have said, 'Twas the broom that swept the booksellers' warehouses.' The numbers of copies involved were extraordinary; for example, 100,000 volumes of *Murray's Family Library* at 1s each, and 50,000 copies of A. J. Valpy's *Delphin Classics*: Frank A. Mumby, *The romance of book selling* (1910) p. 284.

[74] Mumby, *Romance*, p. 295.

[75] Tegg was sometimes challenged on his methods: see *Mawman* v. *Tegg* (1826) 2 Russ 385, where he paid a substantial settlement following alleged taking of material from a copyright encyclopaedia to fill his own rival version.

[76] Chambers, *Memoir*, p. 144. Altick records that 'Tegg's reprints were notorious for their slovenly text and miserly format' – a somewhat different gloss: Altick, *English common reader*, p. 285.

therefore almost inevitable.[77] He was not afraid to be conspicuous, writing several tendentious letters to the newspapers[78] and publishing two signed pamphlets.[79] He also submitted two petitions, the first of which survives.[80] His main argument was that competition in the trade lowered the price of books to the public dramatically, but only once copyright had expired: his technique, which he used in letters and pamphlets also, was to list the published price of titles, and their corresponding remainder price (always hugely deflated). He regarded the retrospective clause with predictable distaste. Talfourd was criticised for his use of Milton and Defoe as examples, authors dating from a time when education was less widespread. Tegg's expressed view was that the measure would frustrate efforts to extend education, and would 'keep books at a monopoly price for the period of 60 years instead of twenty-eight years'.

Tegg signed another petition the following year, which unfortunately was not printed.[81] An astonishing 1,120 signatures were collected, apparently at Tegg's own instigation: 'Not content with getting up petitions in all parts of town and country – that is to say, in all those places where he thought there was any chance of getting a goodly number of persons to petition – he has personally canvassed a host of "M.P.s," proselytising some of his views, and neutralising others who were most strenuous supporters of the learned Sergeant's bill.'[82] He had become one of the public faces of the opposition to Talfourd, and was much reviled by the pro-side as an exploiter of authors. Although he made himself an easy target for such attacks, because of his lack of moderation and his militant philistinism, he never wavered from his opposition to the extension of copyright.

Tegg's very public stance was not copied by many publishers. However, another very independent publishing firm, that of William and Robert Chambers, was prepared to be numbered against Talfourd. The story of these two brothers mirrors Tegg's

[77] 'Mr Tegg is the great champion of cheap literature, and the mortal enemy of copyright bills; not that he cares a fraction of a farthing about literature considered in itself, but that he knows that to prevent the right of republishing interesting works would be to destroy a leading and lucrative branch of his business': James Grant, *Portraits of public characters* (1841), p. 41.

[78] For instance, four to *The Times:* see ch. 6.

[79] See ch. 8.

[80] 2,323 presented 27 February 1839, App. 187.

[81] 13,122 presented 6 May 1840.

[82] Grant, *Portraits*, p. 37.

story in many ways. From very poor beginnings, they built up separate bookselling businesses. William's first stock came from one of Tegg's agents, who allowed him £10 credit in return for his assistance at a trade sale. As their businesses thrived, the brothers became more ambitious and ventured into publishing. Although their earliest attempt at a journal was not profitable,[83] they were keen to provide some alternative to the low-priced serials begun in London and Edinburgh just after 1830. William Chambers dealt in these, but he was exasperated by their irregular publication dates and also by their clearly ephemeral content: 'They consisted for the most part of disjointed and unauthorised extracts from books, clippings from floating literature, old stories, and stale jocularities. With no purpose but to furnish temporary amusement, they were, as it appeared to me, the perversion of what, if rightly conducted, might become a powerful engine of social improvement.'[84]

William thus saw the potential for a journal which would make a contribution to popular education. The result was *Chambers's Edinburgh Journal*, 3½d weekly, which first appeared on 4 February 1832. Sales soon reached 30,000 in Scotland alone, driving out all other cheap Edinburgh papers. With an agent in London, sales exceeded 80,000. The SDUK's *Penny Magazine* was to be its only serious rival, first appearing nearly two months later.[85] The brothers gave up bookselling and began publishing as W. & R. Chambers. The size of the operation was enormous, making it hard to find paper and print locally: stereotype plates were sent weekly to London for the English demand, and another set used in Edinburgh. Steam was to provide a solution.

Related ventures followed; *Chambers's Information for the People* (1833), *Chambers's Educational Course*, *Chambers's Miscellany of Useful and Entertaining Tracts*. The Chambers's material was often in direct competition with the SDUK's productions, and their interest in cheap, educational texts is undeniable: interest in the copyright question is therefore predictable. William Chambers does not mention the subject explicitly in his

[83] *The Kaleidoscope or Edinburgh Literary Amusement*, 6 October 1821–18 January 1827, 3d fortnightly.

[84] Chambers, *Memoir*, p. 231.

[85] First issue 31 March 1832. William Chambers is careful not to suggest that Knight stole his idea – at least not directly: Chambers, *Memoir*, p. 234.

Memoirs.[86] However, it was a matter of such concern that the Chambers brothers wrote a pamphlet and two letters to *The Times* on the subject.[87] Their first letter listed fourteen objections, which encompassed most of the arguments ever used against the bill.[88] They further suggested that the bill would force publishers to insist on being named as author of works which they commissioned, in order to protect their interests.

Although Tegg and the Chambers brothers were unusual in their willingness to court publicity, they did not break the publishers' united front against Talfourd's bill. Unlike the print workers, the publishers were able to campaign on several fronts simultaneously. With the possible exception of the *Publishers' Circular*, which had little external audience, their techniques had been used before. Their effectiveness was reconfirmed: the hated retrospective clause was dropped. Nevertheless, it is possible to detect cracks in the façade of unity, particularly when some of the publishers changed sides in 1840 and petitioned in the bill's favour. The trade underwent a transformation from oligopoly to competitive industry, and there is a sense in which the tensions are visible.

However, general public perceptions of the publishers' views would have been based largely on material in the newspaper press. There the publishers' case was presented with force and conviction, although counterbalancing material was also offered. Editorial opinions were expressed, but much of the material published was factual, and the coverage overall was serious and thoughtful. Newspapers thus provided an important forum for the debate.

86 Although he does deplore the 'extravagant credit system' in the publishing trade which leads to frequent dealings in copyrights: 'valuable literary property, the fruit of ingenious conception and enterprise, is thus constantly undergoing a process of transfer and confiscation'. Note the balance of author and publisher in his description.

87 William and Robert Chambers, *Brief objections to Mr Talfourd's new Copyright Bill* (Edinburgh, 1838). *The Times*, 25 April 1838, 18 May 1838.

88 In précis, these were: that publishers would not pay more for the extended term; they would have no incentive to pay for improvements or revisions of schoolbooks, for example; it would be difficult to make extracts; the 'retrospective' stripping of publishers' rights would be unsettling; copyright was not a natural right, since all authors have studied earlier books, and should be a limited right to repay the author for his trouble – as with patents.

6

THE CAMPAIGN IN THE DAILY PRESS

Parliamentarians involved in the 1842 compromise felt an obligation to consider public opinion: Macaulay's repeated reference to the public interest, and Peel's anxiety that he should not be seen to support 'monopoly', show that this feeling was not confined to radicals. Newspapers were the primary route for the dissemination of parliamentary proceedings, and in some ways act as a barometer – albeit rather unreliable – of public opinion.

After 1832, when the composition of membership of the House of Commons began to change, the House was increasingly influenced by outside opinion. Conduct of ministers and members had already been affected by the greater publicity given to the proceedings of the House. Although members at first resisted publication of reports of their debates, fearing misrepresentation and disliking the publicity, they had tacitly abandoned the right to prevent such publication in 1771. In 1830 the House began to reserve special seats in the public gallery for the use of reporters, resulting in the first series of Hansard's *Debates*. Details of parliamentary proceedings were also available in the newspapers, which published very full reports.[1] Ministers and members thus became accountable to a much wider range of public opinion, and equally began to look to impress public opinion with their speeches and questions.

For a time the House of Commons had preserved the anonymity of members who had voted for and against particular motions. Results but not names were recorded in the *Journals of the House of Commons*, and the strangers' gallery was cleared for a division until 1853. In fact this did not mean that division lists were not

[1] The information available to readers was a testament to the industry and initiative of the parliamentary reporters. William Woodfall was a celebrated early reporter, in the days when proceedings had to be memorised. Reports were not verbatim, nor were they intended to be.

available: they were compiled from information gathered by reporters from members, and did appear in the newspaper reports. But in 1836 the House began to publish official division lists, increasing the pressure on members to respond to their consitu-tents and to lobbying groups.[2]

The serious London daily papers, such as *The Times*, the *Morning Chronicle* and the *Morning Post*, gave very central focus to parliamentary matters. Newspapers were carefully read, and their reports of parliamentary matters were used as material for letters – both those for publication and private ones. Debate on controversial issues was very active and immediate: each newspaper could also provide a non-parliamentary forum for the debate of issues. Comments in one arena were quickly reflected in others, leading to a good deal of interplay not only between the various newspapers and journals, but also with parliamentary debates themselves. Editorial influence was an additional factor: *The Times*'s hostility to the copyright bills was undoubtedly damaging.

Thus, for investigations of attitudes to Talfourd's bill, which did become a high-profile matter, newspapers represent a vital source of material. The press was used unashamedly as a means of general lobbying, but also by those who wished to make very individual points. It thus becomes possible to trace and explain changes in response and attitude – which were often reflected in the versions of the bill. Also, in its purely factual mode, the press logs significant meetings and events, of which no other trace may survive.

Newspapers were not always objective in their coverage of issues, and did not pretend to be. Nevertheless, the factors which had led to a more accountable House of Commons had also affected the press, which was now generally less responsive to ministerial pressure than to the sensitivities of its readers. So, when faced with an issue such as the copyright question, how would the newspapers be likely to react? Various possible editorial lines would have suggested themselves, and the choice between them would certainly have included consideration of the party political loyalties of the paper and its editorial staff; but since

[2] Sir Norman Chester, *The English administrative system 1780–1870* (Oxford, 1981), part II, ch. 3.

copyright was not a party political matter, the editorial stance on other related issues must also be examined.

One such issue was the newspaper stamp. This had been the chief 'tax on knowledge' as far as the radical press was concerned, and the extraordinary campaign against it had resulted in its reduction to 1d in 1836. However, traditional newspapers such as *The Times* had not been at all anxious to see the 4d stamp abolished, and this was well understood at the time: 'the chief representative of the newspaper interests in the House of Commons, Mr. Walter, the principal proprietor of *The Times*, of course opposes a proposal to open the door to competition'.[3]

Although the 1836 reduction dissipated much of the issue's political heat (at least for a time), attempts to characterise copyright as a tax on knowledge would have produced unpredictable results. Spring Rice was the chancellor responsible for the reduction of the stamp, although his handling of this sensitive matter had not been particularly convincing: his compromise solution lay between abolition and retention, but he had angered the more extreme camps on both sides.[4] Spring Rice was one of those sponsoring the copyright bill, and he would scarcely have been hoping for connections to be made.

If Talfourd's plans had been likely to affect newspapers, a self-interested reaction would have been predictable. In the 1820s and 1830s it was common practice for the 2d papers to reprint reports from the stamped papers.[5] The issue was raised during the debates on the 1836 bill to reduce the stamp, by Sir Robert Inglis; he was also to become one of the sponsors of Talfourd's bill. Inglis asked if newspaper copyright was to be included in the new bill. The chancellor of the exchequer reported that he had received a separate draft bill from 'the editors of the London journals', but

[3] Alexander Andrews, *The history of British journalism* (1859), II, p. 230. John Walter was MP for Nottingham, 1841–3.

[4] Birkbeck was one of those who wanted cheap newspapers, and therefore argued for total repeal: he headed a deputation to Melbourne to put this case in February 1836. Of the long list of MPs who accompanied him, several reappear against Talfourd; Warburton, Hume, Grote, Wakley, Strutt. Birkbeck himself petitioned against the bill, and chaired a public meeting at which signatures of those opposed were collected. M. C. Moore, 'The history of the agitation against the stamp duty on newspapers 1830–55' (unpublished M.A. thesis, London, King's College, 1935), p. 145.

[5] Frederick Knight Hunt, *The fourth estate* (1850), I, p. 72.

their plan was 'so imperfect that it was impossible to propose it to the House'.[6] Talfourd wisely did not address newspaper copyright, and the newspapers had no particular axe to grind.[7]

Nor would the newspaper proprietors have been very keen to protect the book trade, which in many ways regarded large-scale newspaper publishing as an inferior relation. Particularly in London, the men who worked on newspapers were paid in a different way, and belonged to a different trade organisation that sought to emphasise the separation of the jobs. However, some of the petitions against the bill were sent from newspaper offices, so the workers evidently perceived some connection.

Viewed from the literary side, many literary men worked for or ran newspapers, and this certainly led to influence being exerted to promote Talfourd's cause. But, equally, journalism was becoming a separate profession, and newspaper proprietors were market-orientated businessmen. In relation to a proposal to extend literary copyright, it would have been foolish to expect from newspapers the same level of support that could have been predicted from the literary periodicals.

In some ways, then, newspaper reaction to the copyright issue was hard to predict. This was not a strictly party question, although party lines and loyalties were a factor. It is not clear that it would have helped Talfourd if it had been: good-quality papers were more interested in their circulation than in fostering a particular political stance. The presentation of issues depended more on the individual characters of the papers, on inter-paper rivalry, on the pressures exerted on the editorial line by those capable of influencing it, and (even) on the issues themselves.

The main London daily papers were *The Times*, and its rival the *Morning Chronicle*. Both were in principle Whig papers, and had achieved much of their pre-eminence because of their connections with the reform ministry. However, by 1834 *The Times*'s fight with Brougham had caused its editor, Barnes, to take a much more

[6] *Hansard, Parliamentary debates* (3rd series), xxxv, 267 (July 1836).

[7] In the 1855 bill which finally abolished the stamp, the chancellor of the exchequer tried to introduce a clause which gave the newspaper proprietor twenty-four hours' copyright of this news, but he had to withdraw it: *Hansard, Parliamentary debates* (3rd series), cxxxvii, 1978–2046. The protection of news stories continues to give trouble: see the long line of case law from *Walter* v. *Lane* [1900] AC 539.

independent editorial line: *The Times* supported Peel's first ministry (1834–5) and followed the Tories into opposition. The main Tory paper was the *Morning Post*, although Theodore Hook's *John Bull* and the high-Tory evening paper the *Standard* should also be mentioned. The *Globe* and the *Courier* were the main evening papers, both Whig.

The provincial press was generally too small to have much influence – although the Westmorland and Cumberland press was an exception. This was managed by the Tory Lowthers, giving them control of the *Carlisle Patriot*, the *Whitehaven Paquet* and – traditionally – the *Kendal Chronicle*. During 1818 the *Kendal Chronicle* began to resist the pressure: early in this important election year it was only neutral, and by 1818 it was hostile. The Lowthers tried to buy the paper outright, a process in which Wordsworth was involved. When the scheme failed, they set up their own rival paper, the *Westmorland Gazette*. Wordsworth was offered the editorship, but declined it.

The details of this episode provide background colour for the copyright debate. Firstly, this was the election at which Brougham was challenging Lord Lonsdale's 'right' to fill the two Westmorland seats. The Lowthers were not expecting any opposition, and Brougham seems to have given them a real fright, although he had most of the Whigs against him as well. In fact Brougham tried and failed three times in Westmorland: this aggressive, upstart behaviour did not endear him either to the Lowthers or to Wordsworth.[8] In addition, it explains why Wordsworth chose to respond to the petition of the Kendal printers (published in the *Kendal Mercury*),[9] and why his own petition was published in the *Westmorland Gazette*.

LONDON DAILIES

The Times

By 1838 *The Times* had become a focal point for opposition to Talfourd. However, this was a position which did not emerge at

[8] Wordsworth wrote two addresses during this election, published in a pamphlet as 'Two addresses to the freeholders of Westmorland': *The prose works of William Wordsworth*, eds. Warwick J. B. Owen and Jane W. Smyser (Oxford, 1974), III, p. 148.

[9] *Kendal Mercury and Westmorland Advertiser*, 14 April 1838, p. 3.

once. In 1837 *The Times* published in full Talfourd's speech introducing the bill, and welcomed it courteously.[10] Readers were referred to Maugham's work on copyright, and he was thanked for his suggestions and assistance.[11] Thomas Hood's letters on copyright in the *Athenaeum* were also praised, for their 'sense, spirit, and humour'.[12]

The Times had access to top-quality writers during this period: Thomas Moore was chief writer of verse, Thackeray wrote book reviews, and Disraeli also contributed.[13] It was not surprising, therefore, that Talfourd did not predict the onslaught to come in 1838. The campaign of opposition started in April, and was clearly planned with reference to the parliamentary timetable. The first sign of this in *The Times* was a report of the master printers' meeting in Fleet Street on 5 April: a draft petition was read and adopted, based on objections to the 'indefinite' period of copyright which would increase piracy, be prejudicial to trade and injurious to the country.[14]

The Times encouraged letters to the editor, and published several which attacked Talfourd's proposals. The first of these came from the influential Edinburgh publishers, William and Robert Chambers, who expounded a comprehensive range of arguments. Their conclusion was that: 'the passing of the bill would strike a greater blow for the perpetuation of human ignorance than anything that has taken place in modern times'.[15]

The worries about the impact on the public were thus raised early in the debate, and not just by publishing firms. 'A lover of cheap books' protested that the bill 'strikes a deadly blow at the progress of knowledge', and 'A book scholar' concluded 'that the bill will sweep away the library of every man whose income is under £500 a year'.[16] Specific exception was taken to the bill's prohibition on the publications of extracts, unless 'fairly and bona

[10] 26 May 1837, p. 3d.

[11] Robert Maugham, *A treatise on the laws of literary property* (1828). Maugham thought the twenty-eight-year term far too short, and argued strongly for perpetual copyright.

[12] See ch. 8.

[13] Henry R. F. Bourne, *English newspapers* (1887), II, p. 108.

[14] 6 April 1838, p. 3a.

[15] 25 April 1838, p. 3c. Robert Chambers wrote again, 18 May 1838, 3b. See ch. 5, p. 127.

[16] 27 April 1838, p. 6c; 28 April 1838, p. 5f.

fide made for the purpose of criticism, observation or argument': this language was attacked as insufficiently specific and easily evaded.[17] The publication of books of extracts was common and profitable practice, although wholesale taking was not permitted. Thomas Tegg was one of those challenged on this, and would have been understandably sensitive.[18]

The Times responded with a provocative leader, deprecating the practice of legislating for a few authors at the expense of the public, which currently enjoyed 'that cheap and easy access to literary works which, in the absence of an unfettered competition among publishers, must necessarily be unattainable'.[19] Authors were divided into two categories – unpopular and popular. Wordsworth was singled out for attack, as someone who had 'for the most part continued to write in a style so uncongenial to the general feelings and taste of mankind, that the public have had little or no sympathy with his abstractions, however profound or original', and who would 'never become more popular than he has hitherto been'. Popular authors were thought to be sufficiently rewarded already, and Scott's troubles were cited, presumably as an example of the general folly of authors. This set the tone of *The Times*'s new position on the copyright bill: personal attacks on those in favour, and selective or inaccurate material on behalf of those lobbying against. *The Times*'s description of 'unfettered competition' in the trade was particularly ironic, given the level of coordination and restrictive practices that actually existed.

Some of the trade reaction was moderate in tone, and raised specific issues rather than attempting to condemn the whole proceeding. One letter from 'booksellers and publishers' expressed concern about the retrospective clause: problems were foreseen

17 This embryonic 'fair dealing' exception appears in much the same form in the Copyright, Designs and Patents Act 1988, s. 30(1), though it was deleted from the 1842 Act. See Appendix II.

18 *Mawman* v. *Tegg* (1826) 2 Russ 385. Proprietors of the *Encyclopoedia Metropolitana* claimed that Tegg's *London Encyclopoedia* copied many of their articles virtually verbatim. However, it was unclear how much had been pirated, especially as there was undoubtedly a good deal of original text, and there were allegations that the *Metropolitana* had itself taken material from prior works – and that this was natural with dictionaries. Lord Eldon V.-C. thought it necessary to refer the case to one of the Masters in Chancery to ascertain the extent of piracy before the court could decide. The suit was compromised 'upon the payment of a considerable sum of money by the Defendant to the Plaintiffs'.

19 9 May 1838, p. 5c.

over improvements to works, and works planned entirely by the publisher. However, there was no objection to extension of the term for authors who currently held their own copyright, or for future authors, and it was stressed that 'the publishers beg distinctly to disclaim any connexion with those whose opposition to this bill arises from their objection to the existence of copyright in any shape'.[20]

A similar line was taken the following week by Longman & Co. They were courteous, if doubtful, about an extended term, but expressed themselves to be happy to acquiesce if parliament decided on a longer term. However, they did provide detailed explanations of the difficulties likely to arise out of the retrospective clause. For the classes of works which needed frequent updating, it was naturally the publisher (holding the copyright) who paid for revisions and improvements. In these instances, if the copyright were later to revert to the author, two conflicting claims would arise:

> [i]n consequence of the changes that are perpetually occuring, it very frequently happens that at the end of 28 years, or at the death of the original author of legal and scientific works, little remains of their primary contributions except that title. That, however, being the designation by which books are known, is of great importance; and, if the families of the original authors are to be entitled to claim it, and any other fragment of the original work that may remain, notwithstanding the sale of every existing and contingent right to it by their fathers, the value of the additions made by the publishers, that is, of the work in its improved state, will be totally destroyed.[21]

This was a very fair point, which future versions of the bill addressed. Talfourd perhaps had not foreseen the problem, which would be much less acute with imaginative works. Another specific issue raised was the ownership of copyright in articles written for encyclopaedias, reviews, periodicals, etc. Longman put the entrepreneur's point of view, namely that it was impractical to regard contributions from numerous individuals to a collective work as anything but contributions purchased outright for payment.[22]

[20] 9 May 1838, p. 6f. [21] 16 May 1838, p. 3f.

[22] Section 21 of the 1838 bill gave copyright in periodical works to the publisher, but made express provision for the editor to be registered as proprietor of the copyright, and for the author to reserve copyright in the article. Later versions of the clause provided that proof of payment to the writer was prima facie

The Times returned to the offensive at the end of the month, with a leader which stated that the extension was 'speciously pleaded for' on grounds of justice to authors, but in fact had been introduced with a view to benefiting one family. Although Sir Walter Scott was not mentioned by name, the reference would have been crystal clear: Scott's bankruptcy, and the efforts to keep Abbotsford in the family, had been matters of unprecedented interest. Further, it was argued that the support of Wordsworth, Southey, Moore and other authors for the bill should be discounted, because of their sympathy for this plan, which would have the effect of returning many valuable copyrights into the family's hands. This was termed 'downright robbery', which would serve as 'a barrier to the publication of cheap editions, whereby the public weal is promoted'.

The bill's defeat at its second reading provided an opportunity to condemn the law officers of the Crown for offering no opposition, but most of all to take a swipe at the Whig government:

> The Melbourne Administration, certainly the most shuffling, irresolute and time-serving that ever disgraced the councils of this country, have, as usual, bilked the confiding Sergeant at the eleventh hour; and now, after having evidenced a tacit and demure concurrence in all the eloquent pleadings expended upon this proposal, forth comes my Lord John Russell to brand it with an official interdict, and to intimate that if it be persisted in, his Lordship will wind the treasury bugles to hunt it down incontinently.[23]

Although much of the pleasure taken from this scene is derived from the discomfiture caused, the basic point concerning the late and unsignalled intervention was a fair one, which Talfourd made himself in parliament. *The Times* implied that the government had been hoping that parliament would vote the measure out, but on hearing that both Longmans and the publishers of the (Whig) *Edinburgh Review* were against it had felt obliged to sacrifice Talfourd in order to prevent an attack from their own side.

During 1839 *The Times* was quiet on the subject of copyright, although Tegg wrote a characteristically trenchant letter, attacking the extension of the 'copyright monopoly' and defending his own

evidence of the publisher's property in the article. This resembles the 'tenth-spear-carrier' problem faced by those involved with performers' rights today. See Appendix II.

23 31 May 1838, p. 4c.

position. He used the rhetoric of the cheap books lobby quite unashamedly: '[t]he learned serjeant – a liberal, a friend to literature, a promoter of education, persists in bringing forward an *ex post facto* law to counteract the advantages of education, to check the diffusion of literature, and to abridge the innocent entertainment of the public, by enhancing the price of books'.[24]

Tegg continued to write letters to *The Times* during 1841.[25] One of his favourite tactics was to list high prices paid by publishers for copyrights of bestsellers, presumably to show that authors were already well rewarded. He gave Scott as one example, alleging that he made £250,000 from his works. This not only supported Tegg's usual point, but also subtly implied that there was no need to provide for Scott's heirs by passing a special measure. Two repetitions of this figure provoked a statement from Robert Cadell, as Scott's publisher, denying any prior knowledge of Talfourd's bill, and refuting Tegg's claim that the bill originated in Scott's representatives.[26]

Tegg also had a sharp eye for the changes in the 1840 version of the bill, and gives a shrewd account of the reasons that lay behind them:

> [Talfourd] felt that as he could not beat the booksellers as enemies, his only chance was to league them with him as friends in this project of fleecing the public; and, therefore, by the second clause of this new bill he gives them a share of the spoil, and has thus bought off these formidable opponents. The bill of 1840 is entirely different, as regards the interest of the booksellers, but identically the same with respect to the pillage of the public.[27]

The Morning Chronicle

The *Morning Chronicle* was a Whig paper, and the other main London newspaper, with *The Times*. Begun in 1779, its first editor, William Woodfall, had made its reputation, especially for parliamentary reporting.[28] John Black, a friend of both the Mills, took over as editor in 1821, and remained there until 1843. Many eminent writers, including Brougham, Thomas Campbell, Albany

[24] 28 February 1839, p. 3f.
[25] 20 February 1840, p. 6b; 2 March 1840, p. 3b; 12 March 1840, p. 5f.
[26] 11 March 1840, p. 5f. [27] 2 March 1840, p. 3b.
[28] Also known as 'Memory Woodfall', a soubriquet linked to his skill in reporting parliamentary debates.

Fonblanque, Lamb and Thomas Moore, wrote for the *Chronicle* at some time during their careers.[29]

The *Chronicle*'s first comment on the copyright bill was in April 1838, in response to Wordsworth's open letter to Talfourd which claimed an author's right in perpetuity to his writings. The *Chronicle* was dismissive of such 'fanciful considerations', instead favouring a pragmatic, almost utilitarian approach: 'the capitalist is as necessary to the author as he is to the capitalist, the protection, as far as the latter is concerned, ought not to extend beyond the term which he considers of importance in fixing the price to be given for the copyright'.[30] Once this period had expired, the work should be placed 'within the reach of the means of the persons in humble life'. Predictably, the retrospective clause was condemned for its likely effect on publishers and printers.

Although this long leader was hostile to the bill, it put forward a thoughtful and argued position which represented the views of many in the book trade. Of all the newspapers, the *Chronicle* was perhaps to provide the most even-handed and extensive coverage in 1838, notwithstanding its own dislike of the measure.[31] This was largely because of the letters it published from 'W.J.F.', which put the opposing case. The identity of this writer is not certain, although to a contemporary reader the initials would immediately have suggested William Johnson Fox, the celebrated and very independent preacher and author.[32] At this time he was a leader-writer for the *Chronicle*.[33] W.J.F.'s first letter appeared only one day after the *Chronicle*'s first leader, and was accompanied by a second leader responding to it. This speed of publication is unusual, and suggests that W.J.F. was well known to the paper.

The first letter acknowledged the public interest in cheap books,

[29] James Grant, *The newspaper press* (1871), I, p. 289. During 1835 Dickens was (briefly) a parliamentary reporter for the *Chronicle*.

[30] 24 April 1838, p. 2a.

[31] Although other newspapers printed a summary of the bill, the *Chronicle* was unique in publishing a careful clause-by-clause analysis with suggestions for improved drafting: 25 April 1838, p. 3c.

[32] 1786–1864. He began as a Unitarian minister; South Place Chapel was built for him in 1824. He contributed to the first number of the *Westminster Review*, and coedited the *Monthly Repository*, which he bought in 1831. His separation from his wife and his subsequent domestic arrangements cost him his Unitarian friends, but he continued to be a popular preacher. Graham Wallas, *William Johnson Fox (1786–1864)* (1924).

[33] Ibid., p. 30.

but made the point that the extended term would only affect the very few books which retained their value beyond the existing copyright period.[34] Two more letters attacked the 'disingenuous' petition from the booksellers, and hit the mark accurately:

> The trade regulations show little of this hatred of monopoly, or this concern for the cheapest supply of the public. Individual booksellers have often been prevented from supplying literary institutions and societies with books at a low commission on the trade prices, by the interference of a trade committee, and the threat of being excluded from the fraternity.[35]

This reference to literary institutions gives credence to the idea that these letters were written by Fox. Unitarians were known for their contribution to education, and Fox himself was strongly in favour of the wide availability of education. Even more indicative is Fox's lecture 'The morality of the press', delivered at the South Place Chapel, probably in 1836. Speaking from his own first-hand knowledge of the press, Fox described the temptations which faced those with a literary vocation:

> works on all the higher topics of thought, and which in their production imply, and in their perusal also, a strenuous and continuous exercise of mental power, are the least acceptable to the world, and the last which are likely to afford anything like remuneration to those by whom they are produced.[36]

In a lengthy assessment, fully supported with examples, he also warned against becoming the dependant of a particular class or faction, and the consequent temptation to prostitute one's literary powers to a 'mere trading literature'. Perhaps unexpectedly, Fox blamed these problems on the 'low estimation' in which the literary vocation was held. He also attacked the taxes on newspapers and advertisements, the extent of the deposit copy system, and the duties on paper and foreign publications.

Even after all this, Fox could still regard the press as 'the great reformer and improver of the world': his sense was that the power of knowledge would prevail over all obstacles eventually.[37] Yet this did not prevent him from appreciating the existing difficulties

[34] 25 April 1838, p. 2g. The next letter dissects the petition (probably 4,821) in detail: 28 April 1838, p. 3e.

[35] *Morning Chronicle*, 27 April 1838, p. 5g. See 28 April 1838, p. 3e, for W.J.F.'s detailed attack on the inconsistencies and contradications in the booksellers' petition.

[36] William Johnson Fox, *Memorial edition of collected works* (1865–8), VII, p. 147.

[37] 'The morality of the press', p. 163.

facing literary men, particularly their lack of status and reward: Fox's arguments throughout acknowledged the complexity of the problem. It seems perfectly possible that he would have welcomed Talfourd's proposals as likely to reward precisely the lasting works that Fox wished to see. Fox, largely because of his connection with the *Monthly Repository*, was a central figure in a literary circle which included Robert Browning and R. H. Horne, as well as other more minor figures.

The W.J.F. of the *Chronicle* was similarly concerned about the prevalence of literature for immediate consumption, and the 'heavy discouragement' which this presents to those 'forfeiting the present rewards of authorship, without any reversion in futurity'.[38] Other similiarities, in the arguments and examples used, support the contention that this was William Johnson Fox. However, a further complication arises from a report of a public meeting, chaired by Dr Birkbeck, to consider the copyright bill.[39]

Birkbeck spoke against the bill on the grounds that it impeded the diffusion of knowledge. Sir George Stevens deprecated the system of legislation for individual interests at the expense of the public, and moved a resolution to the effect that it was very desirable that every facility should be given to the diffusion of useful knowledge. His resolution was seconded by Dr Marshall Hall.[40] Then 'Mr Fox' spoke: he considered that giving a right to an author's family would stimulate him to exertion, and would allow him to write 'under the spirit of independence..instead of their writing, as now, merely for the bookseller'. This speech was greeted with cheers and hisses, and Mr Fox then moved an amendment in favour of the bill 'amidst tremendous confusion, the room having by this time become densely crowded by persons for and against the measure'. Once the 'tumult' had been quelled, the amendment was put to the meeting and was declared to be lost. It is very tempting to surmise that this Mr Fox was in fact W. J. Fox, in a third guise.

[38] 1 May 1838, p. 3e.

[39] The meeting was held held on the evening of 8 May 1838, at the Freemason's Tavern. The *Morning Chronicle*'s report appears on 10 May 1838, p. 5. It appears to have been taken almost verbatim from the previous evening's *Courier*, 9 May 1838.

[40] Petition 5,953 was the direct result of this meeting. Birkbeck and Hall both signed a further petition, 7,254, presented 7 May 1839.

The *Chronicle*'s resistance to Talfourd's plans in effect disappeared with the retrospective clause. Its sympathy with the bookselling interest did not extend to print workers: 'the opposition of printers, type-founders, paper-makers, and others, grounded on the supposed injury their respective trades would sustain from an extension of the copyright, is not entitled to much favour'.[41] Its leaders during 1839 were more supportive, although there was little progress on which to comment: 1840 was even quieter. However, Macaulay's speech in 1841 raised the spectre of suppression, and the *Chronicle* agreed that this was a real danger: 'What has gone forth to the world ought no longer to be subject to the control of any individual. It belongs to mankind.'[42]

A completely opposite view was taken in 1842: 'we know of no manufactured products in which all right of private property ceases as soon as they are forty-two years old'.[43] Mahon's bill was given only a lukewarm reception, as likely to mitigate but not to reform 'the moral order that exists'. The mention of genius, and the references to Bulwer's Dramatic Copyright Act of 1833, perhaps suggest a connection with either Fox or Horne. Certainly the *Chronicle*'s attitude had changed considerably since its unsympathetic 1838 leader.

The Morning Post

The *Morning Post*'s early reputation was as a literary paper: Daniel Stuart was editor, with Coleridge, Lamb, Southey and Wordsworth among its contributors. However, Stuart sold it in 1803 to concentrate on the *Courier*, accompanied by Coleridge, Southey and Wordsworth. Under Nicholas Byrne the *Morning Post* quickly lost its literary reputation and its independence: *Punch* dubbed it the '*Fawning Post*' for its treatment of George IV and the rest of the royal family, although it became much less obsequious after George's death. C. Eastland Michele took over as editor and part-proprietor in 1833. In political matters the *Morning Post* consistently maintained a position behind the aristocratic and landed Tory interest: opposed to reform and in favour of the corn laws, it lost both battles. It did maintain a reputation

[41] 28 February 1839, p. 3a.
[42] 6 February 1841, p. 4b.
[43] 8 April 1838, p. 5a.

as a fashionable paper, which reported on dances and dinners, but it was also proud of its news service, and of its rivalry with *The Times*.

On the copyright question, the *Morning Post* was much more sympathetic than *The Times*.[44] Its first leader on the subject acknowledged (at some length) the problems of authors who did not wish to write for the immediate market, particularly if they wished to see their families provided for:

> [i]t were much better for the respectability of literature, and for the good of general society, that literary men should produce a very few good books, the copyright of which they might bequeath as a property to their children, than that they should be rushing hastily to make hay while the sun shines, and thus cram the world with a kind of 'Brummagem ware' of literature, which is in truth merely 'made to sell', and to sell at the moment.[45]

Scott and Wordsworth were given as examples of those who suffered by the anomalies in the prevailing system. There was more doubt about the appropriateness of a sixty-year term, which was thought 'a very great extension', although the need for a longer period was willingly conceded. A few days later the *Post* addressed the objections of publishers and printers, provoked by a meeting of booksellers and publishers chaired by Longman 'which was attended by Counsel and Solicitors'.[46] Even the retrospective clause was endorsed, on the grounds that publishers had received what they bargained for – the property which the prevailing law allowed them.

Thomas Tegg was the next target. One of Tegg's repeated complaints was the special position of the Clarendon history,

[44] Winthrop M. Praed was chief leader writer 1833–4: he was a vigorous supporter of the copyright bill until his death in 1839. Disraeli succeeded Praed as leader writer: he too supported Talfourd's plans. Derek R. Hudson, *A poet in parliament: the life of W. M. Praed, 1802–1839* (1939); Wilfred Hindle, *The Morning Post* (1937), p. 148.

[45] 6 April 1838, p. 4. The author was probably William Johnston. He wrote to Wordsworth 24 April 1838: 'I knew beforehand from Lord Lowther, that you were in favour of Mr Talfourd's Bill, and I had some thoughts of taking the liberty of writing to you upon the subject, before I published the articles that have appeared in the Morning Post, but I refrained, through a fear of intruding, not knowing whether the interest you took in the matter was much or little'. Quoted by Paul M. Zall, 'Wordsworth and the Copyright Act of 1842', *Proceedings of the Modern Language Association of America* 70 (1955), 135–44 (p. 138).

[46] 10 April 1838, p. 4.

whose copyright was given to Oxford University without time limit. The *Post* trenchantly rejected this example as irrelevant, arguing that cheap, good editions would always prevail over cheap, bad editions:

> if Lord Clarendon's history had been under such a law as Mr Talfourd proposes it would long ago have been public property, and Mr Tegg might have printed it on whity-brown paper, with fifteen mistakes in every page, and have sent it by ship-loads to America or any other place he thought proper, at no expense other than that of the coarse materials and clumsy workmanship employed.[47]

The stream of leaders was maintained. On the morning of the second reading the trade opposition was roundly condemned as self-interested: 'the truth is that these unappointed advocates for the public who complain of monopoly are anxious only to grasp a monopoly for themselves'. The brief summary of the second reading is highly partial. A celebratory leader the next day was filled with abuse of Talfourd's parliamentary opponents: Hume, 'ever stupid, ever imprudent, ever in the wrong, Joseph the swine-headed'; Warburton, 'always harsh, presumptuous, irreverential and eager to destroy'; Pryme and Ward, 'the two silliest, shallowest, and most conceited men in the House'.[48] Wakley was singled out a few days later, in a piece which hinted darkly at his public reputation.[49] The real reason for comment was the publication of Wordsworth's observations on the Kendal printers' petition, which were quoted at some length. Less than a fortnight later, *The Times*'s attack on Wordsworth appeared: the *Morning*

[47] 14 April 1838, p. 2. The point is contentious. The 5s editions (produced by Cadell, Murray and Longman) would have been out of the reach of working-class readers – the targets of the cheap books lobby. Since the SDUK did not produce fiction, Tegg's reprints and remainders were presumably a valuable source for these readers.

[48] 25, 26, 27 April 1838, all p. 2. Disraeli began writing for the *Morning Post* in 1835, and this kind of invective is characteristic, particularly when directed at the parliamentary radicals: '[t]he vast majority of these men . . . are illiterate persons. HUME, for instance, can neither speak nor write English; his caligraphy reminds one of a chandler's shop, and his letters resemble a butterman's bill . . . But the ignorance of WARBURTON rather staggers even these parasites . . . WAKLEY is of a lighter order of mind . . . He would make an admirable cad, or a first-rate conductor of an omnibus' (24 August 1835). Disraeli was in favour of Talfourd's plans, and the 1838 leader has a similar stamp.

[49] 30 April 1838, p. 4. Several dramatic incidents in Wakley's life caused him troubles with the press.

Post responded with staunch defence.[50] Wakley's comments in the second reading were further punished with a doggerel verse, 'PEN versus LANCET'.[51]

A brief period of quiet followed, which lasted only until the committee stage was due. The *Morning Post* turned defence into attack following a hostile *Morning Chronicle* article, and argued that it was rather the publishers' solution that was retrospective, as they had only bargained for twenty-eight years.[52] Then Lord John Russell's late intervention gave the copyright question a new and interesting twist. Unsurprisingly, the *Morning Post* was highly critical, although, unlike Tegg in *The Times*, it did not blame Longman and the *Edinburgh Review*: the problem was traced to 'some Edinburgh publishers'.[53] Russell's arguments were refuted in some detail, both in the leader and in letters, and critical comments from the *Globe* and the *Courier* were reprinted. Russell, like Wakley, also had to endure the versifying of Demetrius Doggerel.[54]

The *Morning Post*, more than any other paper, maintained its interest in the copyright bill throughout its various reincarnations.[55] The reporting of the 1839 bill was nevertheless rather scanty: the solitary leader appears to be a version of one from 1838.[56] Similarly in 1840, only one leader can be justified, deploring existing literature as mere 'Brummagen ware' made to sell quickly: this idea had also been used before.[57]

The defeat of the bill in 1841 was caused largely by Macaulay's speech. The *Morning Post* viewed the Commons' decision with 'unmixed regret', and reminded the Conservative party that literary men 'are not the men to set on the rabble to effect a change in the law by the influence of tumultuary terror. Yet are they not without power in that way if they thought proper so to use it.'[58]

50 10 May 1838, p. 2. 51 11 May 1838. 52 5 June 1838, p. 4.
53 8 June 1838, p. 3. Perhaps the Chambers brothers?
54 7, 8, 9 June 1838, p. 6.
55 Wordsworth to HCR, of the *Morning Post*: 'a journal which by the bye has done itself great honour lately by its zealous and able and praiseworthy defence of the rights of authors in the Copy right qu'. *The letters of William and Dorothy Wordsworth*, 2nd edn, ed. Alan G. Hill (Oxford, 1969–88), VI, p. 606 (18 June 1838).
56 2 March 1839, apparently reworking 27 April 1838.
57 21 February 1840, p. 2. Compare the reference to 'Brummagen Ware' with 6 April 1838, p. 4. See p. 142, above.
58 8 February 1840, p. 4.

This was its final leader on the subject, although the passage of the 1842 bill was charted in the usual way.

EVENING PAPERS

The Globe

The *Globe* was founded in 1803 as a trade journal for booksellers, to give their advertisements more prominence than they could get from the dailies.[59] It gradually became, at least in theory, a liberal ministerial evening paper. It was a recognised channel for ministerial communications, especially favoured by Lord John Russell, although it could be unreliable and even insubordinate on occasion.[60]

It certainly showed a good deal of independence in its opinions on copyright. Its first leader on the subject acknowledged the importance of cheap diffusion of literature, but argued that 'if a man has property in anything, surely he has in the fruits of his own intellect, the products of his imagination – and it is the extreme of injustice to make the very benefit which he has conferred upon the world an excuse for robbing him of all share in the profit from its diffusion'. The problem was seen as one of balance, between national interests and justice to individuals. The *Globe*'s tentative suggestion (intended to 'guard against the evils of monopoly') was that a limited period of absolute copyright should be followed by a payment for every subsequent edition, based on price and number of copies.[61]

However, the subject here was *international* copyright, in particular the introduction of Poulett Thomson's bill. In relation to

[59] Various newspapers had become known for the sort of advertisements which they featured. The *Morning Post* was popular with booksellers. However, when their notices began to dominate the front page, the editor began to delay their insertion, put them on the back page, or to refuse them altogether: he wanted short miscellaneous advertisements, not a 'monopoly' of booksellers. The booksellers responded by starting two rival papers, the *British Press* and the *Globe*. The quarrel bubbled up again in 1838: *Gentleman's Magazine*, May–September 1838.

[60] Bourne, *English newspapers*, II, p. 95. Stephen Koss, *The rise and fall of the political press in Britain* (1990), p. 45.

[61] 21 March 1838, p. 4.

Talfourd's bill, the *Globe* was more cautious: although favourable in principle to the measure, taking into account all legitimate interests seemed more problematic. The meeting of master printers was defended, as the effect of the retrospective clause on vested interests was a cause of legitimate complaint. The *Globe* was convinced that the price of books would indeed rise if the clause stood: it expressed particular concern about revised works, collected works and the dangers of suppression.

Responding to Wakley's notice of a motion to refer both the copyright bill and the international copyright bill to a select committee of the House of Lords, the *Globe* again stated that it was in principle friendly to both bills. It did, however, regard Talfourd's plans as less urgent: 'it is rather a sensitiveness of conscience, a refined feeling of justice, that now seeks satisfaction, than a practically felt grievance', whereas the absence of proper international copyright was described as 'the crying grievance of literature'.[62]

Nevertheless, Talfourd's success in the second reading was welcomed, in a leader which sharply attacked Grote's speech against the bill. Grote had argued that, since the publishing trade was already competitive, any attempt to increase authors' rights would necessarily be at the expense of the public, and that the House should favour public interest above any class interests. The *Globe* called this 'just such a piece of mock-conclusiveness as one expects from Benthamese logic . . . the logic of selfishness-on-system with "greatest happiness" for its pretext', and asked if Grote would insure the public against the loss of valuable works *not* written as a result.[63] Talfourd had made the point that the publishers' trade usage prolonged their monopoly, and this seems to have been well taken.

From this point the *Globe* was noticeably more supportive. In a leader the following day it returned to another issue raised during the second reading. Rejecting the analogy between literary works and inventions, it evidenced a sharp appreciation of the nature of copyright:

> Nothing similar to a patent right is sought for authors; and the whole elaborate fabric reared on that assumption falls to the ground. All that is sought is, that in those works to which their whole or their chief value is

[62] 12 April 1838, p. 2. [63] 26 April 1838, p. 2.

given by the FORM impressed on them by one man's genius, he shall receive the full benefit of having placed ideas in that form . . . Not a single idea or doctrine is locked up by copyright . . . all we seek to prevent is, one man sucking the brains of another without using his own.[64]

More leaders on the copyright bills were published throughout May: they were relatively short and maintained the same line.[65] That of 31 May was a spirited response to *The Times*'s accusation that the bill was introduced solely for the benefit of Sir Walter Scott. When the bill fell at the committee stage, Lord John Russell's late opposition was remarked on unfavourably. The *Globe* suggested politely that he might wish to reconsider, and also objected to his vision of the public interest, preferring to see the public offered good-quality works rather than the greatest quantity at the cheapest price: 'the reign of royal and noble patronage having pretty well come to a close, how are authors to be supported and encouraged in efforts *de longue haleine*? Only by giving them an extended beneficial interest in their results.'[66]

The Courier

The *Courier* had been a Tory paper for thirty years, but changed sides with the Whig ministry of 1830. Its initial position was one of sarcastic and cynical hostility to the copyright bill. Its first leader on the subject appeared in 1837: although rejecting the case for special pleading, it observed with weary certainty that 'with so much clap-trap about it, who can doubt [the bill's] success'.[67] However, by 1838 its attitude was a great deal more positive: whereas in 1837 the bill was regarded as providing little benefit 'except that it gave Mr. Serjeant Talfourd an opportunity to make a speech', his speech introducing the 1838 second reading was considered 'brilliant'.[68]

Although the *Courier*'s coverage of the issues was briefer and more superficial than that of the heavier-weight papers, throughout 1838 the principle of the bill was supported enthusiastically. Even the retrospective clause was defended, on the grounds that the author's family had more claim to the benefit of extended copyright than Mr Tegg's family. There were, however,

[64] 27 April 1838, p. 2. [65] 10, 11, 17, 24, 31 May 1838.
[66] 7 June 1838, p. 2. [67] 19 May 1837, p. 2. [68] 26 April 1838, p. 2.

anxieties as to some of its likely effects, and suggestions for improvements. As with other papers, there was little coverage in 1839. A long and supportive leader followed the 1840 second reading, praising Talfourd for his perseverance in the face of 'the stupid opposition that impedes him'. The article focused on the lack of encouragement and protection for the more enduring branches of literature: 'a high reputation may be the principal object of an author's pursuits, and this cannot be affected by copyright; but it is neither generous nor just that mere tradesmen should reap the benefit of his studies and exertions'.[69] This was to be the *Courier*'s final comment on the matter, although it continued to report on the bill's progress during 1841 and 1842.

CONCLUSION

Newspaper pressure was thus very useful to those opposing Talfourd, especially early on in the campaign. Without this publicity, it would have been much harder to resist the rather technical retrospective clause, and it provided a valuable additional weapon beside that of the petitions. However, once the retrospective clause had been removed from the bill, there was much less reason to object to it, and therefore much less editorial coverage, even from the main dailies. Nevertheless, the regular business of parliamentary reporting was enough to keep the bills in the public eye, and newspapers began to provide a measure of support for a change in the law.

Most of this support was a product of genuine editorial opinion rather than lobbying: for instance, although the *Morning Post* was overtly supportive of the bill, William Johnston's articles were published without the intervention of the campaign managers. Authors turned instead to periodicals, and used this sphere of influence to much greater effect than did the publishers: this gave them their first distinct advantage. However, in other ways authors were much less well marshalled than the publishing forces: they were simply not accustomed to the same level of organisational structure.

[69] 21 February 1840, p. 2.

7

AUTHORS AND THE BEGINNINGS OF AUTHORS' ORGANISATIONS

With some notable but individual exceptions, most authors continued to sell their copyrights outright until nearly the end of the nineteenth century. Authorship was still relatively young as a profession, and attempts to unite it were, on the whole, unsuccessful.

The earliest known authors' organisation was the Society for the Encouragement of Learning, founded in 1735 to give authors a rightful share in the profits of their books.[1] Jerdan's account is of a plan to publish works of 'sterling quality'.[2] The committee of management included 'noblemen and scholars of the highest rank' as well as 'representatives of professional authorship'.[3] It seems to have been a wholly philanthropic organisation, which did its own publishing and gave all profits to the authors. Although this aim proved unsustainable, it apparently alarmed the commercial book trade. Three booksellers were appointed, with a 33 per cent 'allowance', later reduced to 15 per cent. In fact the booksellers would neither buy nor sell the society's books, and putting the sales into the hands of adversaries was seen to be an error. Charles Rivington was an active member but 'as he and his colleagues sustained much injury through it, he withdrew from it'.[4] The

[1] This title mirrors a phrase from the preamble to the Act of Anne 1710.

[2] William Jerdan, *The plan of a National Association for the Encouragement and Protection of Authors, and Men of Talent and Genius* (1839).

[3] One of the latter was James Thomson, the popularity of whose *Seasons* had led to the great case of *Millar* v. *Taylor*, and ultimately to *Donaldson* v. *Beckett*. Thomson and Andrew Millar were old friends, and Thomson's loyalty to his publisher was very great. Even though Thomson was a committee member, Millar remained Thomson's publisher until the poet's death in 1748. Frank A. Mumby, *The romance of book selling: a history from the earliest times to the twentieth century* (1910), p. 233.

[4] Septimus Rivington, *The publishing family of Rivington* (1919), p. 33.

society staggered on for thirteen years, and had a final balance of £24 12s.

The Royal Literary Fund, founded in 1790 by the radical thinker David Williams, was intended to remove authors from 'the discretion and patronage of the government, nobility and opulent gentry'.[5] Williams had hoped that the fund would develop into a wider, more progressive organisation which would work for the protection and advancement of authors' rights, but it remained a charity. By 1806 it had 200 subscribers, although almost none of these were authors. There were many opposed to the fund. Many authors, including Scott, objected to the manner in which the fund distributed mere pittances, and in 1812 Southey launched an attack targeted at 'the absurd purposes of the Literary Fund with its despicable ostentation of patronage'.[6]

In the fund's defence it should be said that applicants were guaranteed anonymity, and by 1833 it had helped over 600 writers. Dickens joined the committee of the fund in 1839: his plans for reform provoked a pamphlet war, although the administrative costs remained just as high, and the fund continued to function as 'an unreformed, unrepentant charity'.[7] Other charitable bodies included the Milton Institute, the Society of British Authors' National Benevolent Institution, and the Artists' Benevolent Fund. None of these achieved much success. Charity was also to be had from individual authors, or via 'testimonial funds'.

The Royal Society of Literature followed the route of patronage. Founded 1820–3 with the support of George IV, it was intended as an English equivalent of the French Académie de Belles Lettres. Ten royal associates were created, and given 100 guinea pensions. However, William IV refused to maintain the royal level of support, which dropped to only £100 a year. The pensions were abruptly discontinued, causing hardship to Coleridge (amongst others).[8] Coleridge's friends intervened to get him a

[5] David Williams, *Claims of literature* (1802) p. 9.

[6] See Southey to Wynn, *Selections from the letters of Robert Southey*, ed. John W. Warter (1856), II, p. 246 (6 April 1821).

[7] Nigel Cross, *The common writer: life in nineteenth-century Grub Street* (Cambridge, 1985), p. 35.

[8] The original ten included Coleridge and Malthus: Sir Edward William Brabrook, *The Royal Society of Literature*, 2nd edn (1879), p. 8. For Coleridge's reactions to the Associateship see *The collected letters of Samuel Taylor Coleridge*, ed. Earl L. Griggs (Oxford, 1956), V, letters 1,382 and 1,392. For the problems which

civil list grant, although these were quite small and scarce. The Royal Society of Literature itself survived, although with more limited ambitions. Another society, this time the Society for the Encouragement of Literature was created in 1825, but soon foundered. William Jerdan's 1838 *Plan for a National Association for the Encouragement and Protection of Authors, and Men of Talent and Genius*, got little further than its prospectus.[9]

All these attempts to help were imposed on authors from those who wished them well. Authors themselves did not appear to think it sufficiently important for them to unite to protect their interests, although their French colleagues began a Société des Gens de Lettres in 1837.[10] The Garrick was the first formal club for writers, founded in 1831, but was focused on dining rather than combining. Campbell's Literary Union Club was started in the same year, although the *Athenaeum* commented that it was 'anything but Literary or United'.[11] One section of the literary world was catered for by the Dramatic Authors' Society, founded in 1833,[12] although serious drama was not flourishing at the time because of the Licensing Act. In 1843 John Petheram published his *Reasons for establishing an Author's Publication Society*, apparently to no response.[13] Leading authors were not brought together until Dickens founded the Guild of Literature and Art in 1851, as

resulted from the ending of the royal endowment, see ibid., VI, letters 1,707, 1,709.

[9] The aim was to raise £200,000 in share capital and thereby 'to rescue the intellectual character of the nation from these degrading and deteriorating circumstances, by providing Capital for the less wealthy, ready access to fair competition for the deserving, adequate compensation for the skilful and industrious, diminished cost and increased emolument to all': Jerdan, *Plan*, p. 33. As to the actual results, Jerdan tells the sad story himself: William Jerdan, *Autobiography* (1852–3), IV, p. 347.

[10] James Hepburn, *The author's empty purse and the rise of the literary agent* (1968), p.37.

[11] *Athenaeum*, 20 March 1830. For Campbell's original vision, which encompassed a 'Britannic Literary Union', see Cyrus Redding, *Literary reminiscences and memoirs of Thomas Campbell* (1860), II, p. 261. Jerdan records that the club was 'overthrown by the bankruptcy of the bankers, after [Campbell] had strengthened it with a host of elevated patrons': *Autobiography*, IV, p. 349.

[12] Founded in 1833 by Thomas James Searle and Douglas Jerrold. Its purpose was to enforce the rights conferred by the Dramatic Copyright Act 1833 (3 Wm. 4 c 15).

[13] *Reasons for establishing an authors' publication society: by which literary labour would receive a more adequate reward, and the price of all new books be much reduced* (1843). Petheram was a writer and second-hand bookdealer.

a frustrated protest in the face of the Royal Literary Fund's refusal to reform. Even then, authors were scarcely united, and the Guild never achieved what was intended.[14] There is also evidence of an Association to Protect the Rights of Authors, started in 1853.[15] The Society of Authors, founded in 1861 by Walter Besant, is the only survivor of all these organisations intended to fight for authors' rights and interests.

From this perspective, authors appear very independent and little interested in putting forward a party line. Heyck has commented of this period that 'men of letters did not become either highly organised or sharply segregated from the rest of society'.[16] A concerted response to Talfourd's bill would therefore have seemed unlikely, and it would be expected that any account of the authorial response to it would inevitably focus on the catalogue of individual reactions. Nevertheless, on sifting through the evidence of the positions of these authors, it becomes clear that there was both a response and a campaign. Talfourd and Wordsworth appear as the prime directors, but there is more than this: an enormous amount of practical help came from others, who gave freely of their time, effort and influence to further the copyright cause. Admittedly there was no existing organisation with formal rules, subscriptions or an office. Instead there were breakfasts and dinners, calls and visits, letters, newspapers and periodicals. The literary world did function as an organisation, however diffuse and however informal its farthest links.

The copyright campaign was built on a network of friends and acquaintances, and it proved robust enough to endure for five weary years. Their approach to the campaigning process reveals a good deal about the emerging profession of authorship, just as the print workers' petitions reveal their own trades' structures. The evidence is less neatly packaged, and it is harder to say that it is

[14] Thackeray and Macaulay, for instance, were very opposed to the idea. Jerdan very respectfully suggests that the Guild of Literature and Art was 'an enlarged and probably more skilfully modelled adaptation of a plan proposed by me to the Literary Fund'. His vision was of Crown-lands and donations 'to found quiet and pleasing retreats for the reception of unsuccessful and worn out authors', which does indeed resemble the Guild's plans: Jerdan, *Autobiography*, IV, p. 37.

[15] Hepburn, *Author's empty purse*, p. 41.

[16] Thomas W. Heyck, *The transformation of intellectual life in Victorian England* (1982), p. 36.

complete, but it does exist: there are few literary figures of a contemporary note with no apparent connection to the copyright question. The copyright campaign – both domestic and international – was perhaps the inaugural dispute of the profession of authorship.

SOUTHEY

Once the dust had settled following *Donaldson* v. *Beckett*, a period of comparative quiet followed, when copyright was no longer controversial. Interest in copyright and related questions grew slowly throughout the early nineteenth century, although at first only a few authors regarded copyright as something worth fighting for. The process can be seen unfolding in the authors whose names came to be associated with complaints about copyright. Southey and Wordsworth were among the first to attribute some of their difficulties to what they perceived to be an inadequate copyright law. This broke the ground for the campaigns of the late 1830s, for changes to both international and domestic regimes.

Southey and Wordsworth were by this time elder statesmen of the literary world: from this position it was possible to demand protection for authorship, for the labour of literary production. Talfourd and his supporters caught this mood of self-worth, and used it to propel the bill through five very difficult years. That the result was only a moderate improvement is less important than the fact that there was still energy left to clamour for international protection. However, when Southey began his literary career, at the turn of the century, the situation was less favourable.

Southey's early political views cost him the support of his relatives, and left him without any of the obvious professions. He began to write for money soon after he left Oxford in 1795, although half-heartedly combining this work with legal studies for a time. He lived in London, where he produced numerous contributions to magazines, reviews and periodicals, as well as his own poetry.

This apprenticeship gave Southey a good understanding of the literary trade. Ill-health took him to Lisbon in 1800, where he finished *Thalaba*. He asked his friend John Rickman to perform the sale:

My private instructions must be vague, – to make the best bargain you can, and on no terms to sell the copyright . . . Longman will probably offer to advance the expense of publishing, and share the profits: this is not fair, as brains ought to bear a higher interest than money. If you are not satisfied with his terms, offer it to Arch, in Gracechurch Street, or to Philips of the *Monthly Magazine*, a man who can afford to pay a good price, because he can advertize and puff his own property every month.[17]

This letter is characteristic of Southey's interest in his own copyrights. He later considered publishing the *Curse of Kehama* in a subscription edition, 'by which means I should receive the whole profit to myself. The bookseller's share is too much like the lion in the fable: 30 or 33 per cent. They first deduct as booksellers, and then half the residue as publishers.'[18] He was also appalled to find that booksellers regarded a half-profits agreement as a surrender of half the copyright in perpetuity.

In 1813 the poet laureateship gave Southey £90 a year, which he invested in a life policy. He was always very anxious for his family's future welfare, and considered the existing law of literary property 'an abominable injustice' because it did not adequately consider them. At this time his friend Wynn was involved in the 1813 select committee on copyright. The trade was asking for a bill to reduce the number of deposit copies demanded of publishers, and (as a concession to the author's interest) to fix the term of copyright at twenty-eight years:[19] this caused Southey to develop his thoughts on these matter in some detail. He did consider that the grant of twenty-eight years absolute would be an improvement on the fourteen plus fourteen term, but:

My opinion is that literary property ought to be inheritable, like every other property; and that a law which should allow you the use of the trees upon your estate for eight-and-twenty years, and after that term make them over to the Carpenters' Company, would not be more unjust than that which takes from me and my heirs the property of my literary labours, and gives it to the Company of Booksellers.[20]

[17] Charles C. Southey (ed.), *Life and correspondence of Robert Southey* (1849), II, p. 121.

[18] To Landor, 2 May 1808: Southey, *Life*, III, p. 143. Southey wrote in similar vein to Ebenezer Elliott, the 'Corn Law Rhymer', advising him to forget booksellers, and to send short poems anonymously to the newspaper, thus keeping the copyrights.

[19] Subsequently the 1814 Copyright Act. Southey provided Wynn with information about 'the law of the trade', and examples of alleged abuse.

[20] To Wynn, 23 May 1813: Southey, *Selections*, II, pp. 320–3.

Southey also thought that booksellers would give no more for the extended term, which would be of little consequence to the great body of authors, 'But to those who really acquire a permanent rank in the literature of their country, the injury is heavy indeed.' He suggested a limited right of sale, to give the author a share of the 'prizes in the lottery' that otherwise went to the bookseller, or a life term.[21]

The 1814 Act did not achieve the results that the book trade had wanted: the number of deposit copies remained unaltered at eleven, and the term of copyright was extended to twenty-eight years or the lifetime of the author (whichever was longer). This was most unsatisfactory to the trade, whose main object had been to reduce the burden of deposit copies; it was little interested in the extended term. The situation remained unstable, and in 1818 another select committee was appointed to look into legal deposit. Although an enormous amount of evidence was collected, the committee could not agree, and nothing was done.[22]

Southey followed the matter closely, helped by Wynn, who sent him the committee's reports. He expressed anxiety at the indifference to the longer term which was expressed by several publishers in their evidence:

> the part of this business which most concerns me is, the term of years which the booksellers seem willing to give up. Now in my case a prolongation of term is of much more consequence than the eleven copies, for my books make their way slowly; they have a steady sale, and there will be a greater demand for them in the first three or four years after my death than there ever has been, or will be, in the same length of time during my life.[23]

This is a shrewd point: Southey's reaction highlights the different interests of authors and of the trade.

These feelings finally took a public form in an article in the *Quarterly Review*.[24] The bulk of the article concerned the question of deposit copies. Southey drew on his readings of the select committee evidence, and on the extensive pamphlet literature which the dispute had engendered. Although his sympathies are

[21] Ibid., II, p. 324.

[22] John Feather, 'Publishers and politicians: the remaking of the law of copyright in Britain 1775–1842. Part I: Legal deposit and the battle of the library tax', *Publishing History* 24 (1988), 49–76.

[23] To Wynn, 7 June 1818: Southey, *Selections*, III, p. 90.

[24] *Quarterly Review* 21 (1819), 196–213.

largely with the publishers on this, he gave a clear-eyed account of the motivation of both sides. It is one of the most readable pieces written on the subject anywhere.

In the last two pages of the article, Southey turned to the wider question of copyright. He poured scorn on Lord Camden's famous remark that Milton 'knew that the real price of his work was immortality, and that posterity would pay it',[25] asking on what principle men of letters were deprived of perpetual property in their own labours, unlike all other workers. Southey regarded the limited term as an unjustifiable form of robbery:

> The last descendants of Milton died in poverty. The descendants of Shakespeare are living in poverty, and in the lowest condition of life. Is it just to these individuals? Is it grateful to the memory of those who are the pride and boast of their country? . . . To have placed the descendants of Shakespeare and Milton in respectability and comfort..simple justice was all that was required; only that they should have possessed the perpetual copyright of their ancestors' works, only that they should not have been deprived of their proper inheritance.[26]

Another of Southey's concerns, the ephemeral nature of the literature which a short copyright term encouraged, was also to figure prominently in the later debate: 'books of great immediate popularity have their run, and come to a dead stop: the hardship is upon those which win their way slowly and with difficulty, but keep the field at last'. Wordsworth and Talfourd both used this argument to argue for a 'life-plus' element to the copyright term.[27]

[25] It was commonly known that Milton was paid £5 for the copyright of *Paradise lost*.

[26] This was a point which would be taken often in relation to Talfourd's bills. Talfourd himself used some of these images when he introduced the 1837 bill. He compared the treatment of Nelson and Wellington, who were given substantial endowments, with that of authors: 'Were our Shakespeare and Milton less the ornaments of their country, less the benefactors of mankind? Would the example be less inspiring if we permitted them to enjoy the spoils of their peaceful victories – if we allowed to their descendants, not the tax assessed by present gratitude and charged on the future, but the mere amount which that future would be delighted to pay . . .?' *Hansard, Parliamentary debates* (3rd series), xxxvii, 874.

[27] They thought that an author's late work was usually his best. Talfourd took Wordsworth as his example, again in his speech introducing the 1837 bill: 'Shall the law, whose term has been amply sufficient to his scorners, now afford him no protection because he has outlasted their scoffs?' *Hansard, Parliamentary debates* (3rd series), xxxviii, 878. This was the basis of Macaulay's argument for a fixed term, since life-plus gave more protection to juvenilia than (superior) late works: *Hansard, Parliamentary debates* (3rd series), lxi, 1363–97. See ch. 3.

Southey was evidently proud of these two pages: in 1829 he reused them in one of his *Colloquies*.[28] This takes the form of a conversation between the ghost of Sir Thomas More and the contemporary Montesinos, in which they discuss many questions relevant to copyright, such as the hugely increased number of books, their accessibility to the public, and the effect this has had. Montesinos claims that only some current literature is of lasting worth. In the rest he detects a corruption of style, whose source he traces to ephemeral literature; written only for present effect, and to dazzle the reader, it is often inaccurate, slovenly and ignorant. More is given Lord Camden's words, and suggests that 'He who labours for posterity in the fields of research, must look to posterity for his reward', but agrees that the desire for immediate reputation leaves some writers indifferent to the consequences of their inflammatory words. More then asks whether the present age has 'done its duty' to the living minds who write for posterity. This sets up the climax of the conversation: Montesino's detailed and technical reply is concerned entirely with defects of the existing system, and the arguments for perpetual copyright. Southey uses much of the *Quarterly Review* material verbatim.

Southey was quick to criticise the existing system, but he also had positive plans, which he revealed in a letter to Lord Brougham.[29] In 1831, through Wynn, Southey met Brougham for only the second time. Given their very slight acquaintance and their very different political views, Southey was very surprised when Brougham shook his hand warmly. He was even more surprised to receive a letter from Brougham, requesting his views on the best means of encouraging scientific and literary pursuits.[30] In 1831 Brougham was still at the height of his popularity, but the Tory poet laureate was deeply suspicious: 'It has a good deal the air of offering me a sop, at which I shall neither bite, nor snarl and show my teeth, but answer him at leisure with sufficient care.'[31] He evidently expected nothing to come of his suggestions, for

[28] Robert S. Southey, *Sir Thomas More; or, Colloquies on the progress and prospects of society* (1829), XIV.

[29] Brougham's role in this exchange has already been considered: see ch. 3.

[30] To Wynn, 3 March 1831: 'Strange things happen in strange times; and that he should write to me upon this subject is one of them': Southey, *Selections*, IV, p. 209. For Brougham's letter, see Southey, *Life*, VI, p. 129.

[31] To Rickman, 12 January 1831: Southey, *Selections*, IV, p. 206.

various reasons, primarily the uneasy state of the country. However, Southey had obvious respect for Brougham's abilities, and he did respond.

Brougham's letter asked firstly whether government had any active role to play in the encouragement of literary pursuits, particularly given the risk that aid would be diverted to party-political purposes. Assuming that there was a role for government, Brougham suggested various possibilities for consideration: financial assistance, societies, prizes and non-hereditary honours. In his reply, Southey took the unsettled state of the country as his background:

> But when better times shall arrive (whoever may live to see them), it will be worthy the consideration of any government whether the institution of an Academy, with salaries for its members (in the nature of literary or lay benefices), might not be the means of retaining in *its* interests, as connected with their own, a certain number of influential men of letters, who should hold those benefices, and a much greater number of aspirants who would look to them in their turn.[32]

Southey sketched a plan for an academy with an annual grant of £10,000, endowing ten £500 appointments, and twenty-five £200 appointments. He was dismissive of prizes and honours, introducing instead a plea for a new law of copyright: 'One thing alone I ask from the legislature, and in the name of justice, – that the injurious law of copyright should be repealed, and that the family of an author should not be deprived of their just and natural rights in his works when his permanent reputation is established.'

Southey maintained a consistent position on copyright law, complaining both about the principle on which it was granted, and his consequent inability to make provision for his family. He could only manage his copyrights as carefully as possible, which he did, particularly with his plans for a posthumous edition.[33] When Peel offered Southey a baronetcy in 1835, anxiety about his financial circumstances led him to consider recycling for Peel the proposals he had made first to Brougham, indicating indirectly that he might be a suitable candidate for one of these 'lay-

[32] To Brougham, 1 February 1831: Southey, *Life*, VI, p. 134.

[33] 'Most of my poems have been carefully collected for posthumous publication, and by witholding all such corrections (which I have done for the last twenty years) they become considerable enough in accumulation and importance to constitute a new date of copyright, so far at least as to put all former editions in disrepute': to Wynn, 25 October 1831: Southey, *Selections*, IV, p. 246.

benefices'.[34] He seems to have been dissuaded from this course, and instead wrote explaining his worries. Peel's response was a generous one: he granted Southey an additional civil list pension of £300.

By 1837, the year of Talfourd's first bill, Southey's health and mental faculties were both failing. Inglis, as one of the bill's sponsors, wrote to Southey in May to ask if he had any suggestions concerning the copyright bill. Southey's account of his response indicates that the 'life-plus' element in the bill was his idea:

> I saw Talfourd in London about the copyright question, and he has taken my suggestion, that the term should commence at the death of the author; otherwise there would be different terms for the works of the same person. When he talked of sixty years I proposed ninety-nine, as a term well-known in leases. However, I shall be thankful for the shorter term, which will not expire, if there be a growing sense of justice in the nation, before the legislature will be ready to grant a perpetuity.[35]

Southey was wrong in this, sadly. Although he lived until the 1842 Act was passed, he was too ill to take any real part in the campaign: his place was taken by Wordsworth.[36]

WORDSWORTH – CAMPAIGN MANAGER

Like Southey, Wordsworth watched the copyright bills of the early nineteenth century with keen interest. In his letters, the first surviving reference to copyright concerns the 1808 Copyright Bill. Although reform of the deposit procedures lay at the real heart of this bill, it did contain a proposal to extend the copyright term.[37] Again like Southey, Wordsworth was most concerned with the term. His opinions are already developed, and well supported with examples:

[34] He thought it proper to refuse the honour, because of Mrs Southey's illness, and because of his own financial insecurity. To Wynn, 3 February 1835: Southey, *Selections*, IV, p. 397.

[35] To Wynn, 31 May 1837, and see also to Rickman, 29 May 1837: Southey, *Selections*, IV, pp. 511–12.

[36] He had been anxious that he would not live to see even this: 'Were I to die before Talfourd's Bill passes, the greater part of my poems, and no little of my prose, would be seized immediately by some rascally booksellers, as property which the law allowed them to scramble for.' To H. Taylor, 2 December 1837, Southey, *Life*, VI, p. 354.

[37] Opposition to the deposit clauses sank the entire bill in a matter of days.

I am told that it is proposed to extend the right from 14 years, as it now stands, after the decease of authors,[38] till 28, this I think far too short a period . . . The law as it now stands merely consults the interest of the useful drudges in Literature, or of flimsy and shallow writers, whose works are upon a level with the taste and knowledge of the age; while men of real power, who go before their age, are deprived of all hope of their families being benefited by their exertions . . . Suppose that Burns or Cowper had left at their deaths each a child a few months old, a daughter for example, is it reasonable that those children, at the age of 28, should cease to derive benefit from their Father's works, when every Bookseller in the Country is profiting by them?[39]

Wordsworth regarded copyright as an appropriate means of rewarding writers, although he rejected others. In 1819 he refused to subscribe to a monument for Burns, arguing that such 'Showy Tributes to Genius' tended to exhaust public spirit unprofitably, leaving more important wrongs unredressed. Southey's *Quarterly Review* article on the deposit copy saga had been published a few months earlier. It is likely that Wordsworth had read it. Now with a full understanding of the deposit question, his views were little changed from 1808:

The attention of Parliament has lately been directed by petition to the exaction of copies of newly published Works for certain Libraries; but this is a trifling evil compared with the restrictions imposed upon the duration of Copyright, which in respect to Works profound in philosophy, or elevated, abstract, and refined in imagination, is tantamount almost to an exclusion of all pecuniary recompense for the Author, and even where Works of imagination and manners are so constituted as to be adapted to immediate demand, as in the case of those of Burns, justly may it be asked what reason can be assigned that an Author who dies young should have the prospect before him of his Children being left to languish in Poverty and Dependence, while Booksellers are revelling in luxury upon gains derived from Works which are the delight of many Nations.[40]

In 1828 the notorious Paris-based publisher Galignani sent

[38] Wordsworth's description is confusing: the term was fourteen years, plus another fourteen if the author was still living to receive it.

[39] To Sharp: Wordsworth, *The letters of William and Dorothy Wordsworth*, 2nd edn, ed. Alan G. Hill (Oxford 1969–88), I, p. 266 (27 September 1808).

[40] To J. Forbes Mitchell: ibid., II, p. 533 (21 April 1819). See also Wordsworth's refusal to contribute to the Shakespeare Society: 'in truth Literature stands much less in need of monuments to the dead than of justice to the living. And while so little attention is paid by the Legislature and by the public also to the principles set forth in Serjeant Talfourd's Copyright Bill, I cannot do more . . . than offer respectfully to the Committee my good wishes': ibid., VII, p. 93 (21 July 1840).

Wordsworth a royal vellum copy of one of his own works, printed without permission of course. Wordsworth thought the gift 'a poor Compensation for his Piracy', but wondered 'how can we expect that foreign Nations will respect our literary property when our laws of copy right are so shamefully unjust?' This episode seems to have awakened his old grievances: he asked Henry Crabb Robinson to reflect on the subject and 'write upon it through the Quarterly or any other leading publication'.[41] He also mentioned it to Lowther, remarking that it was an injustice that must one day attract the notice of parliament.[42]

In fact Wordworth's sales were still low enough that he admitted to being 'rather glad of this practice' as far as the Continent was concerned.[43] Much more damaging were the copies of Galignani's edition apparently available in England. Wordsworth was anxious at the price of the Longman edition, which he thought cost him readers, and would have been happy to see a competing cheap edition: 'I am inclined to think with my friend Mr Southey that shortly few books will be published except low-priced ones, or those that are highly ornamented, for persons who delight in such luxuries.' Nevertheless, he continued to regard the 'extreme injustice of the law of copyright' as the main culprit.[44]

Wordsworth's interest in copyright was reawakened in 1835. Ever anxious about his family, he wished to transfer his sinecure as distributor of stamps to his son, Willy. However, he met with objections that this would set the undesirable precedent of a hereditary claim. Offended, he wrote a defensive protest to Lord Lonsdale:

> I have myself some claim upon my country as a man who in the most disinterested way has devoted his life to the service of sound literature; and now, when the success with which this is done, is generally acknowledged, and a pecuniary return might be expected to be made to my family, the Law respecting copyright steps in, and declares that the greatest part of my productions, shall be public property the moment I cease to breathe; it would be surely therefore hard, if under these circumstances, my wish to resign in favor of my son were not complied with.[45]

[41] Ibid., III, p. 691 (18 December 1828).
[42] Ibid., III, p. 697 (23 December 1828).
[43] Ibid., V, p. 225 (5 April 1830).
[44] To John Gardner: ibid., V, p. 264 (19 May 1830).
[45] Ibid., VI, p. 16 (24 January 1835).

Lord Lonsdale did not manage to dispel government anxieties: Peel still felt unable to agree to the transfer at this stage. He wrote to Wordsworth to express his regret, and asked 'whether there be any thing which I can do to gratify your present wishes, or relieve you from anxiety about the future'. Wordsworth replied at some length, explaining his family's financial circumstances. He raised again his grievance that as an author who chose not to write for immediate effect, 'I have to complain of injury proceeding from the laws of my own Country and the practices of a neighbouring one.'[46]

The perceived injustice of copyright was thus a recurrent theme in Wordsworth's correspondence, its appearance usually triggered by a related event. No action had yet resulted, though, in spite of the request for publicity which was made to Crabb Robinson; but in the summer of 1836 Wordsworth was in London, and his diary of visits indicates that serious plans for a copyright bill were being made.[47] His letters state explicitly that Sir Robert Inglis and Spring Rice were parties to the discussions: both were to become sponsors of the 1837 bill.[48] Wordsworth was later to claim that during this visit he had drawn the attention 'of leading Members of the House of Commons of all parties to the question of domestic copyright'.[49] Wordsworth had been staying with Talfourd, whom he had known since 1815: it seems inconceivable that they would not have discussed (or perhaps planned) these meetings.[50]

Once back at home, Wordworth continued to canvass support, and wrote 'rather a long letter' to Sir Robert Inglis about

[46] Ibid., VI, p. 20 (5 February 1835).

[47] For the suggestion that the campaign to extend the term of copyright might have been Wordsworth's 'attempt to realize his intimations of immortality in legal form', see Susan Eilenberg, 'Mortal pages: Wordsworth and the reform of copyright', *ELH: A Journal of English Literary History* 56 (1989), 351–75.

[48] Wordsworth, *Letters*, VI, p. 257, p. 265 (June 1836): Wordsworth says of Spring Rice that 'He seems determined to take or have it taken up with spirit, so that I have no doubt it (the term) will be greatly extended. Do consider that The Excursion has only 6 years to run if I should die.'

[49] Ibid., VI, p. 36 (February 1837).

[50] Charles Lamb introduced them, with the words 'Wordsworth, give me leave to introduce you to my only admirer': *HCR*, I, p. 120. Talfourd's public championing of contemporary poetry was regarded by many as an important factor in its acceptance: William S. Ward, 'An early champion of Wordsworth: Thomas Noon Talfourd', *Proceedings of the Modern Language Association of America* 68 (1953), 992–1000.

copyright. However, Talfourd seems to have asked Wordsworth to make some sort of public statement of his position, and met with great reluctance and diffidence: 'If I were Master of the facts historically, and had access to the arguments which have been used on both sides, when the question has been brought before the courts of law, or Parliament, I would readily give my best judgment to the consideration of the whole case. As it is, I feel incompetent to treat it in a manner to be of use to you.'[51] In the same letter Wordsworth also made it clear that he would not petition for the bill 'but in the last extremity'. He had previously refused to sign a petition to the American Congress asking for protection for English authors, which many well-known authors had thought it proper to sign. This delicacy must have made Talfourd's task more difficult. However, Wordsworth did send some 'notices', which Talfourd intended to use if he met serious opposition.[52]

Talfourd introduced the first copyright bill in May, but the death of the king ended the parliamentary session abruptly, and the bill with it. Leave to bring in the second bill was granted in December, with the first reading set down for the end of February.

1838

Early in January Wordsworth was confident of the bill's success, and claiming credit for his efforts to interest MPs in it. He now described the extension of term as an essential first step towards 'the other part of the Subject' – reciprocal copyright with America.[53] Confident though he was, Wordsworth did begin to write to people he knew in the House to urge them to attend the second reading, although he and Southey both felt that such friends would attend without any special request.[54] They seem to have been unaware of any formidable opposition, and did not think drastic measures necessary. However, notice of a hostile pamphlet caused Wordsworth some anxiety, which must have

[51] The letter to Inglis has not survived, but Wordsworth mentions it to Talfourd: Wordsworth, *Letters*, VI, p. 321 (16 November 1836).

[52] Ibid., VI, p. 498 (15 December 1837).

[53] Ibid., VI, p. 510 (4 January 1838).

[54] Ibid., VI, pp. 512–15 (January 1838).

been reinforced by the bill's reception at the first reading on 28 February.[55]

Towards the end of March Talfourd reported that 'The Booksellers threaten me with a very strong opposition – and the Doctrinaire party are inclined to support them.' Also, the second reading was down for the Wednesday before the Easter recess, so even a quorum was doubtful.[56] The anxious Talfourd asked Wordsworth to use his influence to rescue the situation. He responded magnificently and began to lobby in earnest, with letters carefully tailored to suit the recipient. Wordsworth told his nephew John that he had written between forty and fifty letters in support of Talfourd's Bill, 'with various success'.[57] Although most of the replies indicated willingness to support any measure that was of interest to Wordsworth, almost all of them asked to be relieved of the duty of supporting it on 11 April, the day before the vacation. The second reading was in fact postponed until 25 April.

Talfourd now knew that considerable forces were being mustered against him, and thought that quiet lobbying was no longer enough. Wordsworth did not hear this from Talfourd directly, but from Philip Howard, member for Carlisle: 'Mr Serjt Talfourd stated to me between ourselves that if Mr Southey and yourself were to send him a petition to present in favour of his Bill it w[d] have weight and be something to show.'[58]

Talfourd had already asked Wordsworth to petition, in 1836, and he had refused. Whereas Wordsworth had been very willing to use his personal influence in a private way, he had strong objections 'to appearing publicly as a Suppliant, for what I consider cannot be denied without the most flagrant injustice to

55 To Moxon: ibid., VI, p. 519 (3 February 1838). The pamphlet was perhaps *Observations on the law of copyright* (1838).

56 'As there is often a thin attendance on Wednesday – the only day when a Bill, not being conducted as a Government measure, can be proceeded with, if opposed – it will be very desirable to obtain the attendance of members favourably disposed to the measure, not merely with a view to a division, but to form a House in the first instance . . . I trust this will reach you in time to enable you to exert any influence you can command to secure attendance and support.' Talfourd's letter is quoted in Paul M. Zall, 'Wordsworth and the Copyright Act of 1842', *Proceedings of the Modern Language Association of America* 70 (1955), 132–44.

57 Wordsworth, *Letters*, VI, pp. 535–52 (March/April 1838).

58 Philip Howard to Wordsworth, 11 April 1838: Zall, 'Wordsworth', pp. 135–6.

the best Authors of the Country, and a correspondent injury to literature'.[59] However, his desire to see the measure passed had gradually eroded his resistance to a public association with the campaign. He had recently written a long letter to the *Kendal Mercury*, commenting in detail on a petition against the bill from Kendal printers:[60] although it was signed 'A.B.', the author's identity became well known. A public petition was only one more step, and Wordsworth agreed to consider petitioning, albeit very reluctantly.

Talfourd responded despondently that he was now afraid that they would be beaten, and appears not to have pressed further.[61] Wordsworth was not able to overcome his scruples, but wrote Talfourd a letter which explained his refusal to petition, stating that he could publish it if this would help. With the second reading only days away Talfourd did publish it, and not anonymously, in the *Morning Post*. Wordsworth stated defiantly that he thought that an author had a right to perpetual copyright, and that he would therefore not petition parliament for a shorter term.[62] On the same day he wrote indignantly to Peel: 'Allow me then to state the fact that if the bill do not pass, or a comprehensive one grounded on its principle, I shall be aggrieved in the most tender points.'[63]

Southey was also considering his position on petitioning. It is probable that Wordsworth had sent him Howard's letter which revealed Talfourd's desire for a joint petition from them. Southey was also reluctant to petition, and had been drafting a letter for Talfourd to use. He was put off even this by the frequency with which his name came up in the debate on the second reading: like Wordsworth, he did not wish to be seen to be arguing for his own personal gain. He even began to favour the attorney-general's plan to vest a power to renew copyright in the Judicial Committee of the Privy Council. Wordsworth tried to encourage Southey to give

59 Wordsworth, *Letters*, VI, p. 553 (14 April 1838).

60 Wordsworth, *The prose works of William Wordsworth*, eds. Warwick J. B. Owen and Jane W. Smyser (Oxford, 1974), p. 309.

61 Talfourd to Wordsworth, 16 April 1838: Wordsworth, *Letters*, VI, p. 554n.

62 Ibid., VI, p. 556 (18 April 1838).

63 Ibid., VI, p. 558. Peel did not vote on the second reading because he had not made up his mind. He wrote to Wordsworth to explain his difficulties, particularly the supposed analogy between copyright and patent, but was not persuaded by the reply: ibid., pp. 568, 572.

Talfourd a letter which could be used during the committee stage. Wordsworth himself disliked the idea of the Privy Council's involvement: 'such a distinction would put those Authors on whom it was conferred in an invidious position. Let the remuneration come from [the] public who would chearfully bestow it.'[64]

Wordsworth continued to cajole weary supporters and pressurise waverers before the committee stage, telling the disheartened Talfourd 'Don't let your hopes down or relax.'[65] There was no House for the first date set for the committee, and the following week the bill came on too late to enter into detailed discussion. The next committee was set for 6 June and, in the interval, Talfourd was forced to drop the retrospective clause. Talfourd himself gave a somewhat circumspect account of this:

> an anxious consideration of the objections of the publishers of London and Edinburgh to the clause whereby a reverting interest in copyrights absolutely assigned was created in favour of authors, convinced those who had charge of the bill that it was impossible by any arrangements to prevent the inconvenience and loss which they suggested as consequential on such a boon to authors. They, therefore, determined to confine the operation of the bill on subsisting copyrights to cases in which the author had retained some interest on which it might operate; and with this, to their honour, the publishers were satisfied.[66]

In spite of this substantial concession, Russell's concerns surfaced here – quite unexpectedly.[67] This stopped effective progress, although the discussions continued. Wordsworth wrote several letters to Talfourd, restating their case at some length, and voicing indignant protests at the behaviour of their opponents.[68] His two sonnets on the theme of copyright date from this time.[69] On 20 June, supported by Gladstone and Inglis, Talfourd agreed to withdraw the bill to avoid the ignominy of its being voted out.[70]

64 *New letters of Robert Southey*, ed. Kenneth Curry (1965), II, p. 474. Wordsworth, *Letters*, VI, p. 565 (30 April 1838).

65 Wordsworth, *Letters*, VI, pp. 575, 579, 568 (May 1838).

66 Thomas Noon Talfourd, *Three speeches delivered in the House of Commons* (1840), p. 67.

67 Probably provoked by the intervention of Tom Longman: see ch. 5, p. 122.

68 Wordsworth to Talfourd, mid-June 1838: Wordsworth, *Letters*, VI, pp. 596–603.

69 *A plea for authors*, and *A poet to his grandchild*, both published in 1838.

70 For Talfourd's explanatory letter to Wordsworth, see Russell Noyes, 'Wordsworth and the Copyright Act of 1842: Addendum', *Proceedings of the Modern Language Association of America* 24 (1961), 380–3.

Gladstone was nevertheless hopeful of getting the bill through eventually, and Wordsworth was similarly optimistic.

Brougham's bill, introduced in the House of Lords, provided a brief diversion in the summer. Wordsworth had no love of Brougham personally or politically, and had already criticised a similar plan. Wordsworth thought the Judicial Committee of the Privy Council unsuited to the task of deciding on the merits of authors, its proper business being the law of the land:

> I see Brougham has brought into the house the Lords [*sic*] a New Copy right Bill – what are its merits? I fear it will prove a milk & water business. He talks about the privy-council – what the deuce can those Stupes know about the merit of works of Imagination – are the judges likely to be better than Jeffrey or B- himself, and yet one of them so late as 22 – had the folly to write in the E. Review, that my productions were despicable without thought, without feeling taste or judgment &c &c See Edin. Review. No^{vr} 1822.[71]

Talfourd allowed himself only a brief respite before making plans for the 1839 bill. In October he told Wordsworth that he intended to reintroduce the bill as soon as the session opened, and proposed that petitions should be produced for the Second Reading:

> Will you just consider it, and let me know your feelings – which first of all by me & by all other friends of the Cause ought to be regarded. If you chose to petition, I presume we might rely on Southey – & Moore – and for most others I could answer. As the prayer of the Petitions would be – not for any individual benefit – but for a general measure of justice for all authors & for all time, I do not see any degradation in proferring them.[72]

In a letter to Lady Frederick Bentinck, which has been dated October/early November 1837, Wordsworth asked her to help drum up parliamentary support.[73] The letter also revealed that the tacticians guiding the bill were anxious at the silence of authors in the face of the booksellers' petitions, and had advised that petitions from individual authors were necessary to counteract this bad impression. Wordsworth wrote: 'I have accordingly drawn up a petition in my own name with a view to have it presented, should the plan be acted upon. But this is all between ourselves, as the thing if done at all, will be in a quiet way.' If this letter is

71 Wordsworth to Henry Crabb Robinson: Crabb Robinson, *Correspondence with the Wordsworth circle, 1806–66*, ed. Edith J. Morley (Oxford, 1927), I, p. 369.

72 Zall, 'Wordsworth', p. 139.

73 Wordsworth, *Letters*, VI, p. 475.

dated correctly, it indicates that Wordsworth had had a total change of mind: one year earlier he had been prepared to petition only 'in the last extremity'. The matter-of-fact tone of the letter is not consistent with this. The discussion of the opposition petitions would represent another oddity, as no petitions were presented until 1838. Other authors who sent petitions did so in 1839, in response to requests organised by the bill's supporters. Wordsworth's own letters at this time indicate that he was only now becoming reconciled to the prospect of petitioning. It seems inherently unlikely that he should have drafted a petition, which he then did not show to any of his friends, as early as 1837: he was confident that the bill would be accepted on its merits. It is submitted that this letter was written in the light of Talfourd's request – in other words, after the close of the 1838 session, in contemplation of the 1839 session to come.

Wordsworth admitted that he was deeply interested in the success of the measure, but less for his own benefit than for his belief in its justice. He also considered its likely effect on literature: 'Authors as a Class could not but be in some degree put upon exertions that would raise them in public estimation – and say what you will, the possession of Property tends to make any body of men more respectable, however high may be their claims to respect upon other considerations.'[74] This reference to the profession of authorship is telling.

1839

In January Talfourd wrote again to Wordsworth, restating his intention to reintroduce the bill as soon as the new session opened in February, and reiterating the need for petitions: he set out the form that such a petition should take, and enclosed a similar letter for Southey.[75] Wordsworth had overcome all his scruples, and was 'quite ready to petition'.[76] Even better, he had shown Talfourd's letter to Dr Arnold, who was also willing to petition.[77] Wordsworth drafted his petition over the next few days, with the advice

[74] To Talfourd: ibid., VI, p. 636 (25 October 1838).
[75] 24 January 1839. Zall, 'Wordsworth', p. 140.
[76] Wordsworth, *Letters*, VI, p. 657 (26 January 1839).
[77] Thomas Arnold was headmaster of Rugby School, and Wordsworth's neighbour for parts of the year.

of Henry Crabb Robinson who was spending the New Year at Rydal.[78] The petition was finally sent to Talfourd in the middle of February, and Wordsworth returned to his task of drumming up support, in contemplation of the second reading on 27 January. Back in London, Crabb Robinson also helped to collect signatures, with mixed success.[79] Wordsworth's own plea to Southey for a petition remained unanswered, but Carlyle's petition made a particular impact.[80]

10 April was finally set as the date of the second reading. This was the first day after the Easter recess, and there was 'no house'.[81] Talfourd was despondent again, and seems to have proposed publishing some of the petitions. Wordsworth thought it better to publish none than to risk offending the authors not selected.[82] The bill continued to make very little progress, to a large extent because of the obstructive tactics of Warburton and Wakley, and then because of Melbourne's resignation.[83] Talfourd nevertheless hoped to keep the matter in the public eye, by publishing his speeches on copyright.

[78] Crabb Robinson's journal is revealing. 28 January: 'I went early to Wordsworth to talk about the Copyright Bill which Talfourd is to bring forward and a petition which Wordsworth and others are individually to send in. Wordsworth has drawn up one in which he is too desirous to express his own impression and cares, too little about the impressions it will excite in others.' 29 January: 'This morning I amused myself by re-writing a petition Wordsworth had drawn up in favour of the new Copyright Bill of Talfourd. Wordsworth adopted a few of my suggestions in himself writing it over again.' Crabb Robinson, *On books and their writers*, ed. Edith J. Morley (1938), II, pp. 566–7.

[79] 'I took charge of Talfourd's Copyright Petition, admirably couched in a very few sentences. I procured for him the signature of Milman, Fonblanque, and H. Taylor: White, Philip Courtenay and Hallam refused me. These at the Athenaeum': ibid., II, p. 568. Courtenay infuriated Wordsworth by saying 'he could not sacrifice his Conscience to vote for such a JOB as the Serjents Copyright Bill': Crabb Robinson, *Correspondence*, I, p. 365.

[80] To Southey: Wordsworth, *Letters*, VI, p. 662 (18 February 1839). For the success of the campaign, see ch. 8.

[81] The House could be counted out unless forty Members were present.

[82] Wordsworth, *Letters*, VI, p. 679.

[83] Talfourd reported the Bill's demise to Wordsworth on 10 July: 'It is put down in the Order Book night after night with the assurance of the Government that they would assist in bringing it on – *now* I have to inform you that the state of suspense is over, and that it is postponed to next Session. Notwithstanding repeated promises from Lord John Russell, and three Thursday evenings provided when it was to have absolute precedence, it has never advanced a step – not even a clause – since that despicable night when Warburton proved the infinite divisibility of matter, on the body of the House of Commons.' Zall, 'Wordsworth', p. 141.

1840

Less of an effort was made with the campaign in 1840, partly because the bill was defeated so early in the session. Wordsworth read one of Tegg's pieces listing the profits made by Bulwer and Scott, and responded that this was not an argument against the extension of copyright, but rather one in its favour: an extended copyright would allow authors to look to the future for their rewards, with a consequent beneficial effect on the quality of literature.[84] Wordsworth was becoming increasingly frustrated with the opposition from senior parliamentaritans, and was still anxiously collecting pamphlets on copyright. He does not seem to have been in very close touch with Talfourd.[85] Rallying letters were not written on the same scale, but Wordsworth did write to Lockhart to ask him to write an article for the *Quarterly Review*.[86] Although the second reading was carried again, the motion for its committal was postponed to the first day after the Easter recess, and the House was counted out again.[87]

1841

1841 was in some ways even worse for Wordsworth. He wrote indignantly to Talfourd asking what should be done: 'I would

[84] To Talfourd: Wordsworth, *Letters*, VII, p. 17 (16 February 1840). Wordsworth develops the argument in a letter to Edward Quillinan: ibid., VII, p. 42 (9 March 1840).

[85] Wordsworth asked Moxon to send him William Dougal Christie's pamphlet *A plea for perpetual copyright in a letter to Lord Monteagle* (1840): Wordsworth, *Letters*, VII, p. 59 (April 1840). He told Gomm, 'I have not lately been in communication with anyone upon the subject so that I know nothing but what the Papers will tell you': Wordsworth, *Letters*, VII, p. 62 (mid-April 1840).

[86] Wordsworth, *Letters*, VII, p. 65 (c. 27 April 1840). Lockhart eventually wrote an important article: see chs. 5 and 8.

[87] Talfourd to Wordsworth, 7 May 1840: 'We had a very good muster of our friends, but a stupid Bill about Mineral Mines, which was not expected to occupy many minutes, lasted until the hungry hour of Seven – our friends dropped off to their engagements – the House trembled on the verge of *forty* – Warburton saw his advantage, and walked out followed by some half dozen Economists – and Wakley, left behind for the purpose, counted out the House, just as the Copyright Bill was coming on . . . I am sure you have done all that can be done to procure attendance – and most successfully – we muster well – several members came to Town on purpose for the last day fixed – but to remain dinnerless all night on the very day in all the week for dinners is too much to hope except from such staunch friends as Inglis, Mahon and Gladstone who never fail. And then our opponents never dine. Warburton is ever there "in his place" ': quoted in Zall, 'Wordsworth', p. 142.

write and publish in my own name a letter addressed to you, in refutation of that trash advanced by Macauley [*sic*] if all that he has said had not been anticipated over and over by yourself and others.'[88] He blamed the loss of the bill on the poor attendance of its supporters, who had preferred a dinner arranged for Hume.[89] Wordsworth's efforts were renewed in the summer, when he was in London again. He secured an interview with Peel to discuss copyright, although the result was disappointing:

> I could not induce him to look favourably upon the Bill; in fact he was obviously afraid of being charged with *monopoly*, if he gave it his support . . . He acknowledged however both the justice and expediency of giving the privilege to particular Persons, and expressed a hope that Parliament would aid in such a measure. – I urged many and I think cogent objections to this scheme; . . . I made, however, little or no impression, none indeed to encourage hope that he would support that or a similar measure.[90]

Indefatigable nevertheless, Wordsworth went on to see Lockhart, where he had more success: Lockhart agreed to write an article for the *Quarterly Review*, 'in support of the cause'. Another matter under consideration was a new sponsor for the bill: Talfourd had decided not to fight the 1841 election, and therefore would not be in the House to introduce the new measure in 1842.

1842

There were several candidates for the job of introducing the new bill. Richard Monckton Milnes, MP for Pontefract and himself an author, had written to Gladstone in January stating his intention to present a modified bill 'if the matter does not fall into better hands'. Gladstone advised him to consult Lord Monteagle, who had been involved in the matter, and reported that Thesiger was rumoured to be interested.[91] In the end it was Lord Mahon, a sponsor of the bill since 1837, who agreed to manage a further attempt to amend the law of copyright. However, Mahon's vision was altogether more modest than Talfourd's: his proposal was for a term of twenty-five years from the author's death.

88 Wordsworth, *Letters*, VII, p. 178 (8 February 1841).
89 Ibid., VII, p. 179 (16 February 1841).
90 To Isabella Fenwick: ibid., VII, p. 214 (10 July 1841).
91 Sir Thomas Wemyss Reid, *The life, letters and friendships of Richard Monckton Milnes*, 2nd edn (1890), I, p. 275.

Wordsworth at first assumed that this plan was based on the French model, rather than the more generous Prussian term. More pragmatic considerations were probably at work, though. Early in the year Gladstone had 'begged Lord Monteagle to propitiate Macaulay', hoping that a moderate term dating from death might be had without violent opposition or the 'confused splutter' of the former proceedings.[92] Another prominent opponent, Lord John Russell, had written to Mahon to state that although he would not oppose the second reading, if the bill was similar to Talfourd's, he would wish to see it much altered in Committee: he thought twenty-five years a long enough term.[93] The influence of both these men was considerable, and Mahon must have been anxious to reach a workable solution. He tactfully secured Wordsworth's support by suggesting that if a short extension were to be granted, a longer term could be secured in the future.[94]

Notwithstanding this element of compromise, Wordsworth welcomed Mahon's involvement, and continued to provide important help and information. Mahon was anxious to deal with Macaulay's very public statement that an extended copyright term could lead to suppression of work by an author's heirs, although he thought that the power of public opinion made this event utterly improbable. Wordsworth agreed that the dangers were exaggerated, and was quick to point out that Talfourd's bill had already dealt with the matter. Wordsworth also gave Mahon a detailed account of his interview with Peel the previous summer. Peel had seemingly abandoned his original worries, expressed in an earlier letter to Wordsworth:[95] he was instead more generally concerned about the evils of monopoly, and had 'dwelt a good deal upon a discretionary power to be lodged in a Section of the Privy Council to reward, in the shape of pensions, meritorious Authors,

[92] Gladstone to Milnes, 19 January 1842: Reid, *Life, letters*, p. 276.

[93] Lord John Russell to Viscount Mahon, 20 February 1842: quoted in Wordsworth, *Letters*, VII, p. 299n.

[94] Wordsworth to Viscount Mahon, 4 March 1842: 'The observation you have made upon your present aim not precluding future improvements reconciles me to what I cannot but think, tho' a prudent, an inadequate measure': ibid., VII, p. 300.

[95] Peel's response is quoted in a letter from Wordsworth to Talfourd: Wordsworth, *Letters*, VI, p. 568 (2 May 1838).

or to confer a privilege upon particular works supposed to be entitled to it'.[96]

Mahon, determined to get the bill through in some form, adopted a pragmatic approach. He consulted leading publishers, particularly Longman and Murray, and worked closely with them to ensure their support. They were given early versions of the bill, and evidently commented on its drafting.[97] In return, Murray and Longman organised petitions from publishers, authors, printers and others – this time in favour of the bill. They were presented at the second reading, although Mahon managed to postpone further debate until the committee stage.

Mahon continued to pacify the publishers, agreeing to reword section 19, a controversial clause concerning the copyright of encyclopaedia articles so as to 'completely meet the views of Mr. Longman as it does Mr. Macaulay'. During the committee stage itself Mahon had to endure the argument between Peel and Macaulay as to the appropriate term, although this never looked likely to defeat the bill. More dangerous was section 24, a clause which would have allowed the common law courts both to grant injunctions and to award damages: the plaintiff had previously been forced to seek these remedies in separate courts. Although Godson, an authority on copyright law, spoke in favour of the clause, Mahon dropped it once it became apparent that there was substantial opposition. The remainder of the bill was agreed to without further difficulty.

Mahon had sent Wordsworth a copy of the bill early in March, and now, early in April he wrote to report his success in the Commons. Although Wordsworth was grateful for Mahon's efforts, and was glad that the principle of a post-mortem term had been conceded, he thought seven years a 'beggarly allowance'. Nor could he conceal his indignation at Macaulay's opposition to this, which he regarded as particularly objectionable since Macaulay 'as

[96] To Viscount Mahon: ibid., VII, p. 299 (4 March 1842).

[97] A letter to Murray from Mahon, 3 March 1842, reveals Murray's concern with international piracies: 'the object you have in view of guarding London publishers from the Paris reprints now brought in by private travellers would be as effectually obtained and much more easily [by including it in Mahon's Bill] than by a separate measure'. Quoted in James J. Barnes, *Authors, publishers and politicians: the quest for an Anglo-American copyright agreement, 1815–54* (1974), p. 122.

is well known, was *jobbed* out to India for the mere purpose of putting money into his pocket'.[98]

In May the copyright bill still had to face more opposition, this time from Lord Brougham in the House of Lords. Mahon had done his best to be conciliatory to Brougham, tactfully sending him an early copy of the bill, and asking for his views, but Brougham does not seem to have been much mollified. Mahon was 'alarmed', and thought that Brougham might have strong support.[99] Wordsworth responded yet again: he visited the House of Lords where he lobbied Lord Monteagle, Lord Clarendon and Lord Aberdeen. He even had an interview with Brougham himself, although the details of this remain tantalisingly vague.[100] Hearing more bad news from Lord Lyndhurst, who was to present the bill in the House of Lords, Mahon turned again to Murray for petitions:

> It would be of very good advantage to the success of this measure if you could obtain four petitions to the Lords similar to those which you sent me for the Commons – namely from authors, publishers, printers and stationers.
>
> Such petitions must be if obtained not later than 4.00 o'clock on Tuesday afternoon [10 May] in the Lord Chancellor's hands. Let me beg of you therefore to see about it immediately – this very evening if possible, or the object of our exertions may yet be lost to us.
>
> The petitions need not be long, but should express satisfaction with the Bill and entreat the House to pass it as it stands.[101]

Murray duly exerted himself to produce the petitions required, which were eventually presented at the committee stage (26 May), Lyndhurst having used the tactical device of deferring the debate on the second reading. In the event, Brougham's views did not find much support, although Wordsworth was anxiously in attendance.[102] The bill passed its third reading in June, and received the royal assent in July.

98 To Viscount Mahon: Wordsworth, *Letters*, VII, p. 323 (11 April 1842). Although predictable Tory abuse of Whig jobbery, such feelings reflect Wordsworth's difficulties in securing his family's future. Macaulay earned £10,000 a year as a member of the Supreme Council of India.

99 Barnes, *Authors*, p. 124. Wordsworth, *Letters*, VII, p. 334.

100 To Viscount Mahon: 'I have just been calling upon Lord Brougham about the Copyright Bill. Even in conversation I could only give you a faint notion of all that he said and in this note it would be absurd for me to enter upon the subject': Wordsworth, *Letters*, VII, p. 333 (8 May 1842).

101 Barnes, *Authors*, p. 124.

102 Crabb Robinson, *On books*, p. 617.

For Wordsworth the 1842 Copyright Act represented a very partial triumph. Although he wrote to congratulate Mahon, he described the measure as 'far short in its provisions of what you, and other enlightened friends of literature wished'. In addition, the debate in parliament had done little to suggest either House's recognition of the status and worth of the author's profession. Wordsworth was also well aware that domestic copyright was now perhaps of less immediate relevance to an English author than the growing threat from foreign piracies. Even as he thanked Mahon for the new domestic protection, Wordsworth's thoughts were on the international problem: 'Could this injustice be stopped, or even materially checked, in Europe, and the same effected in America, Men of letters would take that position in society, in connection with Property which they are entitled to. Of course I mean such as have real merit.'[103]

Wordsworth developed this theme slightly in letters to his American editor, Henry Reed, but the struggle for international copyright was one which others had to take up.[104] His contribution to the passage of the domestic legislation had been enormous: the 1842 Act was a tribute to his efforts, as well as Talfourd's. However, the efforts of the literary world in general should not be underestimated. Authors wrote pamphlets, letters and periodicals, and even overcame an ingrained reluctance to petition for their own requirements.

[103] Wordsworth, *Letters*, VII, p. 348 (late June 1842).

[104] Notably 18 July 1842: ibid., VII, p. 355.

8

THE MAKING OF THE CASE FOR THE BILL

PETITIONS – THOSE IN FAVOUR

Wordsworth's involvement provides a fascinating narrative of the bill's progress: the campaigning played a major part in the bill's eventual success. The petitions themselves are particularly worth studying for what they reveal about the ability of the literary world to unite – contrary to all previous history.[1]

Petitioning was a sensitive matter. There had been adverse comment in parliament about the lack of support from authors, who were supposedly the main beneficiaries of the changes. By 1838 only one petition had been received in favour of the copyright bill. This came from Samuel Wells, 'Barrister at Law and Register of the Honourable the Corporation of the Great Level of the Fens, called the Bedford Level'.[2] Samuel Wells described himself as the author of 'a laborious work called the History of the Bedford Level', a book 'of slow sale and limited circulation'. He was working on another book, 'The History of the Revenue and Expenditure of the United Kingdom', which had already entailed great expense in preparation. His argument was that important

[1] The international petitioning campaign was a partial exception. In 1837 Harriet Martineau organised a petition from English authors to Congress, demanding copyright for their works: she had spent time in America, and knew those involved in the campaign there, who were seeking the support of English authors. She wrote breathlessly to Mary Russell Mitford: 'Everybody is signing; and the case is so clear that I think you cannot hesitate' (9 November 1836). Henry Clay, chairman of the Select Committee of the Senate, submitted five bills between 1837 and 1842, but was defeated each time. Like Talfourd, Clay faced quantities of petitions and memorials from publishers, authors, and booksellers. See John Tebbel, *A history of book publishing in the United States* (1972), p. 558; James J. Barnes, *Authors, publishers and politicians: the quest for an Anglo-American copyright agreement, 1815–54* (1974), p. 60.

[2] 5,956, presented 9 May 1838, App. 456.

works of this nature should be encouraged: 'no property is more legitimate, or more worthy of protection, than the works of authors who spend so many laborious days and sleepless nights in administering to the delight and the instruction of mankind at large'.

Talfourd was probably all too aware of the impression that this was likely to make, and began a campaign to persuade people to petition. Wordsworth was a primary target, although his repeated refusals must have made his cooperation seem unlikely.[3] Talfourd's tact and perseverance were in large measure responsible for Wordsworth's change of heart. Talfourd proposed a widely based approach, couched in judiciously flattering terms:

> We might certainly thus present a formidable array of the greatest names which our age has produced – and if each Author in petitioning would state his own individual case the force of all combined would be the greater. We might obtain not merely the poets, headed by yourself, and the novelists, but many men of science, like Babbage, – Divines like Chalmers . . . and even some eminent publishers, as Smith of Glasgow, Cadell of Edinburgh; and I believe all the lady writers from Miss Martineau downwards or upwards.[4]

In the same letter Talfourd confidently told Wordsworth that he thought he could undertake to obtain the signatures of most other authors, and he did, by using the literary networks to the full. The list of those petitioning in 1839 included the most prominent writers of the day.

Petitions – 1839

The petitions in support of the copyright measure were largely concentrated in 1839: Talfourd presented most of them, as he had intended, at the second reading on 27 February.

[3] Wordsworth had even refused to petition for international copyright, although he was strongly in favour of reciprocal protection. He told Talfourd that he did not sign, both because he had no knowledge of his own works being 'garbled' by American publishers, and also because he thought the strong condemnatory language impolitic. Wordsworth defended his decision in similar terms to the astonished Crabb Robinson: Wordsworth, *The letters of William and Dorothy Wordsworth*, 2nd edn, ed. Alan G. Hill (Oxford, 1969–88), VI, p. 493 (15 December 1837).

[4] Paul M. Zall, 'Wordsworth and the Copyright Act of 1842', *Proceedings of the Modern Language Association of America* 70 (1955), 135–44 (p. 139).

Pride of place was given to Wordsworth's petition.[5] The efforts needed to extract this have already been described. Although Talfourd gave advice as to form, and Henry Crabb Robinson was also consulted, the final petition was drafted entirely by Wordsworth, and submitted by Talfourd unaltered. Wordsworth began with his own case, his copyrights soon to expire, on works only just achieving popular recognition. He contrasted 'the condition of distinguished authors' with that of 'men who rise to eminence in other professions or employments, whereby they not only acquire wealth, but have patronage at command, or obtain the means of forming family establishments in business, which enable them to provide at once for their descendants'. Condensing a point he had made at length in his letter to the *Kendal Mercury*, Wordsworth argued that the interests of copyright holders would ensure that their works were cheaply and readily available, and therefore that fears concerning the availability of books were groundless.

Wordsworth also used the petition to argue that authentic copies were more likely to come from the author's representatives: he took great care with editions of his own works. His reference to the author's last additions or emendations may have been intended to recall Scott's final edition of his own works,[6] or perhaps Southey's concern to leave his family material for an 'authorised' edition. There were certainly echoes of Southey in Wordsworth's final conclusion, although it represented a position which was fully his own, held with great consistency since the earliest copyright bills of the century:

> the Bill has for its main object, to relieve men of letters from the thraldom of being forced to court the living generation, to aid them in rising above degraded taste and slavish prejudice, and to encourage them to rely upon their own impulses, or to leave them with less excuse if they should fail to do so.

Not all petitioners were so individual: Talfourd had drafted a short petition as an exemplar, which was used by several groups of people. It was concisely argued, concentrating on the need for a

[5] 2,324, presented 27 February 1839, App. 188. Wordsworth, *The prose works of William Wordsworth*, eds. Warwick J. B. Owen and Jane W. Smyser (Oxford, 1974), p. 317.

[6] Known as the *magnum*, it was revised and annotated by Scott, with new introductions. See below, p. 193.

longer term as a fair reward for works of lasting value, which (it was claimed) would neither increase the price of books or burden the public. The wording and tone were respectful, moderate and unexceptionable. The names of those signing were much more striking than its content.

The first group had Edinburgh as its geographical centre, in particular the university.[7] In general the signatories were senior figures in the Edinburgh establishment.[8] On the whole they were authors of learned treatises, and not of novels, although several of them were involved in influential magazines. The literary element was probably strong enough on its own to explain their concern with copyright.[9] However, there was perhaps also a thread leading back to Sir Walter Scott. Scott had been at school and university in Edinburgh, and his home, Abbotsford, was nearby. He had been held in great affection, and his extraordinary efforts to repay his debts after 1826 had only served to enhance this. Lockhart's biography of Scott had been published only the previous year, so the matter had been reopened publicly: any discussion of a post-mortem term for copyright must have led Scott's friends to consider how such a law might have relieved his last years.

The same petition was used by a group of signatories from Glasgow, which included the president and treasurer of

[7] 2,325, presented 27 February 1839, App. 189. Edinburgh University Library was a deposit library.

[8] The twenty-one signatories were: John Wood (sheriff of Peebleshire), Patrick Sheen (advocate), Thomas Charles Hope (professor of chemistry, Edinburgh), George Dunbar (professor of Greek, Edinburgh), Adam Ferguson (deputy keeper, Regalia of Scotland), Walter Scott (son of Sir Walter Scott), Thomas Chalmers (professor of divinity, Edinburgh), Alexander Brunton (professor of languages, Edinburgh), John Wilson (professor of moral philosophy, the 'Christopher North' of *Blackwood's Edinburgh Magazine*), James Pillans (professor of humanity), R. Christersom (professor of materia medica), Thomas Stewart Traile (professor of medical jurisprudence), James Horne (professor of practice of medicine), James Gunner (professor of rhetoric and belles lettres), Rev. Archibald Alison, W. O. Anson (professor of the Institutes of Medicine), John Abercrombie (first physician to Her Majesty in Scotland), A. Dunlop (advocate), Henry Glassford Bell (advocate, an author who conducted the *Edinburgh Literary Journal*), George Bowdie (historiographer of her Majesty for Scotland), J. S. Lockhart. Archibald Alison also petitioned separately: 2,328, presented 27 February 1839, App. 191.

[9] John Wilson, the notorious but powerful critic 'Christopher North', was at the heart of a particular literary circle. He also had a Lake District residence near the Wordsworths.

Anderson's University.[10] Anderson's Institution was founded at Glasgow under the will of John Anderson in 1796.[11] A professor at Glasgow University, he had intended it as a rival university, but it was not until 1828 that its range of subjects justified this title. It provided evening lectures aimed at a relatively sophisticated and well-off audience. George Birkbeck, who was professor from 1799–1804, started a rival 'mechanics' class', which in 1823 became the Glasgow Mechanics' Institution. Birkbeck's vision of adult education was very different from that of his colleagues, and the split with Anderson's Institution was not entirely amicable. These differences remained even in the 1830s: as has been seen, Birkbeck was strongly against the bill, whereas key figures in Anderson's University petitioned in its favour.

Three other petitions seem similar. They all came from Glasgow, although there is no record of either their wording or their signatories. However, the Committee on Public Petitions used the same designation as the first Glasgow petition, 'persons interested in or connected with literature or science, Glasgow'. Although it is possible that they came from the same source, this is far from certain. The fact that only the Anderson's University petition was printed suggests that the other signatories were less grand. Two other petitions came from Glasgow, but both of these were individually drafted.

James Thomson was professor of mathematics in the University of Glasgow. In his petition he listed various teaching books he had written, whose sales were at first slow but much later began to provide a reasonable return. He made the interesting point that new text books might be slow to mature into popularity, given the difficulty of overcoming both the resistance of teachers to the unfamiliar, and of booksellers to works which rivalled their current publications.[12] Accounts of difficulties faced by educational books would have been more persuasive in certain constituencies than tales of the problems of modern poets.

The final petition from Glasgow was a very rare thing, as it came from the head of a publishing and bookselling firm, John

[10] 2,329, presented 27 February 1839, App. 192.

[11] Material on the Anderson's Institution is taken from Robert D. Anderson, *Education and the Scottish people 1750–1918* (Oxford, 1995), pp. 158–60.

[12] 2,332, presented 27 February 1839, App. 193.

Smith & Son.[13] Twenty years earlier John Smith had written a pamphlet in which he argued that authors should enjoy perpetual copyright. He took the view that since his own property could be passed on to his heirs, the authors who had enriched him should enjoy the same privilege. He also suggested that no licences above twenty-one years should be enforceable, the property instead reverting to the author or heirs. However, Smith did ask that no clause should be allowed to 'injure the vested rights of any party entitled to claim Copyright under the present law', perhaps a reference to the retrospective element of Talfourd's plans.

The University of St Andrews was also represented in the petitions in favour, and in its corporate capacity. The rector, George Buist, signed 'in name, presence, and by the University of St. Andrews', on behalf of the rector, principals and masters.[14] This petition was another example of individual draftsmanship. The main argument was that the existing copyright term tended 'to encourage superficial productions, and to discourage all works of real and substantial learning'. One of the supporting arguments revealed more about the petitioners' genuine grievances than was typical of most such documents:

> in Scotland, particularly, when the few rewards which used to be conferred on clergymen of literary and scientific merit have been unwisely withdrawn, and when the income of the professors in her Universities have been allowed to suffer great diminution, – these individuals have strong motives to solicit, and additional grounds to expect, that their literary rights be extended and rendered as beneficial as possible to themselves and their families.

The professor of moral philosophy at St Andrews, George Cook, petitioned in his own right.[15] He had published various works, historical, biographical and theological: the nature of the works had made them long in preparation and slow to sell. He argued that an extension in the copyright term would 'secure the

[13] 2,333, presented 27 February 1839, App. 194. John Smith III (1784–1849) was director of the publishing firm founded by his grandfather in 1751. Secretary of the Maitland Club, he had been a college friend at Glasgow of John Wilson, and was also friendly with Scott and Campbell. Wordsworth expressed himself 'particularly pleased' with Smith's petition: Wordsworth, *Letters*, VI, p. 669 (11 March 1839).

[14] 2,335, presented 27 February 1839, App. 196. Again, this was a deposit library.

[15] 2,334, presented 27 February 1839, App. 195.

interest of the authors of extensive and laborious works without the slightest degree interfering with the public good'.

South of the border, Talfourd's sample petition had also been circulating: the campaigners had collected signatures from thirty-four English authors.[16] Even given Talfourd's wide circle of literary friends and acquaintances, it seems remarkable that he could persuade so many authors to sign a single petition.[17] These were important and powerful literary figures, representing an extraordinary range of literary work. Mary Russell Mitford was known for her carefully observed novels. George P. R. James wrote romantic novels, biographies and popular histories, whereas W. Harrison Ainsworth was known for action-packed 'Newgate novels' such as *Jack Sheppard*. Well-established poets such as Thomas Campbell, Samuel Rogers, Thomas Hood and Leigh Hunt signed, as did a much younger poet, Robert Browning. Dickens's writing was already hugely popular. Allan Cunningham and Joanna Baillie represented Scottish poetry and drama. Henry Hart Milman was a former professor of poetry at Oxford, known for his verse dramas and historical writing. John Poole had been a very popular dramatist, and wrote for the *New Monthly*. Henry Taylor wrote verse dramas himself, and was Southey's friend and literary executor. Henry Nelson Coleridge was Coleridge's nephew and literary executor.

In more general literary fields, Carlyle was already an influential essayist and historian. Harriet Martineau began as a reviewer, but

[16] 2,326, presented 27 February 1839, App. 190. The list of signatories is worth repeating in full; Richard H. Horne, Marguerite Blessington, Henry Malden, Thomas Campbell, Thomas Hewitt Key, W. Harrison Ainsworth, Harriet Martineau, Leman Blanchard, Henry Hart Milman, Robert Browning, Henry Taylor, Albany Fonblanque, John Forster, Abraham Hayward, Douglas Jerrold, Henry Nelson Coleridge, W. J. Fox, John Poole, Charles Wentworth Dilke, Leigh Hunt, Thomas Hood, Thomas Carlyle, Richard Cattermole, Charles Dickens, Count D'Orsay, Mary Russell Mitford, Henry Stebbing, George P. R. James, Thomas Roscoe, Samuel Rogers, Joanna Baillie, Richard W. Procter, Allan Cunningham. Although the report indicates that thirty-four signatures were counted, only thirty-three names are listed. In addition, three others seem to have signed a copy of this petition, although their names were not recorded: 2,327.

[17] Impressive though Talfourd's list is, Harriet Martineau collected fifty-six signatures from British authors for the petition on international copyright. The lower response to the domestic petition may reflect a sensitivity to petitioning at home, but it seems more likely that there were differences of opinion on the substantive issues.

was now an essayist and literary celebrity. Marguerite Blessington was a society beauty, known for her glittering literary circle, particularly her friendship with Byron, and later with Count D'Orsay: she herself was quite a talented writer. D'Orsay was an artist, dandy and wit. Thomas Roscoe was an author and translator. Thomas Hewitt Key was professor of Latin in London University, and had written a well-known *Latin grammar*. Richard Cattermole combined his writing activities with the secretaryship of the Royal Society of Literature.

Many of the signatories had very strong connections with literary journalism. Albany Fonblanque was the current editor of the *Examiner*: Leigh Hunt had edited it previously, as well as dozens of other magazines. Charles Wentworth Dilke, the critic and journalist, was editor of the *Athenaeum*. Henry Stebbing had been acting editor of the *Athenaeum* almost from its beginning, and wrote for it himself. Laman Blanchard was a journalist, and had edited several liberal papers: he was editor of the *Courier* at this time. W. J. Fox, R. H. Horne and Leigh Hunt had all been editorially involved in the (now defunct) *Monthly Repository*. Fox and Hunt were both well known for their journalism. John Forster was also a journalist, although he is now remembered for his literary friendships, particularly with Dickens, but also Leigh Hunt, Landor and Bulwer Lytton. Douglas Jerrold was another journalist and author, associated particularly with the *Athenaeum* and *Blackwood's Edinburgh Magazine*, and a regular contributor to *Punch* from its outset.

This petition represents a collective effort of great significance. Many of the signatories helped in other ways, particularly by writing favourable pieces in periodicals.[18] Several also petitioned in their own right, which provided an opportunity for stating a more personal case. For some, copyright was an existing preoccupation. Harriet Martineau had organised the petition in favour of American copyright for English authors, and many of those signing this were to sign Talfourd's petition. R. H. Horne had published a well-known attack on the position of authors in his first book *Exposition of the false medium and barriers . . . excluding men of genius from the public* (1833).[19] For others, such as Dickens

[18] See p. 195.

[19] Horne had proposed a 'Society of English Literature and Art etc, for the

and Browning, Talfourd's bill sparked an interest in copyright which would continue to develop.[20] Dickens came to be most closely identified with the struggle for international copyright: his public statements on this subject during his 1842 tour of America caused great offence. His association with Talfourd, and Talfourd's bill, dates from early in his literary career, and is much less well known.

Dickens's first work on leaving school, aged fifteen, was as a junior clerk to a set of chambers. He taught himself shorthand with the ambition of being a parliamentary reporter, but until a vacancy came up he enrolled at the Doctors' Commons. As a freelance shorthand writer he took notes of evidence and judgments. In 1831 he joined the *Mirror of Parliament*, and was also attached to the *True Sun* where W. J. Fox was editor. Dickens's first writing on his own account was for the *Monthly Magazine*, in the autumn of 1833. The following year he became a general and parliamentary reporter for the *Morning Chronicle*. The successful *Sketches by Boz* appeared in 1835, quickly followed by the *Pickwick Papers* which became a craze. This enabled Dickens to give up his reporting job and concentrate on writing.

In May 1837 he was elected to the Garrick Club, and made his first public speech. In the same month Talfourd introduced the first copyright bill into parliament. They had apparently not been introduced before this, although during his time on the *Morning Chronicle* Dickens had reported Talfourd's speeches in parliament, and some of his court work.[21] By the following August, Dickens was embroiled in a dispute with his publisher, Richard Bentley, over the copyrights of two novels: although Dickens had sold these outright, he sought to reclaim an interest in them. Dickens suggested that Talfourd be

encouragement and permanent support of men of superior ability in all departments of human genius and knowledge'. No further demands were to be made on members, who would receive annuities of between £25 and £150.

20 In 1841 Robert Browning dedicated *Pippa Passes* to Talfourd. Surprisingly, no surviving correspondence mentions Talfourd's bill, although Browning expressed a good deal of anxiety about international copyright from June 1842 onwards.

21 Including the extraordinary *Norton* v. *Melbourne* (1836). Dickens had apparently formed a great admiration for Talfourd: John Forster, *The life of Charles Dickens*, ed. J. W. T. Ley (1928), p. 110n.

appointed as arbitrator, and Talfourd became a trusted advisor for a time.[22]

At the end of August Talfourd sent Dickens a copy of his *Ion*: the generous letter of thanks survives.[23] Even more eloquent was Dickens's September letter to Talfourd, dedicating *Pickwick Papers* to him.[24] This dedication acted as an overt statement of support for Talfourd's efforts, as the letter acknowledged explicitly: 'in thus publicly expressing my deep and grateful sense of your efforts in behalf of English literature, and of those who devote themselves to the most precarious of all pursuits, I do but imperfect justice to my own strong feelings on the subject, if I do no service to you'. Their friendship continued to be warm, although a certain cooling off occurs during 1840 and afterwards.[25] This is one probable explanation for Dickens's relatively small role in the domestic copyright campaign, although his reluctance to be seen to argue for his own interests may also have been a factor.[26]

The final petition presented at the second reading came from Thomas Arnold, who had known Wordsworth since 1818.[27] The Arnolds had a house in the Lake District, and it was on one of their visits there in 1839 that Arnold agreed to petition. A

[22] Dickens, *The letters of Charles Dickens*, eds. Madeleine House and Graham Storey (Oxford, 1965–), I, p. 312n; II, pp. 85, 93.

[23] Ibid., I, p. 229 (30 August 1837).

[24] The opening paragraphs give its flavour: 'If I had not enjoyed the happiness of your private friendship, I should still have dedicated this work to you, as a slight and most inadequate acknowledgment of the inestimable services you are rendering to the literature of your country, and of the lasting benefits you will confer upon the authors of this and succeeding generations, by securing to them and their descendants a permanent interest in the copyright of their works. Many a fevered head and palsied hand will gather new vigour in the hour of sickness and distress from your excellent exertions; many a widowed mother and orphan child, who would otherwise reap nothing from the fame of departed genius but its too frequent legacy of poverty and suffering, will bear, in their altered condition, higher testimony to the value of your labours than the most lavish enconimums from lip or pen could afford': ibid., I, p. 312 (27 September 1837).

[25] The production of Talfourd's play *Glencoe* (first performed 23 May 1840) seems to have been the immediate cause: Dickens took a great deal of trouble over the associated arrangements, but Macready (who had the leading role) found Talfourd's literary sensitivities very trying.

[26] He was possibly also resentful of Wordsworth's commanding role in the campaign.

[27] 2,336, presented 27 February 1839, App. 197.

reforming headmaster of Rugby school, Arnold had a national reputation as a trenchant writer on political and ecclesiastical affairs. Although a fervent Christian, he held many radical views, arguing strongly for democracy and against oppressive laws. His weekly newspaper, the *Englishman's Register*, which he intended should be 'Cobbett-like in style – but Christian in spirit', failed after a few weeks. His articles in the *Sheffield Courant* and the *Hertford Reformer* caused his friends some anxiety. Against such a background, Arnold's support for Talfourd's bill would seem out of character, if it were not for his friendship with Wordsworth.

Arnold wrote on copyright in the *Hertford Reformer*, and although Wordsworth's case must have been in his mind, his argument was broadly based. Arnold saw copyright as a matter of two conflicting rights; those of the author and the purchaser of the book. Society had to resolve the conflict with a compromise. Thus far the parliamentary radicals would have agreed with him. However, Arnold's conclusion was that the existing compromise was unfair, 'Now the property which a man cannot secure even to his own immediate children, is surely scarcely to be called property at all.'[28] Arnold's petition made many of the same points, although he also stressed the unfortunate effect on literature of forcing authors to rely on immediate sales for their remuneration.

More petitions were presented at the committee stage. One extremely terse prayer arrived from the lord provost, magistrates and council of the city of Edinburgh, which showed 'that your Petitioners have observed with satisfaction that a Bill has been brought into your honourable House to amend the Law of Copyright. That your Petitioners regard the measure as founded both on justice to authors and expediency to the public', and asked that it should pass into a law.[29] The seal of the city was affixed, so only one signature was added to the total. One slight note of qualification appeared in the petition from Charles Bucke, gentleman, dramatist and miscellaneous writer. Although in favour of the measure, he suggested the insertion of a clause to the effect that an assigned copyright should revert to the author or his heirs if it remained unpublished for seven years.[30]

28 *Hertford Reformer*, 5 May 1838. Wordsworth, *Prose works*, p. 445.
29 6,970, presented 1 May 1839, App. 663.
30 2,896, presented 7 March 1839.

Several more petitions came from authors of books which required lengthy research, arguing that the period of copyright was too short to allow adequate remuneration for such valuable work and was prejudicial to their families: it seems likely that Talfourd had encouraged this sort of approach, as it is often repeated.[31] Sir David Brewster's petition combined this approach with the political attack seen in the St Andrews petition.[32] Brewster was principal of the united colleges of St Salvator and St Leonard in the university of St Andrews, and was clearly motivated by the same grievances.

Wordsworth had likewise argued that although the public eventually derived benefit from the work of authors who came late to recognition, the author's family often did not. He was disappointed that Southey did not feel able to petition in similar terms. Nevertheless, Coleridge's interests were represented by two important petitions on this theme. One came from Hartley Coleridge, his eldest son, the other from his executor, Joseph Henry Green.[33] Both petitions concentrated on the importance of Coleridge's works, and their steadily growing recognition.

The most talked-of petition of the committee stage came from Thomas Carlyle.[34] Carlyle had little sympathy with the book trade and its customs. His letters during 1838 reveal that he endured repeated frustrations as he negotiated with Fraser, his publisher, over several works.[35] Nevertheless, when Forster approached Carlyle to ask him to petition in favour of Talfourd's bill, he at first refused:

[31] Samuel Thomas Bloomfield DD, presented 15 April 1839, 5,035, App. 511; Patrick Fraser Tytler, 6,969, presented 1 May 1839, App. 662. It seems likely that the petitions from John Bravender (6,968), Rev. Alexander Crombie (6,975) and John Hugh Paisley Polson (12,810) were similar, although they were not printed.

[32] 6,971, presented 1 May 1839, App. 664.

[33] 6,972, 6,973, presented 1 May 1839, Apps. 665 and 666.

[34] 6,974, presented 1 May 1839, App. 667.

[35] For instance, to Ralph Waldo Emerson: 'On studying accurately your program of the American mercantile method, I stood amazed to contrast it with our English one. The Bookseller here admits that he could by diligent bargaining get up such a book for something like the same cost or a *little* more; but the "laws of the trade" deduct from the very front of the selling-price – how much think you? – *forty per cent* and odd, where your man has only *fifteen*, for the mere act of vending! . . . There are "laws of the trade" which ought to be *repealed*"': Carlyle, *The collected letters of Thomas and Jane Welsh Carlyle*, ed. Charles R. Saunders (Durham, NC, 1970), X, p. 229 (2 December 1838).

With regard to the Copyright Bill, I will desire you to assure Serjeant Talfourd, if he yet need assurance, that no person more heartily or gratefully approves of his exertions in that matter than I; or would, as in duty bound, be readier to do any thing and all things that could forward it. But as to Petitioning in my own name, it does appear to me, after all the consideration that I can give it, that neither my age, my position nor pretensions could authorize such a step on my part. Ridicule, it seems to me, and the general inquiry, Who *is* this pretentious 'Single Person'? would be the too probable result.[36]

Carlyle also mentioned a letter (that has since not been traced), 'that atrabilical cynical Utterance which I sent the Serjeant last summer', which he was willing to allow Forster to publish in the *Examiner*: 'the promulgation of this . . . were really producing of *all* the effect I could pretend to, in or out of Parliament, on this business'.

Such reluctance goes some way to explain the relatively small number of petitions in favour of Talfourd's proposals. It is also interesting that the scruples seem to have involved only the specific act of petitioning, since Carlyle was happy to have his support made public in the periodical press. Fortunately for Talfourd, Carlyle quickly overcame his inhibitions: he wrote again to Forster, probably the next day; 'Here, after all, is a Petition, since you have set me on it.'[37] He also gave them freedom to use it as they liked; Talfourd submitted it to the House of Commons, and Forster printed it in the *Examiner*.

Wordsworth wrote to Talfourd that 'Carlyle's petition is like all he does and is, quite *racy*'.[38] Carlyle admitted to Forster that he had found it 'impossible to write gravely on such a subject; demonstrating the tenth-part of a truism, against stolidities without a name'. It would be fascinating to compare the 1839 petition with the first, untraced, letter to Talfourd. They were evidently not the same; Carlyle described the new petition as 'part of the truth', whereas the other 'was the truth and the whole truth according to my sense of it'.[39]

The petition was concise, and seriously argued, although Carlyle sometimes adopted a self-mocking, almost flippant tone. 'Parliamentary' language was used with evident relish to introduce

[36] Ibid., XI, p. 34 (27 February 1839).
[37] Ibid., XI, p. 36 (28? February 1839).
[38] *WW Letters*, VI, p. 678 (8 April 1839).
[39] Carlyle, *Letters*, XI, p. 37 (28? February 1839).

the problem: 'the Petition of Thomas Carlyle, a Writer of Books, Humbly Sheweth, That your petitioner has written certain books, being incited thereto by various innocent or laudable considerations, chiefly by the thought that said books might in the end be found to be worth something'. The body of the text put forward the argument that all useful labour was worthy of recompense, that assuring this was the business of the government and legislation, but that the task was impossible to accomplish accurately. In the particular instance of one whose labour is to write books, Carlyle argued 'that if he be found in the long run to have written a genuine enduring book, his merit therein, and desert towards England and English and other men, will be considerable, not easily estimable in money; that, on the other hand, if his book proves false and ephemeral, he and it will be abolished and forgotten, and no harm done'. This is an elegant and appealing version of an argument that Talfourd often used.

Carlyle's petition had enormous impact, or, rather, the fact that he petitioned was cause for great comment.[40] In some circles the argument was less discussed than the closing paragraph, which was most unusual in naming an individual. Obliged by convention to conclude with a 'prayer',[41] Carlyle returned to the light-hearted tone of the opening:

> May it therefore please your Honourable House to protect [your petitioner] in said happy and long-doubtful event; and (by passing your Copyright Bill) forbid all Thomas Teggs and other extraneous persons, entirely unconcerned in this adventure of his, to steal from him his small winnings, for a space of sixty years at shortest.

Carlyle seems to have followed the bill's progress, but there is only slender evidence of his continuing interest.[42] He was sent Christie's pamphlet on the subject, and wrote to him appreciatively.[43] Carlyle also defended the copyright bill when his visitor, Swynfen Jervis, a known opponent of the bill, began to argue

[40] Carlyle seems to have been not a little pleased with the result: 'Talfourd's people worked a Petition out of me about the Copyright Bill: I wrote it with "hidden satire": the Examiner prints it with a flourish; the D[umphrie]s Herald comes here with it today: – babblement!'. Carlyle, *Letters*, XI, p. 87 (15 April 1839).

[41] Normally a simple request; for instance, 'that the Copyright Bill may pass into a Law'.

[42] Carlyle, *Letters*, XI, p. 42 (11 March 1839).

[43] *A plea for perpetual copyright* (1840). Carlyle, *Letters*, XII, p. 85 (21 March 1840).

against it.[44] Although these isolated incidents indicate that Carlyle was prepared to speak up for the copyright bill on occasion, they do not suggest any very sustained interest in active campaining. Carlyle was busy with his scheme for the London library, and his letters are full of these plans.

However, he read about Wakley's attacks on Wordsworth and others in the committee stage of the 1842 bill, and wrote to Richard Monkton Milnes, who had been staunch in defence:

> Thanks for your castigation of the Vandal Wakley, which I have read this morning. The sound to me is as that of one 'whose speech is of bullocks' – a sound disgraceful to your Commons' House called Honourable. You did well to rebuke him. Nay, the 'natural man' (whose thoughts indeed are emnity to God) regrets rather that instead of the whipping or poliched reprimand it had not been a right leathern dog or horse whip or solid American cowskin; but this I suppose, the forms of your Honourable House would not permit. Mr. Macaulay, too, finds that his last year's excursion was on the wrong tack; that even *at* the risk of smelling of the shop, he had better take the common one. This Bill, not so bad a one, seems likley to pass. Thanks for the day of small things.[45]

Petitions – 1840–2

1840 was a rather quiet year for the copyright bill's supporters: although the second reading was carried on 19 February, it did not pass the committee stage and was dropped in May. There were only five petitions in total, amounting to seventy-four signatures. Only two were printed. Of the three which did not survive, two might have been particularly interesting: both came from lexicographers.[46] One came from David Booth, who had been a brewer and schoolmaster in Fifeshire, and later came to London where he superintended for press the publications of the Society for the Diffusion of Useful Knowledge. In 1835 he had published the first volume of an *Analytical dictionary of the English language*, so

[44] Carlyle reported Jane Carlyle's view that he treated Jervis 'inhumanly, as a bulldog might some ill-favoured *messin* [cur]'. Carlyle seems to have found Jervis generally provoking: in the same letter he described him as 'a dirty little aetheistic radical', and 'a wretched dud': Carlyle, *Letters*, XII, p. 159.

[45] Sir Thomas Wemyss Reid, *The life, letters and friendships of Richard Monckton Milnes*, 2nd edn (1890), I, p. 276.

[46] 11,430 and 11,432, both presented 29 April 1840. The third, 11,431, was from 'Inhabitants of Hawick, Roxburghshire': a petition from this group was printed in 1841, and will be discussed below at p. 191.

he may have had the familiar anxieties of an author whose copyright seemed certain to run out before expenses had been covered. The other was from Charles Richardson, whose chief work was his *New English dictionary*, published between 1835 and 1837: his concerns were likely to have been similar. John Heraud's petition was also of this type.[47] Heraud was a well-known author and critic, which perhaps explains why it was printed.

The remaining petition, from 'Authors, Booksellers and Publishers of London and Westminster', is the most striking of the five.[48] This group had previously reacted to Talfourd's plans with great hostility: there were two well-supported petitions from them in 1838, condemning in particular the retrospective aspects of the bill.[49] The 1840 petitioners referred to their 1838 petition, but were now seeking to update their audience:

> inasmuch as your Petitioners who are publishers, are concerned in the present petition, they beg to assure your honourable House that there is nothing contained in the Bill now before your honourable House, which is in anywise grievous upon them, but that, on the contrary, they are most anxious that the present Bill should pass into a law, and that they will be well satisfied with whatever extended term of copyright your honourable House shall think fit to grant.

The unsettled nature of copyright law was particularly criticised, as harmful to the petitioners' interests. Fifty-six signatures were recorded for this petition, although only three were listed.

1841 was an even sparser year for favourable petitions: there were only three, amounting to forty-two signatures. William Cobbett's, written from H.M. Prison of the Fleet, gave details of a personal grievance concerning Bossange, the famous French bookseller, and a more general objection to 'trade copyrights' and lack of competition in the book trade in general.[50]

A brief petition came from 'Inhabitants of Hawick', and made the now familiar point that the limited copyright period encouraged ephemeral works at the expense of works involving greater labour.[51] The petition's main interest is that it was presented by Bulwer, who had already spoken in favour of the copyright bill

47 1,005, presented 11 February 1840, App. 71.

48 1,755, presented 19 February 1840, App. 131.

49 4,816 and 4,821, both presented 25 April 1838.

50 95, presented 5 February 1841, App. 9. This is not the famous radical William Cobbett, who died in 1835.

51 281, presented 15 February 1841, App. 61.

and had previously persuaded Harriet Martineau to organise the petition for international copyright. Bulwer's interest in this was a personal one. He had an agreement to forward early sheets of all his works to Harper & Brothers in New York, for which they paid £50 a volume. However, this arrangement was precarious, particularly since sheets could be delayed or go missing, allowing other American publishers to nip in before Harpers. In any case, Bulwer considered himself undervalued, and began to talk to Harpers' rivals. When his own publishers, Saunders & Otley, opened an office in New York, Bulwer was faced with a real dilemma. His response was to prevaricate, and back the campaign for international copyright, which would have increased his value and simplified his options.[52]

Rather tantalisingly, a petition from Thomas Hood is also recorded in 1841.[53] Hood was a whole-hearted advocate of copyright reform, writing various poems and pieces in support.[54] He had signed Harriet Martineau's petition for international copyright, and was on the list of signatories of Talfourd's 1839 petition. His enthusiasm was such that in 1839 he wrote an additional petition, for submission in his own name. However, Talfourd thought it 'too richly studded with jests to be presented to the House of Commons', although he printed it in the appendix to his *Three speeches* in 1840.[55] Perhaps Hood wrote a more restrained petition in 1841, or perhaps his original version was now deemed acceptable.

The four petitions in favour of Mahon's 1842 bill were organised by Murray and Longman, as has been discussed. Ninety-eight signatures were collected. Presumably all four were the same, as only one was printed.[56] It is a mere three sentences, including the prayer. The petitioners considered that the bill's provisions were 'most important for the protection of the just rights of your Petitioners, and for the encouragement and promotion of literature and science'.

[52] Barnes, *Authors*, p. 53. [53] 96, presented 5 February 1841.

[54] Notably in the *Athenaeum*: see p. 205.

[55] For instance: 'When your petitioner shall be dead and buried, he might with as much propriety and decency have his body snatched as his literary remains', and 'the fruits of his brain ought no more to be cast amongst the public than a Christian woman's apples or a Jewess's oranges'. Talfourd, *Three speeches delivered in the House of Commons* (1840), p. 141.

[56] 6,252–5, presented 16 March 1842, App. 303. See ch. 7.

There were differing opinions as to the contribution made by the 1842 Act, and thus as to the success of the five-year campaign to amend copyright law in a way more favourable to authors. Whatever the conclusion on this matter, it is undeniable that the campaign brought the literary world together in a way that had not been seen before. There seems to have been little dissent, beyond a concern at the implications of the retrospective clause. Virtually every author of note was active in support. Southey's decision not to petition can be explained by his failing health: his earlier contributions are testament to his views.

Although Sir Walter Scott was dead before Talfourd's first bill was even conceived, his huge success and dramatic reverse in fortunes ensured that his name was mentioned frequently during the debates, and his views on copyright should be examined as far as is possible.

Scott's enormous popularity left him vulnerable to piracy. On the Continent, Gagliani produced a handsome edition of Scott's works, in seven volumes, for a fraction of the original selling price.[57] In the 1820s Scott was one of the few English authors to receive payment from an American publishing firm, Carey & Lea, in return for advance sheets of his works.[58] However, this was merely a modest honorarium: it was not received as of right, nor did it reflect Scott's commercial value in America. Scott might therefore have been expected to take an active interest in the reform of copyright law. However, the crash of 1826 had such disastrous consequences for Scott that he was forced to concentrate on other matters.

The failure of Archibald Constable's London associates, Hurst, Robinson & Co., brought the publishing firm Constable & Co. to bankruptcy, leaving Ballantyne & Co. liable for their debts. Scott was a partner in Ballantyne & Co., and was thus liable personally. Unwilling to escape his obligations by becoming bankrupt, he resolved to pay off the enormous debt entirely by his writings.[59] It was this pressure that resulted in a new edition of his works, revised, with Scott's annotations, and new introductions: he referred to it as the *magnum*. Scott began working on it as soon as

[57] Barnes, *Authors*, p. 95. [58] Ibid., p. 53.

[59] About £120,000. For an excellent account of this episode see Jane Millgate, *Scott's last edition* (Edinburgh, 1987), ch. 1.

he knew that his trustees had secured the relevant copyrights.[60] He set himself a punishing schedule, and his health suffered: two strokes in 1830 were followed by another in 1831, leaving him dizzy, weak and unable to concentrate. He died in September 1832.

The substantial revisions and annotations served to make the *magnum* a copyright work in its own right. Scott was probably too preoccupied and ill to concern himself with an extended copyright term, although in 1830 Wordsworth had tried to interest him in the matter. He wrote to Scott, in contemplation of a possible visit to Abbotsford:

> Among the points many and various which I should like to discuss with you, is one in which surely your family is interested far above that of any other; I mean the short duration of Author's copyright according to the now existing Law. Am I right in supposing that 28 years would put an end to the pecuniary interest of a family in a posthumous work – and that all Works become public property immediately after an Author's death provided they have been published that period of years? If so the law is exceedingly unjust and ought to be altered – but perhaps I am mistaken as to the fact.[61]

There is no record of Scott's response, although the previous April he had written to Peel asking to resign as clerk of session 'upon such superannuation as I may be found entitled to claim for my passd long and constant service'.[62] Scott continued to monitor his liabilities and likely receipts, but an extended term of copyright does not seem to figure in his schemes. He was dead before Talfourd's campaign was even underway.

It is ironic that the effect of Talfourd's Act was to increase the value of the copyrights, as Scott's sole publisher, Robert Cadell, noted in his diary: the bill received the royal assent on 1 July 1842, a date only 'one week before the first 28 years of Waverly had

[60] He took an understandable interest in the sale of these copyrights: it was essential for Scott that he retained control over them. It was agreed that Cadell would be co-proprietor with Scott and his sympathetic and far-sighted trustees. Cadell secured the copyrights at auction for £8,500, after brisk bidding. See Scott's journal for this period: *Journal 1825–32*, revised J. G. Tait (Edinburgh, 1939–46). See also letters to John Gibson, 19 November and 21 December 1827, and to John Gibson Lockhart, 21 December 1827: *The letters of Sir Walter Scott*, ed. Herbert J. C. Grierson (1936), X, pp. 314, 340–4.

[61] Wordsworth, *Letters*, V, p. 306 (20 July 1830).

[62] Scott, *Letters*, XI, p. 332 (14 April 1830).

expired'.[63] The copyright on the first edition of *Waverly* was thereby extended to 1856: the textual revisions, *magnum* introductions and annotations enjoyed copyright until the 1870s. Cadell estimated the total worth of the new bill to him, at a conservative estimate, to be ten or twelve thousand pounds.[64]

Scott's place in the copyright campaign was taken by his relatives and friends, chiefly his son-in-law, John Gibson Lockhart. He was one of those who realised that petitioning, important though it was, was not the only means of pressure. With such an array of figures in support, it is not surprising that many of them used their influence in other ways – either personally, or through articles in magazines and periodicals. It can be argued that this more subtle pressure proved the most effective in the end.

THE ARGUMENT IN THE PERIODICALS

Contemporary periodicals sought both to entertain and to inform, often providing an important public forum for serious debate of contemporary issues. They form an important source of materials relevant to copyright, and reveal a homogeneity of response which seems surprising, particularly given the range of reactions from newspapers. Periodicals were by their nature sectional, aiming at different target audiences. Some engaged only with current politics and international affairs, some were specifically literary, and others addressed a very specialist audience. The attention paid to the international copyright question reflects this to some extent: much less contentious than domestic copyright, some periodicals concentrated on the international dimension exclusively.

The *Monthly Chronicle*, for instance, was among the first to welcome Poulett Thomson's 1838 international copyright bill, and urged the public to support it.[65] The *Foreign Quarterly Review*, as might have been predicted from its name, was also more con-

[63] National Library of Scotland MS 21032, p. 212, quoted by Millgate, *Last edition*, p. 51.

[64] Millgate, *Last edition*, p. 213. The changed situation probably influenced Cadell's decision not to retire, which he had been considering seriously at the beginning of 1842.

[65] April 1838, pp. 163–8. This article has been attributed to a collaboration between David Brewster and Edward Bulwer Lytton: this would be consistent with Bulwer's continuing interest in both domestic and international copyright.

cerned with international copyright than domestic.[66] A much more surprising silence was that of the *Edinburgh Review*, which scarcely addressed the subject of copyright at all.[67] Writing to its editor, Macvey Napier, with news of the 1842 compromise, Macaulay noted that copyright was one of the few matters on which they did not agree: the depth and nature of those differences is unclear.[68] Another *Edinburgh* reviewer, Sydney Smith, apparently opposed the retrospective clause, although his views on an extended term are not known.[69] Perhaps silence was the most positive response that could be offered.

Although a certain amount of interest was generated by the question of international copyright during this period, it was not such a topic of public controversy as domestic copyright came to be. Only a few radicals objected to international protection, and the 1838 International Copyright Act passed easily. Although this authorised agreements for reciprocal protection, little came of it: it was not until 1842 that pressure was exerted for progress to be made in that arena. Talfourd's bills, in their various versions, generated much more opposition, both in and out of parliament. This made domestic copyright a suitable topic for both general and literary periodicals. Some of these visited the issue once only, others, particularly the very literary periodicals, followed the progress of the measure more closely. With very few exceptions, these articles expressed broad support for Talfourd. In very real ways, they were substitutes for petitions.

Early notices

In 1837, when the bill was still uncontroversial, relatively little comment appeared. A notable exception was the *Monthly Repository*, which did address the copyright question in a short article which was highly critical of Tegg and strongly supportive of

[66] *Foreign Quarterly Review* 26 (1840), p. 95. Talfourd's bill was referred to briefly but even-handedly in this article on 'Printing and publishing at home and abroad': American piracies were seen as a very great problem.

[67] In its review of the 1839 session, the negotiations for an international law of copyright were given favourable mention, although only in passing. *Edinburgh Review* 70 (1839), p. 279.

[68] To Macvey Napier: *The letters of Thomas Babington, Baron Macaulay*, ed. Thomas Pinney (Cambridge, 1974–81), IV, p. 25 (7 April 1842).

[69] Moore, *Journals*, ed. Dowden, p. 1969 (May 20 1838).

Talfourd.[70] The article on Talfourd's bill was a product of Leigh Hunt's editorship: it has been confidently attributed to Thornton Leigh Hunt, Leigh Hunt's eldest son.[71] The topic was clearly one which preoccupied this whole circle. Leigh Hunt was an author himself, indebted to Talfourd in many ways: he was to sign the 1839 petition. R. H. Horne, the previous editor, had published a well-known attack on the position of authors in his *Exposition of the false medium and barriers . . . excluding men of genius from the public*: in 1838 he was to research the history of copyright for Talfourd, and he too would be a petitioner in 1839.[72] Evidence of W. J. Fox's interest in copyright, and its apparent expression in a series of letters to the *Morning Chronicle*, has already been discussed.

Two early opponents should be addressed and dismissed here; the *Age* and *Tait's Edinburgh Magazine*. Edited by Molloy Westmacott, the *Age* had an unenviable reputation for unscrupulousness, even blackmail: 'It was Tory in its politics, and whenever it thought a Liberal of note could be seriously damaged it never hesitated to assail him in his private character.'[73] Although Talfourd was not exposed to blackmail, he and his friends did suffer considerable abuse in its pages. In relation to the copyright bill, Talfourd was styled a 'bungling juggler', although the *Age* briefly favoured it, hoping that 'many of our automaton contemporaries, who with faces of brass pilfer all their intelligence and wit from the AGE, must soon be extinct'.[74] However, by early 1838 the publishers' arguments had proved convincing: the *Age* was attacking the retrospective clause, and urging Talfourd not to persist 'in this most untoward measure'. The hostility was maintained,

70 *Monthly Repository*, XI–I (1837) p. 14. Founded in 1806 to advance the Unitarian cause, the *Monthly Repository* of 1830 was still strongly associated with Unitarianism. However, under the editorship of W. J. Fox it was to become sufficiently radical to alarm the more moderate Whig Unitarians. By 1836 Fox's other commitments left him little time for the *Repository*, and R. H. Horne took over the editorship in 1836. The circulation continued to drop, and in June 1837 the magazine was given to Leigh Hunt as a free gift: it lasted only nine months more.

71 Francis E. Mineka, *The dissidence of dissent: the Monthly Repository, 1806–38 under the editorship of Robert Aspland, W. J. Fox, R. H. Horne, & Leigh Hunt; with a chapter on religious periodicals, 1700–1825* (Chapel Hill, NC, 1944).

72 Ann Blainey, *The farthing poet* (1968), p. 91.

73 James Grant, *The newspaper press* (1871), II, p. 10.

74 3 December 1837, p. 380.

and in 1842 a leading article was highly critical of the waste of public time in legislating for three or four cases per century.[75]

Tait's Edinburgh Magazine was unreservedly hostile to Talfourd's plans. A literary and radical magazine, its editor and publisher was William Tait. Tait's view, relying on an analogy with patents, was that there was no case for perpetual copyright.[76] Predictably, particular objection was taken to clause 5, the retrospective clause. However, Tait's clear statement of an assignee's loss by the clause was unusual, revealing as it did the extent of the book trade's concerted practices: 'True, their copyright, so far as regarded the right of excluding others, does not extend beyond [the twenty-eight-year term]; but they have a right to go on printing, themselves; nay, they have an honorary copyright, – not without considerable advantages by the custom of the London trade – of which the bill would deprive them.' Tait also dismissed as 'balderdash' Poulett Thompson's plans for international copyright: a 'scheme of extending book monopoly over space, as Serjeant Talfourd's bill does over time'. Serious consideration of the issues was left to the reviews.

Reviews

Reviews were a very popular form of periodical literature. They commonly took a text, or often a series of texts, as a starting point for an article or essay. In the best reviews, such as the *Edinburgh Review* and the *Quarterly Review*, the standard of the writing was very high: both review and reviewer had a good deal of influence, and could enjoy considerable prestige. There was a well-known link between these reviews and party politics: Brougham and Macaulay both made their names as *Edinburgh* reviewers, and they were not unique. Although articles were usually anonymous, at least formally, in practice the author's name was often no real secret in certain circles. As a result, review articles were an

[75] 8 April 1838, p. 110; 10 April 1842, p. 4.

[76] *Tait's Edinburgh Magazine*, May 1838, p. 332. The article is playfully indexed by Tait under 'Copyright Bill, Talfourd's mischievous'. Tait seems to have forgotten his debt to Talfourd, whose speech in defence of *Tait's Magazine* (*Richmond* v. *Tait* (1835)) was considered to be one in which he particularly distinguished himself: Laman Blanchard's 'Memoir of Mr. Serjeant Talfourd, M.P.', *New Monthly* 51 (1837), 213.

excellent means of ensuring that an issue was publicised and discussed.

In relation to copyright, the reviewer had a large number of texts to work with. Discussion of the eighteenth-century great cases had resulted in numerous pamphlets, and the disputes over deposit copies had produced a further series. This pattern continued during Talfourd's bills: the prolonged controversy led to the production of publications on both sides of the debate. Talfourd himself published all of his speeches in a deliberate attempt to gain publicity.[77] One of the earliest pamphlets to appear was *Areopagitica Secunda: or speech of the shade of John Milton on Mr Sergeant Talfourd's Copyright Extension Bill* (1838). It argued strongly that forcing writers to write for immediate profit would ultimately result in a degraded national literature. Although published anonymously, it seems clear that this twenty-eight-page pamphlet was written by Wordsworth's nephew, Christopher Wordsworth.[78]

Another fairly common way of expressing support was to write what was ostensibly a private letter to someone involved, but in fact always intending it to be published. One pamphlet using this device was *A proposed new law of copyright; of the highest importance to authors, and to the inhabitants of Great Britain and Ireland in a letter addressed to Mr Serjeant Talfourd M.P. by a friend to authors*: it argued for perpetual copyright, and railed against the 'vile practices' of the booksellers. The same useful mechanism was used for William Dougal Christie's pamphlet, *A plea for perpetual copyright in a letter to Lord Monteagle* (1840): this time the author allowed himself to be named.

One of the earliest pamphlets to argue against Talfourd's proposals was *Observations on the law of copyright*.[79] Its arguments and language both suggest an author with radical sympathies. It

77 *Three speeches*.

78 Christie's *Plea for perpetual copyright* attributes this *Areopagitica* to Landor: p. 10. However, see Wordsworth to John Gibson Lockhart: Wordsworth, *Letters*, VI, p. 260 (November 1841).

79 *Observations on the Law of Copyright; in reference to the Bill introduced into the House of Commons by Mr Serjeant Talfourd: in which it is attempted to be proved, that the provisions of the Bill are opposed to the Principles of English Law; that Authors require no additional protection; and that such a Bill would inflict a heavy blow on Literature and prove a great discouragement to its diffusion in this country* (1838).

was dedicated to Lord John Russell, and quoted his declaration that 'it is the paramount duty of the Government to provide education for the whole body of the people'. The main thrust of the pamphlet was that an extension of copyright threatened the public availability of books at a reasonable price, and could not be justified. However, the author suggested a scheme to create an order of fifty 'Literary Associates', a plan which appeared to owe something to the discontinued Royal Literary Fund associateships, although more ambitious (with fifty grants) and more elaborate in its details.[80] Other hostile pamphlets included two from Thomas Tegg and one from the Chambers brothers.[81]

One of the first to address the copyright question, the *Eclectic Review* had only a limited range of materials to consider: the bill itself, Talfourd's speech introducing it, and the Tegg and Chambers pamphlets. Although entirely supportive, the reviewer adopted a rather lofty stance, focusing on works of genius and dismissing the productions of 'literary drudges, writing hacks, book making mechanics, mere jobbers'. Such a point of view left little room for understanding either the publishers' practical desire for a return on capital, or the claims of the public to cheap books: 'The public are not obliged to buy.' The article added little to Talfourd's speech, which it quoted at length.[82]

In contrast, the *British and Foreign Review* published a long and carefully reasoned article assessing Talfourd's claim to a term of life plus sixty years.[83] Talfourd's speeches formed the main texts for consideration, although the supporting references were wide-ranging and scholarly. In many ways sympathetic to a change in copyright law, the writer was nevertheless critical of Talfourd's arguments and approach, and concluded that the proposed extension was excessive. This is one of the most balanced and compelling pieces written in opposition to Talfourd: it is unfortunate that the author remains unknown.

80 See ch. 7.

81 *Remarks on the speech of Serjeant Talfourd* (1837) and *Extension of Copyright proposed by Serjeant Talfourd* (1840). William and Robert Chambers, *Brief objections to Mr Talfourd's new Copyright Bill* (Edinburgh, 1838). See also *Objections to and Remarks upon Mr. Serjeant Talfourd's Scheme* (1841).

82 *Eclectic Review* 67 (1839), p. 693. Another much briefer article noted Talfourd's decision to drop the retrospective clause, and was still unwaveringly in favour of the measure: *Eclectic Review* 69 (1839), p. 434.

83 *British and Foreign Review* (1839), 333–59.

Drawing on the writings of the French lawyer Foucher,[84] the writer characterised copyright as a special right of re-publication, which should acknowledge not only the interests of the author, but also those of the community at large. Although any claim to perpetual copyright was therefore rejected, the question of the appropriate term remained. The preferred solution was a term which was long enough to benefit the author's widow and children, but not his grandchildren. The means suggested was a twenty-eight-year term, commencing not at publication but at the author's death: 'This creates a certain provision for the immediate survivors; it obviates the possibility of a man's dying with the consciousness that his literary fortune dies with him, though he should have been only overtaken by success upon the verge of the grave; and it renders the privilege more certain and equal.' This was a serious and thoughtful contribution to the copyright discussions. Its influence can be detected in William Dougal Christie's pamphlet, which seems to have attempted to respond to some of the points made in this article.

Even more influential was Lockhart's article in the *Quarterly Review*.[85] As has been seen, this was the result of several requests from Wordsworth. Writing after the 1841 election and between parliamentary sessions, Lockhart knew that Talfourd was no longer in charge of the bill's passage. This article marked an important punctuation point in the debate, published as it was in an influential Tory periodical. Peel, the new Tory prime minister, had been lobbied repeatedly, but appeared undecided.[86] The main thrust of Lockhart's article was that the 1842 bill 'ought to be a new one in its general arrangement as well as very many of the details'. In particular, although he carefully did not advocate any specific scheme, he did suggest that it should be remodelled along the lines of the French and Prussian codes: 'Why should the Englishman's protection . . . terminate with his life – while France, in every case, prolongs it to his widow and children for twenty, Prussia for thirty years after his death?' This set the scene for Mahon's plan.

84 Victor Foucher, *De la propriété littéraire et de la contrefaçon* (Paris, 1836).

85 *Quarterly Review* 69 (December 1841), 186–227.

86 Lockhart was icily polite: 'down to a very remote period we understand him to have professed that he had not found leisure to make himself master of its merits'.

Lockhart made good use of his impressive reading list, drawing the historical background of domestic copyright legislation, and surveying the contemporary international context. The luxurious expanse of a *Quarterly Review* article gave him the space to work through the objections in some detail, and to provide clear explanations of some troublesome concepts. The general failure (or sometimes refusal) to understand some of these concepts had allowed a garbled understanding of copyright's effects to gain currency in some quarters. In particular, it had been stated repeatedly that an extended copyright would act to restrict the transmission of knowledge. Lockhart therefore concentrated on the difference between idea and expression, and the difference between the patent right (restricting use) and copyright (restricting only copying): 'You are welcome to take the fact and my opinion of its bearing into your mind, and make your own use of it, in the composition or revisal of your own book. The only claim here is that it shall not be allowed to transfer one man's bodily labour to another.' It must have been good for the bill that these points could be made at length and in such an influential publication.

In terms of attacks on the bill's opponents, the heaviest guns were reserved for Macaulay's speech. To support his own onslaught Lockhart quoted extensively from an article in the *Examiner*, also written in criticism of Macaulay's speech. Macaulay had used real authors as illustrations of various points in his arguments. Lockhart took particular exception to Macaulay's references to Dr Johnson, Boswell and Milton, spending a good deal of the article refuting in detail various statements made about them, and thus by extension Macaulay's arguments. Macaulay was also taken to task for his immoderate comments on the dangers of suppression of works, which were made in the face of an existing clause in Talfourd's bill which dealt specifically with this concern.

Lockhart's conclusion was that a change in the law was essential. He did consider and reject several alternatives: the idea of a royalty, payable to the author's heirs by any publishing house which chose to issue the work, was considered unenforceable; a power in the Privy Council was thought to revive patronage in one of its worst forms. He was, however, adamant that, unless something was done, 'Literary and scientific eminence must become a prize reserved for the exclusive ambition of the rich.' In support of his case, a revised version of Wordsworth's letter to the *Kendal Mercury* was printed as an appendix to the article. In total Lockhart's piece ran to over forty pages: it stands as one of the most substantial articles written during the entire debate.

The article in the *Examiner*, quoted at some length by Lockhart, is of significance in its own right. Although founded by the Hunt brothers as a radical political journal, the *Examiner* under Albany Fonblanque had become much less radical. Literature and arts now featured prominently, with Forster as literary editor. The *Examiner* was in favour of Talfourd's plans from the outset and, as a weekly publication, it could provide a more sustained level of comment than either the monthlies or the quarterlies. In 1838 each stage of the bill was carefully noted, with positive comments, albeit relatively brief ones. The first editorial appeared in 1839, commenting on the petitions presented by Talfourd: lengthy extracts from Carlyle's and Landor's petitions were also printed.[87] It was a wonderful piece of journalism, cleverly argued and hard-hitting. The assumption that cheap books were necessarily the best for the public was strongly attacked: 'Whatever the Solicitor-General and the Mechanics' Institute may think of the question, we, the public, can very clearly distinguish between the interests of "literature" and the interests of "printing"; between the diffusion of "knowledge" and the diffusion of "paper".'

The bill's fortunes continued to be traced during 1840, although there is no editorial material of much length. However, in 1841 the *Examiner* published a blistering attack on Macaulay, provoked by his late intervention in the copyright debate. Aspects of the bill were criticised, and Talfourd himself was not spared, although this served rather to heighten the effect. The criticisms were unabashedly personal: Macaulay's arguments were 'contemptible', he took 'commonplace for his premises and paradox for his conclusions; and the richness of a fertile memory conceal[ed] the meagreness of a most defective logic'. The speech itself was demolished in some detail. In particular, Macaulay had made much of the fact that most authors of note had sold their copyrights outright. In response, a very telling point was made: 'We

[87] *Examiner*, 7 April 1839, 214. Perhaps by Fonblanque himself, a petitioner in favour of the bill, or perhaps by Forster, who collected signatures for Talfourd's petition.

venture to say that at this time there are very few authors of eminence who do not sell their copyrights, and whenever they have done so, ere reputation had given permanent value to their works, their first object is to re-purchase them.' This was certainly true, and authors generally were becoming more aware of the value of their copyrights.

The 1841 *Examiner* article had a tremendous impact, and not just on Lockhart: Peel certainly read it, and Wordsworth described it as 'spirited'.[88] Its refutation of Macaulay's arguments impressed others. John Stuart Mill asked Albany Fonblanque, as editor of the *Examiner*, if the author of the article would consider producing a statement of the case for the copyright bill: Mill explained that he was acting on behalf of supporters of the bill, who were offering remuneration – 'for which purpose a subscription is spoken of'.[89] The article was by Bulwer, who wrote it at Forster's request. Although Forster had worked tirelessly for Talfourd's bills, the 1841 collapse left him furious and frustrated. Provoked equally by Macaulay's behaviour and Talfourd's lofty demand that Members should vote with him or reject the bill outright, he wrote to Bulwer:

For God's sake don't spare Macaulay. Fonblanque quite agrees with me in thinking his arguments below contempt – and he tells me that his conduct has been baser than his argument. Is it true that he promised to take no active part against the Bill. And he, a cabinet minster, with his Cabinet colleagues voting in its favour, moves its rejection! What a paltry business.

And oh! paltrier Talfourd! Don't spare him either – if it is true, as Fonblanque tells me, that *you* offered to answer Macaulay and were prevented by his request. That could only be the meanest envy.

Such an exhibition altogether was surely never seen. Not to have a word to say for himself! To give the matter up like a plaything! To declare, as he did in effect, that he had taken the subject up for a few fine tawdry speeches, and that as to the positive thing in issue, he hadn't a word to fling to even such a dog as the nasty Mr Macaulay.

In my life I never knew a man cut so contemptible a figure. For heaven's sake put in a word for the real interest at stake. At the head of the literary men of the day, say one word on their behalf. Expose the

88 Wordsworth to J. G. Lockhart (November 1841), Wordsworth, *Letters*, VI, p. 260. Ibid., V, p. 678 (8 April 1839).

89 John Stuart Mill to Albany Fonblanque, 1 January 1842. Mill, *The earlier letters of John Stuart Mill, 1812–48*, ed. Francis E. Mineka (Toronto, 1963), II, p. 495.

absurdity of Talfourd as well as Macaulay, and show how the whole thing has failed.[90]

Mill's letter to Fonblanque is preserved in Bulwer's papers, confirming that the article was by Bulwer: this would certainly have been perfectly consistent with his supportive remarks in parliament. The savagery of the piece is also characteristic.

The *Examiner*'s main competitor for the weekly periodical market was the *Athenaeum*, which achieved a circulation of about 18,000 during the late 1830s. Politically moderate, it concentrated on literature, art and science. The *Athenaeum* demonstrated an early interest in copyright matters: there were calls for relief from international piracies as early as 1835, and again in 1836 and 1837.[91] Also in 1837, a brief notice appeared, expressing pleasure at Talfourd's plans to consolidate the law of domestic copyright. His first speech was likewise welcomed, although there was little official editorial comment on it. Instead, the magazine published three long signed letters from Thomas Hood, in effect essays, with the title 'Copyright and copywrong'. Hood had become known through his poetry, and his contributions to journals, especially the *Athenaeum*, of which he had been joint proprietor for a time. His biggest success had been with his *Comic Annual* for 1830: he had been enraged to see rival annuals, such as *The New Comic Annual*, attempting to capitalise on his efforts.[92]

Hood's essays put forward a strongly argued case for changes to copyright law, although his tone remained light-handed. He expressed an unashamedly literary point of view with real balance and detachment. It is significant that his main preoccupations were with the profession of authorship, and the dignity of his work, and he thought that Talfourd's bill had important repercussions for these:

the Legislature will not only have to decide *directly*, by a formal act, whether the literary interest is worthy of a place beside the shipping interest, the landed interest, the funded interest, the manufacturing and other public interests, but also it will have *indirectly* to determine whether

90 Forster to Bulwer, no date (Feb 1841?), Herts Record Office, Bulwer Papers, XV, quoted in Barnes, *Authors*, p. 121.

91 *Athenaeum* 1835, p. 376; 1836, p. 817; 1837, pp. 65, 122, 141, 249.

92 For a very helpful account of Hood's early career see Peter Thorogood, 'Thomas Hood: a nineteenth-century author and his relations with the book trade to 1835', in *Development of the English book trade, 1700–1899*, eds. Robin Myers and Michael Harris (Oxford, 1981), pp. 106–72.

literary men belong to the privileged class, – the higher, lower or middle class, – the working class, – productive or unproductive class, – or, in short, to any class at all.[93]

Hood noted the ferocity with which the libel law had been used against authors, whilst copyright left them in practice unprotected against assaults on their own literary property. Hood's examples of plagiarism and parodies clearly stem from his own experience, particularly when he describes the pirates who use his name on works not his own: 'for the literary man, thus doubly robbed, of his money and his reputation, what is his redress but by an injunction, or action against walking shadows'. In the second essay Hood deplored the low esteem in which literature was held by the state, and in the third defended the literary character against some common accusations – such as improvidence and poverty.[94] Hood saw the copyright bill as a solution: 'instead of being nobodies with nothing, we shall be, if not freeholders, a sort of copyholders, with something between the sky and the centre, that we can call our own'.

Although happy to publicise Hood's views, the *Athenaeum*'s official editorial response remained low key until May 1838, when it defended Talfourd against the charge that there were no authors in favour of his scheme. In his support, three items were reproduced. The first was Southey's letter to Brougham, written in 1831, asking for a new law of copyright which acknowledged the rights of the author's family. The second was a poem, 'The grand dinner of Type & Co.': the tone is light, but there is more than a little edge in the descriptions of the publishers' feasting like cormorants on folios and drinking port out of poets' skulls. The author was again Thomas Hood, although this was not publicly admitted here. Finally, Wordsworth's public letter to Talfourd was reprinted.[95]

Although the *Athenaeum* was generally supportive, it did not favour the retrospective clause, as was made clear in its comments on Longman's objections to the bill.[96] There were no notices in 1839, but reports of the bill's progress resumed in 1840. Robert Cadell chose the *Athenaeum* as one of the places in which he

93 *Athenaeum* 1837, p. 264. 94 Ibid., 1837, pp. 285, 304.

95 Ibid., 5 May 1838, pp. 323–4. Moore mentions the poem in his journal, (ed. Dowden), p. 1965 (May 1838). Wordsworth, *Letters*, VI, p. 556 (18 April 1838).

96 *Athenaeum*, 19 May 1838, p. 359.

denied that he, or any of Scott's representatives, had been involved as originators of Talfourd's bill. Macaulay's 1841 speech was noted briefly, and scorn poured on his arguments, although the failure of the bill was attributed also to its lack of party interest: 'they were fighting for an abstraction, and wanted fit audience'.[97]

The eventual success of the bill in 1842 was welcomed, although the *Athenaeum* was increasingly concerned with the revival of demands for satisfactory international copyright protection. Thomas Hood had not forgotten Talfourd's efforts, however, and in 1842 he completed his 'Copyright and copywrong' series with two more essays. In the first he reviewed and answered the arguments used by the bill's opponents. In the second, he too looked forward to the international question.[98] He was now editor of the *New Monthly*, where he continued to agitate on the subject of copyright, domestic and international.[99]

Legal periodicals

It might have been expected that debate on a legal matter such as copyright would have raged in the legal arena, as in the literary world. This is not evident from the two main legal periodicals, the *Law Magazine* and the *Legal Observer*.

The *Legal Observer* adhered to a strictly factual brief, and was steadfastly informative rather than polemic. It was a weekly magazine, which concentrated on providing current information for its professional readers. The page was divided into two columns, suggesting a newspaper rather than a magazine. It was largely composed of case notes, discussions of new or topical legal points, and notices of parliamentary business: the progress or

[97] Ibid., 14 March 1840, p. 219; 20 February 1841, p. 155.

[98] Ibid., 11 and 18 June 1842, pp. 524, 543. One anecdote bears repeating. Hood was asked to write for a new journal, intended to be sold very cheaply to benefit the public. He agreed to write for virtually nothing on condition that he could persuade his own suppliers to accept similar terms. 'It will be sufficient to quote the answer of the butcher: – "Sir, Respectin your note. Cheap literater be blowed. Butchers must live as well as other pepel – and if so be you or the readin publick wants to have meat at prime cost, you must buy your own beastesses, and kill yourselves. I remane, &c. John Stokes."'

[99] See in particular Hood's mockery of Wakley's presumptuous criticisms of Wordsworth: 'Mr Wakley and the Poets', *New Monthly* 65 (1842), p. 136.

content of bills were common items. Items tended to be very brief, reinforcing the newspaper style. There was little editorial material, although each weekly part began with a rather longer article which did offer the opportunity for comment.

The copyright bills did not feature in this editorial section until 1842, after Mahon's bill had passed its second reading in the House of Lords.[100] There was a very warm acknowledgment of Talfourd's originating role, and of his efforts since 1837. The writer appeared generally supportive of the measure, and accepted that it would provide encouragement to authors of 'useful and laborious works', including legal works. However, some anxiety was expressed about the drafting of the clause concerning extension of copyright for works published before the bill. The power to license publication, to be given to the Judicial Committee of the Privy Council in the event of a work's suppression, was particularly welcomed, as were the modifications to the registration requirements.

The *Law Magazine* appeared four times a year, and its brief editorial 'Events of the quarter' was supportive of Talfourd. There were only a few sentences regretting the bill's loss in 1837, but in May 1838 an article was devoted to the question.[101] Lockhart termed it 'short but comprehensive'. The writer emphasised that an author had had a perpetual copyright before the Act of Anne, and suggested that the publishers' fears were groundless, since the bill would affect few cases. The supposed analogy with patent was carefully demolished. The *Law Magazine* continued to monitor the bill's progress, although the final outcome was welcomed only in the most lukewarm terms: 'seven years is a paltry boon at last'.[102]

Analysis of the periodical literature shows that the copyright question was of real interest, and hotly debated. It is clear that these articles were widely read, particularly by those in power, and there is evidence of interplay with the wider debate. The periodical press ranks with other lobbying levers, such as newspapers and petitions: its significant influence should not be underestimated.

100 *Legal Observer* 23 (1842), p. 33.

101 *Law Magazine* 19 (1838), 365–78. The article has been attributed to Mr Henry Sheppard Q.C.

102 Ibid., 28, (1842), p. 513.

However, interest waned as Talfourd's plans were cut down: reaction to Mahon's compromise plan was relatively muted. The only attempt to sum up the results came from Archibald Alison, writing in *Blackwood's*: the 'Maga', perhaps surprisingly, had not considered the copyright question before.[103] Alison, a petitioner for Talfourd's bill, was highly critical. He argued that the booksellers' resistance to the essential extension of copyright represented a greater threat to the public than the longer term itself, because it promoted only ephemeral literature:

> It is the national character which is really affected by the present downward tendency of our literature; it is the national interests which are really at stake; it is the final fate of the empire which is at issue in the character of our literature. True, an extension of the copyright will not affect the interests of a thousandth part of the writers, or a hundredth part of the readers in the present age; but what then – it is they who are to form the general opinion of mankind in the next; it is on that thousandth and that hundredeth, that the fate of the world depends.

Alison regarded the 1842 bill as 'a disgrace to British legislation' and thought that his successors would come to regard it as 'evidence of the barbarism of the nineteenth century'. His strongly felt fears echo Talfourd's concerns. Alison was summing up after five difficult and disappointing years for Talfourd's supporters, and found it hard to look forward positively. His concerns were for the quality of national literature – an intangible – so his prediction is hard to test. However, the 1842 Act remained influential into the twentieth century, and provided a platform for future developments. An attempt to assess its ongoing contribution is essential.

[103] *Blackwood's Edinburgh Magazine* 51 (1842), p. 107.

9

CONCLUSION

Although Archibald Alison considered it 'a disgrace to British legislation', legal commentators throughout the nineteenth century responded warmly and positively to the 1842 Copyright Act. Godson's *Practical treatise* had devoted considerable space to the exposition of Talfourd's proposals, as yet unpassed.[1] The 1844 supplement to this declared the law respecting copyright in books to be 'much improved' since the last edition, 'by acts of Parliament, for which the public owe great thanks, as to copyright, to Mr Serjeant Talfourd'.[2] Burke, who provided a further supplement to Godson's textbook in 1851, was still entirely supportive of Talfourd, to whom the public owed 'the happy amelioration of our Copyright law'.[3] Another near-contemporary, Blaine, writing in 1853, described how the Statute of Anne 'cut down' the perpetual right in literary works to a short fourteen-year term, and noted that 'since that time instalments of justice have with the greatest difficulty been wrung from the Legislature'.[4] A footnote attributed the 1842 Act to 'the generous and unwearied exertions of one of the most distinguished authors of modern times, Sir Thomas Noon Talfourd'.

In the 1870 first edition of Copinger, now a standard work, it was emphasised that the contemporary law of literary copyright depended on the 1842 Act. Again Talfourd's contribution is recognised: 'To Mr Serjeant Talfourd is due the honour of

[1] Richard Godson, *A practical treatise on the law of patents for inventions and of copyright*, 2nd edn (1840), pp. 305–6, 316–18.

[2] *A supplement to the second edition of A Practical Treatise* . . . (1844), pp. vii–viii.

[3] Peter Burke, *Supplement to Godson's practical treatise on the law of patents* . . . (1851).

[4] Delabere Roberton Blaine, *On the laws of artistic copyright and their defects* (1853), p. 11.

obtaining this piece of legislative justice.'[5] Later commentators likewise emphasised the continuing reliance on the 1842 Act.[6] They also began to point out drawbacks in the copyright system, some of which Talfourd had once hoped to correct. Writing over half a century after the 1837 bill, Scrutton bemoaned the fact that Talfourd's agenda of consolidation had still not been addressed: 'The whole patchwork and piecemeal collection of Acts waits and has waited for years for a codifying and simplifying measure which Parliament cannot find leisure to bestow.'[7] The rest of Scrutton's account was brief and factual, although he appeared sympathetic to Talfourd and even to perpetual copyright.

Nineteenth-century commentators, then, regarded Talfourd's contribution as a positive one; they speak of 'justice' and 'improvements'. In terms of the Act's specific provisions, this may well have been true: the extended term, clearer definitions and improved registration system would certainly have been helpful. Yet none of these assessments addresses the question of how far the 1842 Act provided anything constructive in terms of the rationale for copyright. After the passage of the 1911 Act there is even less comment on the 1842 Act, which is generally dismissed as of minor historical interest, in spite of its importance as a precursor for the new Act.[8]

Modern theorists have tended to regard the eighteenth-century great cases, particularly *Donaldson* v. *Beckett*,[9] as pivotal for the

[5] Walter Arthur Copinger, *The law of copyright in works of literature and art* (1870), p. 18. This sentence reappears in the latest edition, although no longer unqualified: the Act's 'faults both in substance and in drafting' are also noted. Edmund P. Skone James, *et al.*, *Copinger and Skone James on copyright*, 13th edn (1991), p. 8.

[6] John Camden Hotten's quasi-theoretical account, published within a year of Copinger's, provided one dissenting voice: 'Though the Parliament of 1842 refused to legislate for authors' interests merely, the influence of authors, who were, of course, more active than any other class in impressing their views on the legislature, is clearly traceable in the Copyright Act to secure for the public benefits which were in theory intended to be conferred upon them; and generally it cannot be said that the doctrine of public policy laid down by the Government as the condition of giving their support to the measure was strictly followed in all its provisions': *Literary copyright* (1871), p. 31. However, Hotten was not a lawyer, but a publisher.

[7] Thomas E. Scrutton, *The law of copyright*, 2nd edn (1890), p. 47.

[8] See, for instance, Richard Rogers Bowker, *Copyright: its history and its law* (1912), p. 28.

[9] See pp. 14–15, above.

definition of copyright's purposes. Woodmansee and Rose both site copyright at an intersection between legal-economic and aesthetic realms of discourse, and both have detected links between copyright and the emerging concept of authorship. Woodmansee defines 'author' 'in its modern sense' as 'an individual who is solely responsible – and therefore exclusively deserving of credit – for the production of a unique work'.[10] She sees this as a relatively recent invention, a product of the transition from the limited patronage of aristocratic society to the democratic patronage of the market place – which inevitably involves copyright. Rose's discussion of *Donaldson* v. *Beckett* develops this idea in more detail. For Rose the distinguishing characteristic of a modern author 'is that he is a proprietor, that he is conceived as the originator and therefore the owner of a special kind of commodity', with copyright 'a crucial institutional embodiment of the author–work relation'.[11]

Rose divides into two categories the arguments put forward in connection with *Donaldson* v. *Beckett*. The historical claim to the right perpetual was rehearsed many times, by those arguing on both sides. The theoretical arguments, often based on the claims of natural law, interest him more. Even though perpetual copyright did not survive *Donaldson* v. *Beckett*, Rose argues that the representation of the author as proprietor, and the book as product, remained – thanks to the wide dissemination of the particular theoretical arguments presented by the London booksellers. Here the intersection of realms can be seen clearly: the development of copyright law is linked to various cultural developments – the emergence of a mass market for books, the valorisation of original genius and the development of a Lockean discourse of progressive individualism.

Rose states, almost in passing, that copyright is now regarded as a balancing exercise in the face of conflicts between individual needs and the needs of modern society: the resulting compromise

[10] Martha Woodmansee, 'The genius and the copyright: economic and legal conditions of the emergence of the "Author"', *Eighteenth-century Studies* 17 (1984) 425–48 (p. 426). Woodmansee develops these ideas in wider contexts in *The author, art and the market: rereading the history of aesthetics* (New York, 1994).

[11] Mark Rose, 'The author as proprietor: *Donaldson* v. *Becket* and the genealogy of modern authorship', *Representations* 23 (1988), 51–85 (p. 54).

is a long but limited term.[12] He uses this as a base state with which to contrast the eighteenth-century view of copyright as an abstract concept, susceptible to reason and scholarship. His article is concerned largely with the eighteenth century, and much of his assessment provides valuable insight into the eighteenth-century context for copyright.[13] However, Rose proceeds to the more sweeping conclusion that the ground was prepared for Romanticism by the long debate over copyright, and argues that the theoretical problems raised by the copyright struggle were 're-solved' by Romantic theory. This raises the question of the impact of *Donaldson* v. *Beckett* on nineteenth-century copyright.

In one sense copyright law does form a continuity – a progression of positive laws beginning with the Statute of Anne. But Saunders is right to object to the portrayal of copyright as a continuity with inevitability, inextricably linked (or even subordinated) to the Romantic aesthetic.[14] There are many rationales for copyright, and the early ones had little to do with the author as an aesthetic personality. However, positive law – unlike natural law – is capable of change and of change which reflects societal pressures. Once it was accepted that copyright was not entirely a creature of natural law – and this was essential after *Donaldson* v. *Beckett* – change was possible, even if problematic.

In practice, *Donaldson* v. *Beckett* offered copyright law only discontinuity. The historical claim to a perpetual right was trumped by the Statute of Anne, which was held to have abrogated the common law right. The theoretical lines of argument, which Rose stresses, were not reflected in the outcome of the case: the book trade's Lockean rhetoric did not prevail, at least not immediately. Furthermore, the unusual circumstances of the judgment, typified by Lord Mansfield's unexplained silence, contributed to the sense of cloudiness and confusion. Although it unquestionably resulted in a decision, *Donaldson* v. *Beckett* in no sense resolved the perennial problem of copyright's rationale. Furthermore, if copyright was governed by statute, it could not be regarded as immutable: it had to be capable of response to social and cultural developments.

12 Ibid., p. 59.

13 Rose's ideas in this article are worked out more fully in *Authors and owners: the invention of copyright* (1993).

14 David Saunders, *Authorship and copyright* (1992), p. 2.

This is the legal context in which the 1837 bill was presented. Although Talfourd argued strongly for one particular view, he was in effect asking for the entire copyright question to be reopened. This could be achieved only by legislative intervention. This fact had its own impact on the terms of the debate, and changed the dimensions of the problem. This was no longer a judicial matter, a consideration (however weighty) of legal interests. Publishers, printers and authors – those customarily interested in copyright – demanded and deserved attention. In addition, parliament was obliged to consider the views of other powerful groups, notably the radicals both in and out of parliament, who had come to regard themselves as interested. The resulting claims and demands introduced themes of national significance: attitudes to monopoly, the availability of knowledge, definitions of cultural worth. Legislative decisions which affected these areas had consequences for the general public good and, in a time when Bentham's views were influential, this was widely accepted. Once this extensive context had been sketched, copyright became hugely problematic. The debate from which the 1842 Act emerged was characterised by conflict, and parliament struggled in its attempt to perform just the sort of balancing exercise that Rose takes so much for granted. Rose's assertion – that the theoretical arguments finally prevailed in modern copyright law – is a rather facile gloss.[15] It took five years for the balancing process to reach a conclusion which was arguably arbitrary, and certainly calculated with an eye to political and parliamentary expediency.

Various rationales for copyright were, however, offered to parliament. Given the temporal intersection with the development of the author, it was natural and tempting for Wordsworth and others to regard copyright as an aspect of their own conceptions of authorship.[16] Wordsworth saw the bill as 'a general measure of justice for all authors & for all time'.[17] This aesthetic rationale

[15] Rose, 'Author as proprietor', p. 59.

[16] Rose suggests (p. 70) that 'The booksellers had promulgated the representation of authorship that writers such as Southey and Wordsworth now adopted as their own.' This seems to imply a linear and causal relationship which is far too simple: Wordsworth and Southey were not relying on concepts born of copyright law, but on concepts of much more general literary application.

[17] Quoted in Paul M. Zall, 'Wordsworth and the Copyright Act of 1842', *Proceedings of the Modern Language Association of America* 70 (1955), 135–44.

claimed copyright as the natural and rightful reward of genius, and asked parliament for its rubber stamp. Nevertheless, they failed to convince parliament of the primacy and inevitability of the author's claims – the 1842 Act does not embrace this vision of the author, often characterised as Romantic.

Although this rationale for copyright was implicitly rejected, no clear substitute emerged. An opposing economic pole saw copyright as a rightful return on investment. Tegg's position was extreme, perhaps, but he was not alone in regarding the book as an unromantic commodity, first and last. Others, such as Hume, presented copyright as an economic incentive; the correct term was that which induced the author to provide instruction or amusement for the public.[18] The influence of the free traders, and consequent fear of monopoly, cost Talfourd Peel's support, and certainly affected the result. Macaulay's views bear further witness to this, but could scarcely be presented as copyright's new rationale.

It is the nature of public debate that extreme positions are adopted. Parliament provided the forum in which decisions of principle could – and should – have been taken. However, political reality finally swamped the theoretical discussions: those attempting to achieve a considered solution were faced with a network of arguments and issues which touched and diverted copyright. Copyright was no longer a limited concept, relevant only to certain interest groups: the explosion of print culture had thrust it into an environment where immense political, social, cultural and economic forces were operating. Print offered a range of intellectual freedoms to a rapidly growing constituency, and access to it was regarded as essential. Countervailing pressures from many sides, some only tangentially related to copyright, left copyright law exposed to public and unprecedented buffeting. Even the interest in *Donaldson* v. *Beckett* was exceeded: more people felt affected, and more people had access to the debate. Public interest thus began to weigh in the balance, in competition with trade interest and authors' rights.

Issues and interests of such complexity are not easily 'resolved', and parliament's failure to do so is understandable. To those faced with the entrenched views represented by Talfourd on the one

[18] *Hansard, Parliamentary debates* (3rd series), xlii, 567.

hand and Wakley on the other, compromise perhaps seemed the only way forward. Mahon's political and practical decision to settle for a lesser term than Talfourd had demanded provided a result, but (like *Donaldson* v. *Beckett*) offered no resolution. Parliament – as led by Peel and Macaulay – can be criticised for its failure to address its real task, which was to provide a considered rationale for copyright protection in nineteenth-century society. The very audacity of Talfourd's back-bench scheme offered the opportunity to debate this question in a non-party-political context. It is unfortunate that the heat generated by wider forces led those involved to confine copyright to a simple issue of term, and to reduce even this to an arbitrary figure determined by political pragmatism.

Nevertheless, the discussions surrounding the 1842 Act did contribute something of significance to authorship. Rose and Woodmansee concur with many in setting the birth date of the individual 'author' in the eighteenth century. The nineteenth century sees the birth of the profession of authorship, and copyright is the first issue around which the new profession coalesces. The copyright issue became high profile and controversial, and came to intersect many planes of argument that had been apparently unconnected. When measures to address international copyright law were discussed, much ground had already been covered in terms of publicity and familiarity with the arguments.

The legal contribution of the 1842 Act should also be recognised.[19] Although it was not the reforming Act that Talfourd had hoped for, its rites of passage helped to create an environment in which the international protection which Talfourd had once envisaged could be realised. In 1908 the Berlin Revision of the Berne Convention required signatories to offer a mimimum term of protection of copyright; it was to be at least the author's life plus fifty years. Within the European Community, the copyright term for literary works has recently been harmonised: all Member States are obliged to protect works for the author's life plus seventy years. It is not merely ironic that the requirements of the Berne Convention approach Talfourd's ideal of protection, and may before long exceed it: the ground was broken by the debates which preceded the 1842 Act.

[19] For a detailed account, see Appendix II.

Britain's desire to ratify the Berlin Revision of the Berne Convention ensured that the march of positive law continued. The 1911 Copyright Act had to perform many functions. Although its primary purpose was to make the changes necessary to allow ratification, the opportunity was at last taken to consolidate the various existing copyrights in a single statute. In addition, producers of sound recordings were given their own exclusive right to prevent reproductions of their recordings. This is the kind of entrepreneurial right which continental theorists would term a 'neighbouring right', and not a copyright at all. The 1956 Copyright Act added three further entrepreneurial rights; in films, broadcasts and the typographical format of published editions. There was no attempt to clarify copyright's rationale: Professor Cornish has described the 1956 Act as 'a complex piece of draftsmanship which elaborated many rules at perplexing length while neglecting to spell out basic principles in the clear order appropriate to a real code'.[20] The 1988 Copyright, Designs and Patents Act added rental rights to the entrepreneurial catalogue, although it did also introduce certain limited moral rights for authors.

This mushrooming of entrepreneurial rights exemplifies the problems faced by a copyright regime which lacks a coherent rationale. Unfortunately, one thing that the 1842 Act emphatically did not provide was an accepted rationale for the law of copyright. Many interest groups argue that their entrepreneurial investment deserves legal protection. Knowing that *sui generis* protection is difficult to obtain, a niche is sought in existing schemes of protection. The patent, trade mark and design systems resist incongruous developments: their rationales are relatively clear. Copyright, however, is regarded as inherently flexible and responsive, and thus as an ideal home for apparently deserving cases. Deserving they may be, but the appropriateness of a long period of copyright protection is not self-evident in all cases. Ideally, individual claims for copyright protection should be screened for their compatibility with the scheme of copyright. Without an agreed theoretical basis for copyright, this is not possible. Claims are inevitably judged in a piecemeal fashion. Much may depend

[20] William R. Cornish, *Intellectual property*, 2nd edn (1989), p. 251.

on lobbying strength, which may well not take account of, say, wider educational interests.

The problem is a complex and intractable one, which has in the past proved insoluble in both judicial and parliamentary contexts. The 1842 Act provides an important case study. Although debate continued for five years, in the widest public and parliamentary circles, the resolution was only partial: years of complex political negotiations were reduced to a limited decision on copyright term. This should serve as a spectacular example for contemporary legislators. So many of society's interests are touched by copyright that it can seem impossible to address in its entirety. Now that the context is even wider, and the dangers correspondingly increased, repetitions of Talfourd's failure seem almost inevitable: copyright's complexity leads to legislative compromise. The European Community has so far tried and failed to provide a comprehensive harmonisation of the main body of copyright, being forced – like Talfourd – to confine itself to the upward harmonisation of term. The recent TRIPS agreement provides much for right holders in terms of incentives and enforcement, but little by way of rationale.[21]

Further challenges are imminent. So far copyright has been able to respond to new copying technologies, which threaten the very rights it protects. This may not be possible for much longer, as international telecommunication links give unprecedented and often uncontrolled access both to copyright works and to copying technology. With this technology has come a new attitude to copying. Users wish to enjoy the extraordinary opportunities offered to them, and may even be hostile to the idea of protection. It is scarcely surprising that copyright is regarded by some as limiting, old-fashioned and irrelevant. It now seems impossible to summarise – as Talfourd could have done – what should be protected and why. A case-by-case approach to copyright law risks leaving it diluted and distorted to the point that the rights which it grants can neither be supported nor enforced. The justification for copyright law must be better defined and more widely understood. If copyright law is to retain any coherence, much work remains to be done, and quickly.

[21] Agreement on Trade-related Aspects of Intellectual Property Rights, including Trade in Counterfeit Goods.

Appendix I

CHRONOLOGY OF THE BILLS

1837

18 May – leave to introduce
7 June – presented and read
14 June – second reading deferred
28 June – second reading: committee stage set this day three months

1838

14 December 1837 – leave to introduce
28 February – first reading
27 March, 11 April – dates set down for second reading, but postponed
25 April – second reading
9 May – committee
15 May – committee deferred
6 June – committee pro forma, to sit again
20 June – bill withdrawn

1839

12 February – leave to introduce
13 February – presented and read
27 February – second reading (Talfourd introduces petitions)
10 April – no house for committee

11 April – committee deferred repeatedly until 8 July, when deferred three months

1840

4 February – leave to introduce
11 February – first reading
19 February – second reading
26 February – committee deferred repeatedly until 8 July, when deferred three months

1841

27 January – leave to introduce
29 January – first reading (in spite of radical tactics)
5 February – second reading, deferred three months (Macaulay's first speech)

1842

3 March – leave to introduce
4 March – first reading
16 March – second reading
6 April – committee (term decided), completed 20 and 21 April
26 April – third reading
8 May – second reading: House of Lords
26 May – committee: House of Lords
29 June – House of Lords amendments agreed by House of Commons
1 July – royal assent

Appendix II

SUCCESSIVE VERSIONS OF THE BILL

Talfourd endured a great deal of public criticism during the copyright debates, some directed at his plans, but also a considerable amount directed at him personally. Parliamentary opponents and pamphleteers did not hesitate to mock his florid speeches and his partisan enthusiasm. Talfourd was left dispirited and frustrated by the many reverses his bill suffered, and Mahon's safe political hands were certainly welcome in the closing stages. It is easy to carry away from the contemporary squabbling an impression of Talfourd the 'bungling juggler', the warm-hearted but wrong-headed literary amateur. Yet this is to do Talfourd a great injustice.

Analysis of the various drafts of the bill makes it plain that Talfourd's knowledge of copyright law was practical and extensive. Many of the elements of modern copyright law were already in place by 1837, although not necessarily in statutory form. The various pieces of copyright legislation had been enacted piecemeal, in response to demands for protection from particular groups, and the results varied in coherence and quality. The absence of international copyright was an admitted and glaring problem. Talfourd's plans for revision and improvement were coherent and careful, though avowedly ambitious. These bills are not the work of an unbalanced fanatic with large ideals and no substance. They contained carefully drafted clauses intended to address various practical problems which had emerged from the existing web of statutory and case law protection. Of particular interest to a modern lawyer is Talfourd's far-sighted but unsuccessful attempt to include a statutory 'fair use' clause.

There were many versions of the original bill, which was very considerably modified.[1] The changes were often the result of

[1] These were published in the House of Commons papers on the following dates;

profound disagreements as to the nature and purpose of copyright, and reveal starkly the political pressures which were brought to bear. Any oscillations were not the result of Talfourd's indecision, but reflected the hostile political climate which these copyright bills faced. The House of Lords was responsible for the removal of several of the more ambitious provisions, notably the 'fair use' clause. Although the supporters of the bill were in some measure pleased to see it become an Act, the concessions from the original plan were considerable. Some of the points conceded in 1842 were reintroduced and accepted in the scheme of the 1911 Act. This perhaps serves as a more objective assessment of Talfourd's overall vision than did Macaulay's crowing victory claim for his own efforts in the House of Commons.[2] The detailed changes to the individual clauses reveal a good deal about how this vision was originally underpinned, and how it was finally undermined.

PREAMBLE

Talfourd's grand aims were immediately apparent in the preamble to the 1837 bill:

> Whereas it is expedient to consolidate and render uniform the Laws relating to Copyright in Printed Books, Musical Compositions, Acted Dramas and Engravings, and to afford greater encouragement to the Authors and Inventors thereof, by extending the term of their exclusive right therein; Be it therefore enacted . . .

This wording echoes the Act of Anne, particularly with its aim of encouragement of learning.[3] Although consolidation was perhaps

6 June 1837, 27 February 1838, 6 June 1838 , 12 February 1839, 11 February 1840, 29 January 1841, 4 March 1842, 23 March 1842, 21 April 1842. The 21 April version was reprinted unchanged after its first reading in the House of Lords on 28 April: *HL Papers* 1842 (88). A first batch of amendments was reported 14 June: *HL Papers* 1842 (133). Further amendments were made on 24 June, and the bill was passed and sent to the House of Commons. The complete list of amendments was printed in *HC Papers* 27 June 1842. These were agreed to and returned on 30 June. The Act received the royal assent 1 July 1842. For brevity, the House of Commons versions of the bill will be referred to by year, plus lower case letters where necessary.

2 Macaulay, *The letters of Thomas Babington, Baron Macaulay*, ed. Thomas Pinney (Cambridge, 1974–81), IV, p. 25 (7 April 1842), and see above, ch. 3, p. 60.

3 'Whereas printers, booksellers and other persons have of late frequently taken the liberty of printing, reprinting and publishing, or causing to be printed, reprinted and published, books and other writings, without the consent of the authors or

expedient, it did not prove possible.[4] The clauses concerned with engravings did not appear in the 1838 versions, nor did the provision for international protection. The 1838 preamble is laconic to the point of timidity.[5] By 1839 the Act of Anne's plangent reference to authors had been deleted, to be replaced by the utilitarian aim of affording 'greater encouragement to the production of Literary Works of lasting benefit to the World'. This preamble survived unchanged in the 1842 Act.

INTERPRETATION CLAUSE

All versions included a series of carefully wrought definitions, which reflected case law where relevant. For instance, the 1710 Act had covered 'books or other writings', a phrase which had been held to include a single sheet of letterpress, and also sheet music.[6] A new bill offered a convenient opportunity to adopt this view explicitly, and this was done in all versions of the bill.

Yet the definition of this seemingly elementary term was drafted and redrafted, the pattern of continued change reflecting the difficulties involved in delineating the scope of copyright. Later

proprietors of such books and writings, to their very great detriment, and too often to the ruin of them and their families: for preventing therefore such practices for the future, and for the encouragement of learned men to compose and write useful Books' (Copyright Act 1710).

4 'These statutes are without exception of most involved and inartistic draftsmanship, and present to the legislature a suitable, even an urgent, case for codification, though nothing has been done to attain this desirable end since the Report of the Copyright Commission in 1878': Thomas E. Scrutton *The law of copyright*, 2nd edn (1890), p. 2.

5 'Whereas it is expedient to amend the Law relating to Copyright, and to afford greater encouragement to authors; Be it enacted . . .' (1838, 1838b).

6 *Hime* v. *Dale* (1803) 2 Camp 27n; 11 East 244n, where the words of a song had been published on a single sheet of paper. Lord Ellenborough was inclined to think that this was not within the Act of Anne because 'book' suggested a plurality of sheets, but he later changed his mind. See also *Clementi* v. *Golding* (1809) 11 East 244; 2 Camp 25 and *White* v. *Gerock* (1819) 2 Barn & Ald 298. On music see *Bach* v. *Longman* (1777) 2 Cowp 623, *per* Lord Mansfield (observing that the case was so clear and the arguments such that it was difficult to speak seriously on it): 'The words of the Act of Parliament are very large: "books and other writings". It is not confined to language or letters. Music is a science; it may be written; and the mode of conveying the ideas, is by signs and marks. A person may use the copy by playing it, but he has no right to rob the author of the profit by multiplying copies and disposing of them to his own use.'

versions of this same clause attempted to bring parts of volumes within the definition of 'book', perhaps hoping to avoid questions about the nature of infringement when only sections of a work were copied.[7]

Modern copyright law uses the concept of 'literary works', expansively defined and requiring only an elementary level of originality. Early nineteenth-century decisions did help to establish the sort of work in which copyright could subsist. Although there was concern that copyright should not be used to sequester information that was in the public domain, the more audacious piracies were certainly restrained. For instance, road books (a guide-book to the roads of a district) were a lucrative form of publication, the more so if the information they contained could be taken from others without payment. In *Taylor* v. *Bayne* several pages of the plaintiffs' map book, which had been compiled from their own survey, were copied into an almanack published by the defendant. In the face of 'an evident piracy' the defence that this was simply a list of stages and distances, and thus not capable of protection, was rejected.[8] Another popular product was a themed calendar, containing a selection of relevant lists, dates and other information. Although the theme itself could not be monopolised, the court would intervene to prevent a mere copy with colourable variations.[9] These definitional questions overlap with those concerning infringement, which will be discussed below. Here it is

[7] 'Book': 'every volume, pamphlet, sheet of letter-press and sheet of music, map, chart or plan' (1837, 1838a); 'every volume, pamphlet, part of any work separately published, sheet of letter-press and sheet of music, map, chart or plan' (1838b, 1839); 'every volume, part or division of a volume, pamphlet, sheet of letter-press, sheet of music, map, chart or plan separately published' (1840, 1841, 1842). The wording 'map, chart or plan' was transplanted from the 1766 Engraving Copyright Act. This was a significant change, since registration was required for protection under the 1842 Act, whereas the Engraving Copyright Act required that the proprietor's name and the date appear on the engraving. See *Stannard* v. *Lee* (1871) 6 Ch App 346, confirming that maps were 'books' not 'engravings', so needed to be registered. However, compare *Stannard* v. *Harrison* (1871) 24 LT 571, where one of the plaintiff's enormously popular lithographed bird's-eye views of Paris was held to be a landscape within the Engraving Copyright Act, so did not need to be registered.

[8] (1776) Mor 8308

[9] *Matthewson* v. *Stockdale* (1806) 12 Ves 270 (the *East India Calendar*). Lord Chancellor Erskine voiced personal doubts about the wisdom of protection in such cases, but felt bound to follow established law.

sufficient to indicate that although the term 'book' covered a wide area, it did have definite boundaries.

TERM

As is plain from the main text of the book, the clauses concerned with the term of copyright proved hugely controversial. The wide variety of philosophical, economic and policy arguments used, both to support and to attack Talfourd's proposals, have already been discussed.[10] Although the length of term came to be regarded as the central issue, in fact opposition to the transitional provisions on term – including the so-called 'retrospective clause' – proved extremely damaging. The bill as originally drafted would have resulted in a considerable extension to copyright term, far exceeding the English historical precedents.[11] The Act of Anne had given a fourteen-year term, after which 'the sole right of printing or disposing of copies shall return to the authors thereof, if they are then living, for another term of 14 years'. The 1814 Act consolidated this term by granting a definite twenty-eight years from date of publication 'and also, if the author shall be living at the end of that period, for the residue of his natural life'.[12] Little case law had been generated on this issue, largely because book trade practice rendered disputes unlikely and unnecessary.[13]

[10] See ch. 1, pp. 19–26.

[11] Life plus sixty years would have exceeded most European terms also. Prussia granted life plus thirty, Russia life plus twenty-five, Holland and Belgium life plus twenty. A French decree of 1810 gave copyright to the author for life, the widow for her life, and the children for twenty years. The United States term was twenty-eight years plus another fourteen if the author or the family was still living at the original term's expiry. Lowndes states that Norway, Sweden and Spain gave perpetual rights, but does not quote a statutory source. All figures from John James Lowndes, *An historical sketch of the law of copyright* (1840), Appendix.

[12] Copyright Act 1710, ss. 1, 11; Copyright Act 1814, s. 9

[13] The rare exceptions under the 1710 Act include *Carnan* v. *Bowles* (1786) 2 Bro CC 80, where an author sold the rights in his road book to Carnan, and yet sought to issue an improved edition with copper-plates at the expiry of the inital fourteen-year term. It was held that an author had no rights against his assignee, and the letter press of the new version therefore infringed, although the additional copper-plates were regarded as a new work. The wording of the 1814 Act did generate one transitional matter. It was held that an author was not entitled to the benefit of section 9 if the work had been published more than twenty-eight years before the Act passed, since the Act was intended to extend

Talfourd sought a term of life plus sixty years, and this figure did not change until Mahon took over in 1842. Talfourd's indefatigable tenacity was remarkable given the levels of opposition, both inside parliament and outside it. The 1840 and 1841 versions distinguished between works published during an author's lifetime (where the term was life plus sixty years) and those published posthumously (where the term was sixty years from publication). Mahon changed the figures in the 1842 bills, proposing to give a standard term of life plus twenty-five years, increased to thirty years for posthumously published works.[14] A revised version published after the second reading added a requirement 'That in no case shall the whole term be less than Twenty-eight Years'.[15] The final result was a term of life plus seven years, with a minimum period of forty-two years. Books published after the author's death received forty-two years from publication.[16]

The transitional provisions proved even more problematic. The book trade's enormous and public resentment of the 'retrospective clause' almost destroyed the bill. The questions for those drafting the bill were, firstly, whether the proposed extension should apply to books published before the passing of the Act, and, secondly, assuming that it did apply to these, who should benefit from the windfall. Again, there were models to follow. The Act of Anne gave authors of books already printed twenty-one years from the date of the Act, unless they had transferred the 'copy' or 'share' of the book. Those who had purchased or acquired the 'copy' enjoyed the same term. Although this was less than the potential twenty-eight years available to new books, it was a valuable offering. The 1814 Act (section 8) stated that 'it is reasonable that Authors of Books already published, and who are now living, should also have the benefit of the Extension of Copyright'. The longer period was granted to the personal representatives of an

existing rights, not to recreate expired rights: *Brooke* v. *Clarke* (1818) 1 Barn & Ald 396.

14 'In proposing this reduction of the period which Mr Serjeant Talfourd originally claimed, I wish to guard myself against it being supposed that I for a moment consider the former demand in the least degree unjust. I and those with whom I act ask for it because that reduction of the demand affords the best chance of carrying the measure': *Hansard, Parliamentary debates* (3rd series), lx, 1356 (6 April 1842).

15 1842b, s. 3.

16 Copyright Act 1842, s. 3.

author who had been living at the time of the Act, but had died before the expiry of the first fourteen-year term. The author's original assignees (if any) were protected by their right to sell any copies printed within the first fourteen years and, in addition, their rights under any contract with the author were preserved. Any author of books published before the 1814 Act who was still living at the end of twenty-eight years, was then also granted the sole right of publication for the remainder of his life (section 9). Again there was a saving to allow the author's assignees to sell copies printed within the earlier term, or to enforce the terms of any contract.

Some of these techniques were adopted, but the drafts also show some novel ideas. Talfourd was plainly concerned to ensure that any benefit would reach those for whom it was intended – the author or the author's family. The 1837 bill gave the full extension to authors who had retained any part of the copyright in subsisting copyright works, subject to any licence or partial assignment. This increase was extended to various categories of people, all of whom would have been holding a subsisting copyright as a result of the author's death.[17] The aim was to prevent publishers from enjoying what Talfourd regarded as a windfall, since they had bargained on the basis of a twenty-eight-year term. Even more controversially, authors who had previously assigned their copyrights were nevertheless to have the benefit of the full extension once the twenty-eight-year period of assignment had expired (section 5). Although the assignee's fixed term was explicitly preserved, this reversion to the author would have obliged any publisher of a work still in print to open new negotiations with the author or their family. If the work was notably successful, the bargaining power would have been very much with the author. This was too much for the publishers, who were accustomed to quite different conditions of business.[18]

[17] '. . . such Copyright shall, either absolutely or subject to any licence or partial assignment thereof, belong to the personal representative, or to the legatee, widow or next of kin of such Author, or other person who may have acquired the same in the course of the administration of the estate of such Author, such Copyright shall continue for the residue of the term of Sixty Years, commencing at the time of the death of such Author' (1837, s. 4).

[18] A contemporary legal commentator noted that 'it would appear that by the practice of the trade, the term of Copyright was in reality generally prolonged beyond the legal term; no respectable publisher, from motives of mutual

The first 1838 draft adopted the same strategy as the 1837 bill, but changes were inevitable in the face of the overwhelming protests from those affected. Talfourd was obliged to go into committee pro forma, to allow the alterations to be printed. He was unrepentant as to the principle of giving the extension to the author and not the publisher, but admitted that 'he had received from most respectable parties and eminent publishers so many complaints of practical inconveniences resulting from granting an extended term to authors who had assigned their whole interest' that he had been forced to amend the clause.[19] The new version (printed in June 1838 and used unchanged for the 1839 bill) was scarcely much of a concession. The list of those given the extended term was expanded to include 'any person to whom such Author may have assigned [the copyright] in consideration of natural love and affection'. Again the wording attempts to include family but exclude the book trade. The change was presumably necessary to ensure that assignments made before death to family members would be within the ambit of the changes. The extension likewise applied where the copyright had been assigned in part, and the residue remained with the author's family. In such a case all parties were now to enjoy the full sixty-year term, in proportion to their respective interests. However, where an author had assigned the copyright in its entirety, 'for other consideration than natural love and affection', the term was to cease after the old twenty-eight-year period: the spectre of a reversionary interest was thus laid to rest.[20] Nevertheless, since publishers usually did take an assignment of copyright in its entirety, they still had cause for

convenience, printing upon another. But however this might answer their purpose among themselves, and be compatible with justice and equity, as far as they were concerned, it was far otherwise with regard to the author and the public, neither of whom profited by this tacit understanding. But the publishers feeling that if this Bill were passed, they would either, in the case of a valuable work, have to purchase the remainder of the term, or be prevented on the death of an author from enjoying this implied copyright any longer, tried every means to oppose a measure which would deprive them of this source of profit': Lowndes, *Sketch*, p. 85.

19 *Hansard, Parliamentary debates* (3rd series), xliii, 554 (6 June 1838).

20 1838b, ss. 4–6 (repeated in 1839). Lowndes objected to this distinction, thinking it unfair on the author who 'not having the same means or good fortune, has assigned away all his interest'. He suggested the even more impractical expedient of allowing the author to assign the future interests only to the original assignee, and providing that the term would expire if the parties could not agree terms. Lowndes, *Sketch*, p. 106.

complaint in relation to subsisting copyright: in such cases they were not to receive the extension.

The 1840 bill condensed three clauses into one, but the underlying approach was little changed. Proprietors of subsisting copyright were in principle to have the benefit of the proposed Act, but where copyright had been acquired for other consideration than that of natural love and affection it would not be extended. However, there was an important potential exception to this rule. If the author (or his personal representatives) and the proprietor of the copyright agreed in writing to 'accept the benefits' of the Act with respect to a particular book, then copyright would endure for the full term. This approach left room for the renegotiation of terms, where appropriate. Some scrupulous authors had spoken against the original proposals on the grounds that they believed they had parted with their copyright for good, in honour if not in law: this scheme allowed them to give their publishers the windfall benefit if they so chose. In 1841 the clause was slightly amended to provide that the terms of the agreement should be minuted in the book of registry.[21] The arrangements remained controversial, being challenged in committee, and in the House of Lords, where the Lord Chancellor made a specific defence of the clause in his opening speech.[22] No further changes were made.

Early versions of the bill had attempted to preserve some residual rights for the assignee even after the copyright was again in the hands of the author. The 1837 bill (section 5) provided that, where copyright had been assigned before the 1814 Act, 'nothing herein contained shall prejudice the right of the assignee thereof to sell or dispose, after his interest shall have expired, of any copies of such Book printed during the continuance of his interest in the same'. The 1838 bill added a further significant concession, allowing the assignee to continue to print and sell where a book had been stereotyped. Perhaps fortunately, once the reversionary aspects of the bill had been abandoned, these clauses could likewise be excised. Given the nature of the book trade, it would seem unlikely that such a scheme could have achieved anything other

[21] Enacted as Copyright Act 1842, s. 4 (and Schedule 1).

[22] *Hansard, Parliamentary debates* (3rd series), lxiii, 785 (26 May 1842).

than the complete sabotage of any reversionary interest, at least where a successful book was concerned.[23]

LICENCE TO REPRINT

As has been explained, the proposed sixty-year copyright period represented a considerable increase on the existing term. There was genuine fear that books would go out of print and then become unavailable for an extended time, because the copyright proprietor would not or could not reprint them. This might result in useful or valuable books being, in effect, withheld from the public. The question of censorship was a sensitive one, and the accusation that books would be suppressed was damaging.[24] Talfourd attempted to forestall such arguments by providing a mechanism for the authorisation of reprints. There were no direct precedents for this.[25]

The 1837 bill (section 6) provided that, five years after the expiry of what would have become the old copyright term, if the book was out of print, any person could take steps to have it reprinted. Notice in writing had to be left at the place of publication or the proprietor's address. After one year (or two years if the

[23] A similar situation was generated by contract in *Howitt* v. *Hall* (1862) 10 WR 381; 6 LT 348. The plaintiff sold the defendant the copyright of a particular work for four years from 1854. The defendant produced three editions in that time, including a cheap edition in 1857. In 1862 the plaintiff sought to bring out a uniform edition of juvenile works, but found that the defendant was still advertising and selling the cheap edition. It was held (*per* Wood V.C.), referring to section 15 of the 1842 Act, that 'the Copyright Acts were directed against unlawful printing; and, when, as in this case, the defendant had acquired the right of lawfully printing the work, he was at liberty to sell at any time what he had so printed'. The vice-chancellor also commented that 'a publisher was not likely to incur the useless expense of printing copies enough to exhaust the demand for all time, and have them lying on his hands unprofitably. Besides this, even if the effect of a sale for four years might operate in this way to deprive the author of all copyright in his work, the answer was that he had not guarded himself against such a contingency.' The point was, surely, that the publisher of a successful work would not incur *useless* expense in printing a large edition, because the copies would sell well, undermining the author's own sales and extending the effective copyright period beyond that bargained for.

[24] See ch. 3, pp. 65–6.

[25] Though compare the Copyright Act 1710, s. 4, which gave the archbishop of Canterbury, certain legal officers and others the power to settle the prices of books following complaint that these were unreasonable.

book exceeded 500 pages) the petitioner could apply to the lord chancellor, master of the rolls, or vice-chancellor, for permission to reprint. This could be granted for whatever period and on whatever terms seemed just. The Court of Session and lord ordinary were added to the list in the first 1838 bill. This expensive and cumbersome approach was rethought in the final 1838 bill. The would-be publisher was now to give notice in the London *Gazette* for three successive weeks, and also to write to each proprietor named in the register. The courts were removed from the process entirely. The bill stated that one year after the final advertisement it would be automatically lawful for that person to reprint. Even more surprisingly, the publisher acquired the unexpired portion of the copyright term in the work on re-publication.

This draconian approach would have made failure to reprint extremely risky for the original proprietor, and allowed no room for explanations or even for reasonable conditions. The 1840 and 1841 versions nevertheless retained it, although they dropped the explicit statement that the remainder of the copyright term would go to the new publisher. Lowndes, writing after the 1839 bill had been lost, reported that this clause was 'much objected to, on account of the difficulties it is supposed in practice it would present'.[26] In his 1841 speech, Macaulay had made much of the dangers of suppression of works, hinting darkly of civil turmoil if the bill was passed unmodified. Mahon remained unconvinced of the danger, but agreed to include a provision to guard against its remote likelihood.[27] In his hands the clause was transformed into

[26] Lowndes's own suggestion, even more unwieldy, was that proof of demand at the publishers for several successive years would stand as a prima facie case entitling a person to reprint. This would be rebuttable by proof by either the author or the assignee that a new edition was being prepared, or that it was in fact in print. 'Such a clause would protect the owner of Copyright; at the same time it would not check enterprize, by obliging publicity and thus awakening competition. It is absurd to contend, as has been done, that a publisher, not wishing to reprint himself, nor that others should reprint, might keep some copies by him to show that it was not out of print; for if the work was worth reprinting, a sale would be found for these remaining copies and he could not refuse to sell': Lowndes, *Sketch*, p. 107.

[27] During the committee stage Mahon observed that 'there really would be no danger of a desire to suppress published works, unless, indeed, they were works of an immoral or anti-social tendency, the suppression of which would, of course, as we should all admit, be a public benefit. But to guard against all possibility of such a danger, a clause has been inserted in the present bill, giving

a power in the Judicial Committee of the Privy Council to license re-publication, its stated aim 'to provide against the suppression of Books of importance to the public'. As in Talfourd's original draft, conditions could be set as was thought fit.[28]

DEPOSIT COPIES

The history of the law relating to deposit copies is full of battles and controversies.[29] The 1710 Act included deposit clauses: section 5 required printers to deliver nine copies of every book, on best paper, to the warehouse-keeper of the Stationers' Company before publication. This created nine deposit libraries in the United Kingdom: the Royal Library, the university libraries of Oxford and Cambridge, the libraries of the four universities in Scotland (St Andrews, Edinburgh, Glasgow, Aberdeen), Sion College, and the Faculty of Advocates Library, Edinburgh. There were heavy financial penalties for non-compliance.

Notwithstanding the possible fines, the book trade was extremely resistant to the concept, and the libraries often did not receive their due. The Copyright (Ireland) Act 1801 added Trinity College and King's Inn Dublin to the list of deposit libraries, so demanding eleven copies in all. In 1806 Edward Christian, the Downing professor of the laws of England at Cambridge, began a well-publicised effort to ensure that the law was clarified and properly enforced. Christian's attempt to get a bill passed failed after a good deal of argument, but in *Cambridge University* v. *Bryer*, the court confirmed Christian's position; all books were subject to the deposit requirement, whether or not they had been registered.[30] Statutory clarification came in the 1814 Act. Eleven copies had to be delivered to the warehouse-keeper on demand in writing within one year of publication. The

the Privy Council Judicial Committee power to license works for publication, by other parties, in the case of suppression, being attempted by the proprietors of the copyright': *Hansard, Parliamentary debates* (3rd series), lx, 1354 (6 April 1842).

28 Section 5 was not modified during the passage of the bill, and was enacted unchanged.

29 See Robert C. B. Partridge, *The history of the legal deposit of books throughout the British Empire* (1938); John Feather, *Publishing, piracy and politics* (1994), ch. 4.

30 (1806) 16 East 317.

only concession was that second editions did not have to be delivered if the additions were printed and delivered separately. Again the penalty was the value of the volumes, plus £5 per volume, plus costs. The book trade continued to regard this as an intolerable tax on their business, and in 1818 secured a select committee which conducted a detailed investigation. However, the committee was divided and made no recommendation about the number of deposit copies.

In 1836, the radical MP James Silk Buckingham brought in a bill to abolish legal deposit entirely. After amendments in committee, the privileges of the British Museum and the English universities were reinstated, as were those of the Faculty of Advocates Library and Trinity College Dublin.[31] This was the situation which Talfourd inherited. His approach was to confirm the existing position, but he attempted to refine and clarify some of the procedures. He also gave the British Museum a unique privilege: delivery to the British Museum was made compulsory, whereas the other libraries had to make demand in writing.

The 1837 bill treated all the deposit libraries together in a single clause. Five copies (for the usual libraries) were required on demand within twelve months of publication. The publisher could deliver to the libraries themselves or to the Stationers' Company. The penalty for each default was again £5 plus the value of the book. The British Museum's copy was to be on the best paper on which the work was printed, the others to be on the paper on which the largest number of copies of the work was printed. The obligation did not extend to subsequent editions unless they contained changes. If there were changes, it was acceptable to deliver 'a printed copy of such additions and alterations only, printed in a uniform manner with the former edition of such Book'.

The 1838 and 1839 versions were more demanding in their details. There were now two clauses, distinguishing between the British Museum and the other four libraries. The British Museum was to receive one copy of every book, now including new editions containing additions or alterations. It was to be bound, sewed or stitched, on best paper, 'together with all Maps, Prints or other Engravings belonging thereto, finished and coloured in the same

[31] Legal Deposit Act 1836, 6 & 7 Wm. 4 c. 110.

manner as the best Copies of the same shall be published'. The requirement that copies should be bound was new to English copyright law. Presumably it was intended to prevent the expense of binding from falling on the British Museum. The timings were also tightened: delivery had to be within one calendar month after the book was first sold, published, or offered for sale within the bills of mortality, or within three months if the book was exclusively sold, published, advertised or offered for sale in any other part of the United Kingdom. The book had to be delivered to the Museum between ten and four (not including Sundays), and given to a librarian, officer or other authorised person, who had to give a receipt in writing.[32] These timings were altered several times. In 1840 the periods were extended to three and six months respectively. They reverted to one and three months in the remaining versions, with a new twelve-month period if the book was first sold elsewhere in the British Dominions.

This clause was redrafted in the House of Lords, as a result of amendments suggested by the archbishop of Canterbury, William Howley. The archbishop was *ex officio* one of the principal trustees of the British Museum, and his separately printed amendments were all concerned to safeguard the museum's interests.[33] The new version of this clause did not represent a radical change, but the drafting of the requirements was made even more specific. For instance, a new edition was now explicitly defined to include additions and alterations whether or not these appeared in the text or in any associated maps, prints and engravings. This reflects a sharp, practical understanding of the publishing trade. The basic obligation was to deliver one copy of every book, including new editions containing additions and alterations, regardless of whether the first edition was published before or after the Act, and including new editions of every book where a previous edition had not been delivered, to the British Museum.

The other four copies were to be delivered to the Stationers' Company within a month of a demand in writing to the publisher (up to twelve months from publication). Delivery to the individual libraries was permitted. These copies did not have to be on best

[32] Good Friday and Christmas Day were added to this list from 1840, and Ash Wednesday was added in the Act itself. It seems that 'letter-of-the-law' compliance was expected.

[33] *HL Papers* 1842 (133a).

paper. The penalty for non-compliance was £5 plus the value of the book, as before, but it was now stated 'to be recovered by the Librarian of the Library for the use whereof such Copy should have been delivered'. Final versions of the clause added a requirement that copies should be delivered 'in the like condition as the copies prepared for sale by the publisher thereof'.

REGISTRATION

Although there was an early link with censorship, the Stationers' Company register's chief practical use was in infringement actions. As a result, the works registered were often simply those most susceptible to piracy, notably plays, poems, sermons and pamphlets. Partridge records that after the 1842 Act 'almost as many trade labels and catalogues were registered as were books'.[34] Nevertheless, registration was of obvious use for evidential matters such as date of publication and transfers of ownership. Failure to register did not affect copyright as such, but it was a necessary preliminary to an action at law for copyright infringement. Later attempts to combine registration and deposit came to nothing, and were ultimately rendered unneccesary by the United Kingdom's accession to the Berne Convention (1886), which required the abolition of the registration system.

The legal system of registration had begun with the Act of Anne, although the Stationers' Company had been keeping its own register book for some considerable time. The 1710 Act (section 2) provided that a copyright holder could not sue for the statutory penalties 'unless Title to the Copy of such Book or Books hereafter published shall, before such Publication, be entered in the Register Book of the Company of Stationers, in such Manner as hath been usual.' It was also possible for anyone printing a book to register the proprietor's consent, and thereby guard against the statutory penalties. It cost 6d to make an entry, and the register could be inspected for nothing, although a certificate of an entry was 6d.[35] Under the 1814 Act (section 5),

[34] Partridge, *Legal deposit of books*, p. 92.

[35] There was also a severe £20 penalty for a clerk who refused or neglected to make an entry when required to do so: s. 3.

registration was required within one month of the book's being sold, published or offered for sale within the bills of mortality, or within three months if sold elsewhere in the United Kingdom. The fees were now 2s per entry, 1s to inspect, and 1s for a certificate of entry. Failure to register rendered the publishers liable to a penalty of £5 plus eleven times the price of the book (i.e. the number of deposit copies), though copyright was stated to be unaffected by such failure.[36]

Talfourd did little to alter the underlying system of registration, although the layout of the schedules was formalised. The copyright proprietor could make an original entry in the registry book listing title, date of first publication, name and place of abode of proprietor, according to the forms in Schedules 2 and 3. Assignments were dealt with in Schedules 4 and 5. All the bills provided that no original entry could be made without the written consent of the publisher, again in the form given in a schedule, but this requirement was deleted in the House of Lords. No mention of the cost of an entry was made in the 1837 bill, but the first 1838 version set the fee at 2s, quickly rising in the second version to the 5s figure that was enacted. The fee for inspection of the register remained at 1s, though a cost of a certified copy of entry rose sharply to 5s. As in the past, the entry served as prima facie proof of proprietorship or assignment of copyright or licence. After 1841 the clause was expanded to cover dramatic and musical pieces, so that a register entry also provided prima facie evidence of the right of representation or performance. False entry was an indictable misdemeanour. Anyone aggrieved by an entry in the registry book could apply for an order for it to be altered or expunged.[37] Talfourd had intended that application could be by petition or motion, but the reference to petitions was deleted in

[36] This clause was enacted to confirm *Beckford* v. *Hood* (1798) 7 TR 620 and *Baller* v. *Walker* (cited 2 Atk. 94). These cases held that failure to make an entry in the register did not affect copyright, since the remedies were cumulative: although the special action on the case for statutory remedies was precluded, the civil action for damages was not.

[37] Unfortunately, lack of foresight in the drafting left the courts without the power to reinstate an entry once deleted, which made them extremely reluctant to expunge entries where there was an unresolved dispute as to title. If necessary, however, the courts could rule that the plaintiff could not use the entry as prima facie evidence of title against the defendant at trial: *Chappell* v. *Purday* (1843) 12 M & W 303; *ex. p. Davidson* (1853) 2 E & B 577.

the House of Lords. As before, there was no obligation to register, although this was a precondition to an action for infringement.[38]

INTERNATIONAL COPYRIGHT

Foreign 'piracy' of British books was an old problem, but it became much more urgent as the market for books in English expanded in the nineteenth century.[39] Publishers and authors felt understandable annoyance as their books were sold and reprinted elsewhere in large numbers without any right to compensation. On the Continent, publishers such as Galignani, Baudry and Baillère first sought to service the market for British travellers, but soon expanded their horizons to the American market. In 1830 Baillère even opened a shop in London, producing predictable resentment among the native publishers. In so far as he sold foreign books his trade was quite legal, but there is evidence of considerable sales of foreign reprints of British books. This was not only a breach of copyright, but a serious customs offence.[40] Another famous continental publisher, Tauchnitz, was unusual in his efforts to obtain permission for his reprints. American publishers were also reprinting popular British books as soon as they could get them. A few publishers would pay authors for early copies of the sheets, but this was not an obligation. It was perfectly legal for American publishers to reprint British works without permission or acknowledgment, the only illegality occuring on the rare occasions when the reprints were imported into Britain.

All these issues could have been dealt with by a functioning

[38] Perhaps surprisingly, it was held to be sufficient simply to register before issuing the writ: *Warne* v. *Lawrence* (1886) 54 LT 371. Here the plaintiffs had registered their title earlier in the day on which they issued the writ. This had the obvious drawback that the defendant had no way of discovering the plaintiff's title in the register before the act of infringement. In contrast, no copyright was acquired by registration before publication: *Correspondent Newspaper Co.* v. *Saunders* (1865) 11 Jur (NS) 540.

[39] For a full account, see Simon Harcourt Nowell-Smith, *International copyright law and the publisher in the reign of Queen Victoria* (Oxford, 1968).

[40] The troubles of Wordsworth and Scott in this regard have already been mentioned. See also Giles Barber, 'Galignani and the publication of English books in France from 1800 to 1852', *The Library*, 5th ser., 16 (1961) 267–86; James J. Barnes, 'Galignani and the publication of English books in France: a postscript', *The Library*, 5th ser., 25 (1970), 294–313.

system of international copyright. Talfourd sought to address part of the problem in his 1837 bill (section 11, Schedule 4). This would have allowed authors outside the British Dominions to register their works, if they named a publisher within the British Dominions. On publication by this British publisher, the author would have had copyright within the British Dominions with remedies as for a native author. This would have reversed the decision in *Clementi* v. *Walker*, where it was held that to gain the protection of the statute, first publication had to be made in Britain.[41]

However, the clause was dropped after pressure from the government, which regarded international copyright as a matter of public policy, and an unsuitable subject for back-bench legislation. Also, the government was itself planning to introduce an international copyright bill, and this was done in 1838. Recognising the futility and potential harm to domestic industry which would result from a unilateral stance, the bill proposed simply that the government should be authorised to make agreements with other countries willing to offer reciprocal copyright protection to British authors. Although there was some opposition, the government's position prevailed and the bill was passed.[42] It gave the government the power to negotiate agreements with other countries, and validate them by Order in council. In fact this power was not used until 1846, when an agreement was made with Prussia. After this the network of bilateral and even multilateral agreements began to grow. It finally found fruition in the Berne Convention.

INFRINGEMENT

The definition of infringement is crucial for any copyright statute, since it draws the boundary between what is protected and what is public. The Act of Anne made it illegal to 'print, reprint, import, or cause to be printed, reprinted or imported' books without written consent signed in the presence of two 'credible' witnesses. Knowing sale without consent was likewise prohibited. The

[41] (1824) 2 B & C 861. cf. later *Jeffereys* v. *Boosey* (1854) 4 HL Cas 815.
[42] International Copyright Act 1838, 1 & 2 Vict. c. 59.

statutory penalty was forfeiture of the infringing copies to the proprietor, 'who shall forthwith Damask and make Waste Paper of them', plus a fine of 1d a sheet, half to the Crown, and half to whoever sued for it.[43] These fines were increased to 3d per sheet in 1801. There was a new £10 fine for importing books first published in the United Kingdom and reprinted elsewhere, and a new power to reward customs officers for seizing such books. There was, however, an exception for books not printed in the United Kingdom in the previous twenty years, and also for books reprinted abroad but inserted in a collection which was largely first composed and written abroad.[44] The list of infringing acts remained unchanged by the 1814 Act, as did the penalties, although the reference to 'credible' witnesses disappears.

The infringement clause in Talfourd's 1837 bill was to a large extent modelled on earlier Acts. The prohibited acts were printing or causing to be printed within British Dominions any book (or any portion of a book) in which there was subsisting copyright without consent of the proprietor; importing such a book; selling, publishing, exposing to sale, causing to be sold, published or exposed to sale, or possessing for sale such a book knowing it to have been unlawfully printed or imported.[45] The proprietor's rights could be defended by bringing a special action on the case, to recover minimum damages of 40s, plus costs. Again there was a special penalty for importing foreign reprints of U.K. books: the fine was £10 as before.[46] The exception for books brought in as part of a collection was likewise reproduced, but was deleted after 1839.

A notable innovation was the reference to 'any portion of a book'. As with the attempt to include parts of volumes within the definition of 'book', this phrase sought to remove doubt in cases

[43] To damask is to deface or destroy by stamping or marking with figures or lines (*Shorter Oxford English Dictionary*).

[44] Sections. 1, 7.

[45] Note the prohibition of secondary infringement, with a requirement of *mens rea*. There was a common law right to prevent unauthorised publication of an unpublished manuscript, so Talfourd (understandably) did not address this. See, e.g. *Burnett* v. *Chetwood* (1720) 2 Mer 441; *Webb* v. *Rose* (1732) cited Amb 695; 2 Bro PC 138; *Forrester* v. *Waller* (1741) cited Amb 695; 2 Bro PC 138; *Macklin* v. *Richardson* (1770) Amb 694; *Duke of Queensbury* v. *Shebbeare* (1758) 2 Eden 329.

[46] Importing for hire was added to the list of prohibitions in 1842, and the fine was specifically divided between the customs officer and the copyright proprietor.

where only part of a book was copied. Later versions only prohibited the printing of a portion of a book 'to such extent as shall be injurious to the property therein'. The phrase was deleted entirely in the House of Lords. One 1838 modification proved extremely controversial, when Talfourd added abridgements to the list of prohibited acts (section 19). This would have represented an about-turn in approach, and Talfourd was eventually forced to concede this point. Another late change, again effected by amendments in the House of Lords, was the decision to add hiring to the list of prohibited acts.[47]

The stance on abridgements seems to have been part of a larger attempt to define with more precision those parts of a copyright work which were available for public use. Remarkably, Talfourd's original bill included a clause easily recognisable as a 'fair use' exception, saving 'the publication of any extracts fairly and bona fide made from any Book for the purpose of criticism, observation or argument, or to any translation into another language, or abridgment fairly made of any book' from the infringement provisions. Talfourd thought that he was enacting the case law much as it stood, but the clause was changed significantly on several occasions, and did not survive the House of Lords amendments.[48] A survey of the relevant precedents in copyright generally is helpful in explaining this apparent conundrum. There was a clear acknowledgment that copyright material should be protected, but only within certain limits.

The courts were alert to the dangers of recognising copyright in particular ideas or subjects, and were extremely reluctant to intervene if unoriginal or trivial material was involved. In *Longman* v. *Winchester*, the plaintiff's *Imperial calendar* was copied verbatim. Lord Eldon granted an injunction, 'but I have said nothing, that has a tendency to prevent any person from giving to the public a work of this kind; if it is the fair fruit of original labour: the subject being open to all the world'.[49] Simi-

[47] 1842c, s. 15.

[48] A similar clause, recognisable to modern lawyers, reappeared in the 1911 Act: s. 2(1)(i) permitted 'any fair dealing with the work for the purposes of private study, research, criticism, review or newspaper summary'. See now Copyright, Designs and Patents Act 1988, s. 29.

[49] (1809) 16 Ves 272, and see also *Matthewson* v. *Stockdale* (1806) 12 Ves 270, *Schove* v. *Schimnke* (1886) 33 Ch D 546. This line of case law is crowned by the famous case of *Kenrick & Co.* v. *Lawrence & Co.* (1890) 25 QBD 99.

larly in *Trusler* v. *Murray*, discussing an alleged piracy of *Trusler's Chronology: 'Time's Telescope'*, the court acknowledged that any chronological work must necessarily relate the same facts, and that these were free for use.[50] Trusler won because he was able to show that although parts of the defendant's work differed, in general it was the same, and fourteen pages were copied without a single alteration. Lord Chancellor Erskine, commenting on this case in *Matthewson* v. *Stockdale*, stressed that Trusler would have had no case if the defendant had been endeavouring to make improvements and additions.[51] Lord Ellenborough's approach in *Cary* v. *Kearsley* was much cited:

> That part of the work of one author that is found in another is not of itself piracy, or sufficient to support an action; a man may fairly adopt part of the work of another: he may so make use of another's labours for the promotion of science, and the benefit of the public: but having done so, the question will be, Was the matter so taken used fairly with that view, and without what I may term the *animus furandi*? . . . While I shall think myself bound to secure every man in the enjoyment of his copy right, one must not put manacles on science.[52]

The law on substantial taking was not yet particularly well developed, since the early reported cases generally involve obvious piracies. In *Tonson* v. *Walker* the defendant had printed *Paradise lost* with a total of 1,500 notes assembled from all the former editions (Tonson's being still in copyright): twenty-eight new notes were held insufficient to excuse him.[53] Nor was it arguable that Pope and Swift's *Miscellanies* could be published freely because they contained many pieces which were out of copyright: an injunction was granted to protect the compilation as a whole.[54] In his 1823 treatise on copyright Godson stated that 'a compilation may be different from a treatise published by itself; but certain limits must be fixed to the transcripts. It must not be allowed to sweep up all modern works, or an Encyclopaedia would completely destroy all literary property.'[55] Even where there was

[50] (1789) 1 East 363n.

[51] (1806) 12 Ves 270. See likewise *Sayre* v. *Moore* (1785) 1 East 361n.

[52] (1802) 4 Esp 168. [53] (1752) cited Amb 405.

[54] *Motte* v. *Falkner* (1753) 4 Burr Rep 2353; 1 Bla Rep 331. See also *Mason* v. *Murray* (1777) Dick 536.

[55] Richard Godson, *A practical treatise on the law of patents for invention and of copyright*, 2nd edn (1840), p. 233.

obvious taking, there remained difficulties and grey areas. In *Planché* v. *Braham* the plaintiff had written the English libretto for Weber's opera *Oberon*, which was performed at Covent Garden with the defendant in the main role. The defendant then had another libretto written for the same opera, and this was performed at his own theatre. He used the plaintiff's words for 'two or three of the most striking airs', and faced an action under the Dramatic Representation Act 1833. A sympathetically directed jury found that there had been a representation of part of the plaintiff's production.[56] The potential uncertainty perhaps explains Talfourd's efforts to include 'portion of a book' within the statute.

Another troublesome issue was the use of quotations from a copyright work. Lord Eldon acknowledged that it was hard to draw the line between legitimate and illegitimate quotation: 'There is no doubt, that a man cannot under the pretence of quotation, publish either the whole or part of another's work; though he may use, what is in all cases difficult to define, fair quotation.'[57] There was generally considerable sympathy for the defendant when quotations were used in a review of a work, even if these were fairly extensive.[58] In contrast, where a short cut was taken in the production of a saleable work, the courts were less tolerant. In a case decided in the February before the 1842 Act was passed, the defendant published a 790-page volume, comprising 34 pages of his own critical essay, and 756 pages of pieces and extracts, allegedly to illustrate points in his essay: 733 lines were taken from copyright works by Thomas Campbell, including six entire poems. An injunction was granted, the court fully

[56] (1837) 4 Bing NC 17. [57] *Wilkins* v. *Aikin* (1810) 17 Ves 422.

[58] See, for instance, *Whittingham* v. *Wooler* (1817) 2 Swan 428. The publishers of a cheap periodical, the *Stage*, published extracts from a farce. Less than seven pages out of forty were used, no entire act or scene was taken, and only 160 copies were sold. Sir William Grant M.R. clearly thought the action too trivial for words, and refused a perpetual injunction. The test was later refined in *Chatterton* v. *Cave* (1878) 3 App Cas 403 at 492 (H.L.). Lord Hatherley's approach became standard: 'Books are published with an expectation, if not a desire, that they will be criticised in reviews, and if deemed valuable that parts of them will be used as affording illustrations by way of quotation, or the like, – and if the quantity taken be neither substantial nor material, if, as it has been expressed by some judges, "a fair use" only be made of the publication, no wrong is done and no action can be brought.'

recognising that it was the 'mass of pirated matter, which, in fact, constitutes the value of the volume'.[59]

There were philosophical differences concerning the correct approach to abridgements, and it is possible to perceive a change in attitude later in the nineteenth century. In early cases, abridgements are regarded with favour, as original works in their own right. Lord Chancellor Apsley explained 'That to constitute a true and proper abridgment of a work the whole must be preserved in its sense: and then the act of abridgement is an act of understanding, employed in carrying a large work into a smaller compass, and rendering it less expensive, and more convenient both to the time and use of the reader. Which made an abridgment in the nature of a new and a meritorious work.' This case involved Newbery's abridgement of Dr Hawkesworth's voyages. Newbery had consulted Blackstone J before making his abridgement: 'They had spent some hours together and were agreed that an abridgment, where the understanding is employed in retrenching unnecessary and uninteresting circumstances, which rather deaden the narration, is not an act of plagiarism upon the original work, not against any property of the author in it, but an allowable and meritorious work.' Given this weight of support, it is unsurprising that the abridgement was protected.[60] Abridgements were part of publishing practice, and were rarely challenged.[61]

The courts were certainly aware that an incompetent abridge-

[59] *Campbell* v. *Scott* (1842) 11 Simons 31. For an earlier example see *Roworth* v. *Wilkes* (1807) 1 Camp 98, where 75 of the 118 pages of a work on fencing were transcribed into an encyclopaedia. This was found to be piracy, Lord Ellenborough holding that the author's intentions were irrelevant: 'it is enough that the publication complained of is in substance a copy, whereby a work vested in another is prejudiced'. See also *Mawman* v. *Tegg* (1826) 2 Russ 385, where the plaintiffs could show that Tegg's encyclopaedia took articles verbatim from their own. There was doubt as to whether the similiarities merited an injunction against the entire work, since they amounted only to a small fraction of the whole.

[60] *Newbery's case*, Lofft Rep 775.

[61] This practice worked against Johnson's publishers in *Dodsley* v. *Kinnersley* (1761) Amb 403. They had produced a two-volume edition of *Rasselas*, and objected when the defendant printed part of the narrative in a magazine. Tonson and several other booksellers were examined for the plaintiffs, and all agreed (unsurprisingly) that the sale of the book was prejudiced by the magazine. However, the defendant called evidence to show that it was usual to print extracts of new books in magazines without the permission of the author – and often at the request of the author to help the sale of the book. The plaintiffs' own actions showed this custom and usage, and there was held to be no prejudice

ment could work to the detriment of an author, and were also ready to prevent palpable piracies under the name of abridgements.[62] Nevertheless, there was a strong belief that the process of abridgement was a legitimate one:

> Where books are colourably shortened only, they are undoubtedly within the meaning of the Act of Parliament, and are an [*sic*] mere evasion of the statute, and cannot be called an abridgment. But this must not be carried so far as to restrain persons from making a real and fair abridgment, for abridgments may with great propriety be called a new book, because not only the paper and print, but the invention, learning and judgment of the author is shewn in them, and in many cases are extremely useful, though in some instances prejudicial, by mistaking and curtailing the sense of an author.[63]

There are few early nineteenth-century cases. An injunction was granted to prevent publication of opera airs arranged for dancing, held to be insufficiently distinct from the plaintiff's arrangement for piano. Even so, the making of true abridgements and digests was still regarded as legitimate, since they 'are in their nature original'.[64] The practice of publishing abridgements was mushrooming in the hands of Thomas Tegg and his ilk, and it is understandable that Talfourd would have wished to address the subject in his bill. Cases after the Act show a greater reluctance to condone abridgement, and distinguish more sharply between legitimate use and unfair taking. Given the part that Dickens had taken in the copyright campaign, it seems little coincidence that an abridgement of *A Christmas carol* was challenged soon after the 1842 Act, Talfourd appearing as counsel for Dickens.[65] The

to the plaintiffs since they had published an abstract themselves in the *London Chronicle*.

62 e.g. *Butterworth* v. *Robinson* (1801) 5 Ves 709, where the publication of a colourable abridgement of the *Term Reports* was restrained. Lord Chancellor Loughborough described the abridgement as 'an extremely illiberal publication'. However, on law reports compare *Sweet* v. *Benning* (1855) 16 CB 459.

63 *Gyles* v. *Wilcox* (1740) 2 Atk 151, *per* Lord Hardwicke. Nineteenth-century commentators in general agreed: Godson, *Treatise*, 2nd edn, p. 238; Robert Maugham, *A treatise on the law of literary property* (1828), p. 129. However, Copinger expresses doubt in certain cases: 'It seems a very unsatisfactory answer to an original author, who has been injured by an abridgment, to say that because the wrongful taker has exhibited talent and ingenuity, both in the taking and in the use which he has made of it, the original author has no remedy': Walter Arthur Copinger, *The law of copyright in works of literature and art*, 1st edn (1870), pp. 101–2.

64 *D'Almaine* v. *Boosey* (1835) 1 Y & C Ex 288.

65 *Dickens* v. *Lee* (1844) 8 Jur 183.

defendant had published 'A Christmas Ghost Story, re-originated from the original, by Charles Dickens Esq., and analytically condensed expressly for this work'. He argued that his colourable alterations amounted to abridgement, but Knight Bruce V.-C. showed considerable resistance to this approach: 'I am not aware that one man has the right to abridge the works of another.' The defendant's argument that his penny text was no competition for Dickens's five shilling edition was also rejected: this was 'mere borrowing' of a valuable property. The line between fair and unfair abridgement nevertheless remained shadowy.[66]

Translations were another rather grey area. It was clear 'That every person, who employs his time and abilities in making translations from the ancient classic authors, justly acquires a copyright in the productions'.[67] In one case a translation in English of a contemporary work written in Latin was restrained, since 'the book was only intended to the learned and for that reason was wrote in Latin'.[68] Translations into English from other languages generated little discussion, because often there was no English copyright holder to protest.[69] If the English translation was itself copied, the courts could intervene. In *Wyatt* v. *Barnard* the plaintiff printed selected patent specifications in a magazine, some of which had been translated from French and German. The defendant copied them, and filed an affidavit that 'stated the usual practice among publishers of magazines and monthly publications was to take from each other articles translated from foreign languages, or become public property, as having appeared in other works'. Lord Eldon was not sympathetic, but some of his

[66] See *Sweet* v. *Benning* (1855) 16 CB 459 at 483. The publishers of the *Monthly Digest* took head notes and marginal notes from all the law reports, and arranged them under analytical heads. They were challenged by the publishers of the *Jurist*, whose material amounted to about a twentieth of the *Digest*. The decision was three to one that this was a piracy, but all four judges emphasised how difficult it was to draw the line between fair use and piracy in such a case.

[67] Godson, *Treatise*, 2nd edn, p. 241, and see Yates J in *Millar* v. *Taylor*.

[68] *Burnett* v. *Chetwood* (1720) 2 Meriv 441n: arguably the injunction was granted because of the work's contents.

[69] Though see *Wright* v. *Tallis* (1845) 1 CB 893. Here the plaintiff had published a book which fraudulently purported to be a translation of a work by Sturm, an eminent German religious author whose works enjoyed great popularity when translated into English. This book was then pirated by the defendant. The publication was characterised as a transaction *crimen falsi*, so there was no valid and subsisting copyright.

resentment may have been generated by his perception that the booksellers were trying to make their own concerted practices replace the law.[70] He refused to distinguish translations from other works, concluding that every translation was an original work.[71] It was assumed from this decision that translation of an English copyright work could not therefore be piracy, although this view was not universally accepted.[72]

A review of the various draft provisions concerning abridgement and related exceptions shows how much uncertainty these topics generated. In the 1837 draft (section 13) an abridgement 'fairly made' was within the special saving, although the proposed statutory power to grant injunction in case of piracy could not be used where part of a book was copied 'for the purpose of criticism, argument or observation thereon' (section 27). In the first 1838 bill (section 19) abridgement was added to the list of prohibited acts. In the second bill it returned to the special saving, as regards 'any abridgment of a book fairly and bona fide made', where it remained during 1839. In 1840 the reference to abridgement was deleted from the special saving, and from that point it was not mentioned.

The other aspects of the special saving were not altered so significantly. Talfourd intended to give the 'publication of any extracts fairly and bona fide made from any Book for the purpose of criticism, observation or argument' statutory legitimacy, in effect enacting the case law.[73] It was likewise legitimate to

[70] (1814) 3 Ves & B 77. For more of Lord Eldon's views on book trade practice see *Hogg* v. *Kirby* (1803) 8 Ves 215: 'with reference to the interests of the public therefore I should not be inclined to make a decree upon the understanding among booksellers'. Holdsworth is extremely critical of some of Lord Eldon's decisions on copyright: Sir William Holdsworth, *A history of English law*, XIII, p. 637.

[71] (1814) 3 Ves & B 77. See also *Murray* v. *Bogue* (1853) 1 Drew 353. Bogue started a series of guides to rival Murray's, and used a translation of a German guide admittedly based on Murray's but found to be substantially original. It was acknowledged that if Murray's book had been literally translated by the German author, and then translated back by Bogue, that the court could have restrained the indirect piracy of Murray's work.

[72] Copinger, *Law of copyright*, p. 47. Cf. Scrutton's opinion that: 'There is no market in England for the translation into a foreign tongue of an English work' but that in principle this would amount to a clear infringement of copyright in the original: Scrutton, *Law of copyright*, p. 128.

[73] During the second reading of the 1838 bill Talfourd explained that the prohibition of extracts made purely for the compiler's gain was merely declaratory of the present law, but the prohibition of unauthorised abridgements was

translate a book into another language. In addition, versions from 1838 onwards also clarified the status and ownership of the translation: 'the Copyright in every translation shall be deemed to be the property of the Translator thereof and his assignees as though it were an original work'. However, Talfourd's sense that a statutory saving would be more secure than the slightly diffuse case law did not prove a sufficiently weighty argument in favour of adopting his clause. As has already been noted, it was deleted in the House of Lords, leaving both extracts and translations subject to existing precedents. A similar clause was eventually enacted in the 1911 Act, after a considerable body of case law had been decided.[74]

As well as addressing these general issues, Talfourd also sought to rationalise the law in certain specific categories of work. The government's resistance to his plans for consolidation meant that some of his ideas were shelved (notably those for engravings), but he was still able to make some useful improvements.

PERIODICAL WORKS

Talfourd was concerned to clarify the copyright position with regard to periodical works. He had an extensive knowledge of this subject himself, being a veteran contributor to literary magazines. There was little case law of direct relevance.[75] The clause as first drafted was surprisingly insensitive to authorial feelings. The

new. There was immediate opposition in the House, even from those in favour of the principle of the bill. Wakley was later to object to the clause on the grounds that it 'would prevent elegant extracts being put into school-books', and protested that the existing law was already 'very stringent'. In response, Godson, the author of a well-known treatise on copyright, spoke in favour of the wording. Mahon confirmed that 'it was desired by the clause to re-enact the existing law with reference to extracts. It was quite evident, that any extracts for criticism, observation, or argument would not come within the law as it at present stood; but it was necessary to adopt some measure for the prevention of the artifices which are constantly resorted to in order to profit by extracts from popular works': *Hansard, Parliamentary debates* (3rd series), lxii, 890 (20 April 1842).

[74] Section 2(1)(i).

[75] Though for related disputes see *Hogg* v. *Kirby* (1803) 8 Ves 215; *Brooke* v. *Chitty* (1831) 2 Coop 216; *Sweet* v. *Cater* (1841) 5 Jur 68.

publisher of a periodical work which included contributions from others was 'deemed to be the author' of it, although any author could reserve copyright in a particular article with the publisher's written consent, and subject to its continued publication as part of such a work.[76] The next version was considerably expanded and more explicit. It provided that if a publisher had employed someone to compose something for publication in the periodical, and had paid for it, then he would have a property in the piece. This property would give him 'the same rights and advantages as if he were the actual Author thereof', notably the same term of copyright as for books. It was specifically stated, however, that an author could reserve (by express or implied contract) the right to publish his contribution in a separate form, and that he would then be entitled to the copyright in that separate publication, without prejudice to the original publisher's right. In early versions the author's receipt for payment was made prima facie evidence that the copyright had been supplied under employment, and was vested in the publisher without formal assignment.[77] This provision was deleted after 1840.

The version enacted (section 18) added a further complication. After twenty-eight years, the right of publication in a separate form automatically reverted to the author for the remainder of the full copyright term. Nor could the publisher publish the essay separately without the author's prior consent. The provision allowing the author to make specific advance reservation of the right of separate publication remained unchanged. A separate clause (which became section 19 of the Act) granted the proprietor of the copyright in 'any encyclopaedia, review, magazine, periodical work, or other work published in a series of books or parts' the right to register the title, either on first publication, or (for existing titles) on first publication after the Act.

[76] 1838a, s. 21. The reference to 'publisher' was later extended to include projector and conductor also.

[77] This made little difference in practice, since the courts were prepared to imply an agreement where necessary. See *Sweet* v. *Benning* (1855) 3 WR 519 where barristers writing reports of cases for the *Jurist* were paid by the sheet, with no explicit reference to the copyright. The defendant here argued that the plaintiff publishers had no copyright within section 18. It was held to be an implied condition that the publisher, having paid for the reports, acquired copyright therein. If it had been otherwise the author could republish the following day in a separate form without the publisher having any benefit.

These sections appear to have worked tolerably well, although one area of doubt was caused by use of the word 'property' to describe what the publisher was given. Talfourd later argued successfully that before the 1842 Act copyright could pass only by assignment, and that section 18 did not alter this: section 18 intended only to allow proprietors of periodicals to protect themselves from the piracies of strangers, and therefore granted a licence for the particular purpose but not an assignment.[78] It was also necessary to take care to address the specific requirements of section 18: a defendant publisher who was taking articles from a Longmans publication escaped an injunction when the affidavit showed only that Longmans paid the editor, and not that the editor paid the contributors.[79]

One important category of periodical publication was not specifically addressed in the Act – newspapers. Newspapers generally appeared very little concerned with claiming or defending copyright in their articles.[80] It was part of life in the industry that the provincial papers would borrow news and articles from the London dailies, and there would have been little sympathy from the courts for an action to restrain the publication of old news. It took the injured feelings of several eminent engineers to bring *Bell* v. *Whitehead* to court, and even here the lord chancellor plainly considered the issue to be a waste of his time. There had been a controversy concerning the velocity attainable on railways, with Mr Brunell and Dr Lardner taking opposing positions. The *Monthly Chronicle* had published an article on the subject, called 'The Great Western Railway enquiry'. The *Railway Times* had published a different article, containing an extract (in fact written by Lardner) from the *Chronicle* article. Although this amounted to about a quarter of the original article, *The Times* also published reports from other engineers including Brunell, and added

[78] *Bishop of Hereford* v. *Griffin* (1848) 16 Sim 190. Followed in *Smith* v. *Johnson* (1863) 4 Giff 637. An extension of this argument was used in *Stevens* v. *Benning* (1854) 1 K & J 168. An author signed an agreement with a publisher allowing him to publish a particular work. When this publisher went bankrupt, all his rights were sold to Stevens. The agreement was held to be personal contract with the original publisher and not an assignment of copyright, so Stevens was not entitled to publish.

[79] *Browne* v. *Cooke* (1846) 11 Jur 77.

[80] There were few petitions against the copyright bills from newspaper men. See ch. 4, p. 74.

comments and observations. The lord chancellor held that the extract was clearly published for the purpose of criticism, in the tradition of the *Edinburgh* and *Quarterly* Reviews. He refused an injunction, apparently in contemplation of the floodgates argument: 'If I were to entertain this application of the plaintiffs, how could I decline to entertain a similar application in the case of those newspapers from the columns of which articles have been extracted and printed in other newspapers, for the purpose of questioning or criticising the opinions expressed therein?'[81]

Talfourd's Act did provide an interesting legacy for the newspaper trade though, on the question of registration. In 1870 the *Field* brought an action for piracy against another journal. Astonishingly, Sir Robert Malins V.-C. held that a newspaper was not a book for the purposes of section 2 and that, although it was a work published in a series and therefore within section 18, it did not need to be registered. His view was that (somehow) the proprietor had sufficient property in all its contents as would entitle him to sue for piracy, although he refused an injunction for this particular 'insignificant matter'.[82] However, in *Walter* v. *Howe* Lord Jessel M.R. held that a newspaper was indeed a 'book' under section 2, and also a periodical work under section 18. He refused to follow the earlier decision, saying that it was opposed to the plain wording of the Act, and that a decision in accordance with it would be 'virtually overruling the Act'. This approach defeated the plaintiff editor of the unregistered *Times*.[83]

DRAMATIC AND MUSICAL WORKS

Bulwer Lytton's Dramatic Copyright Act 1833 granted authors of dramatic works 'the sole liberty of representing [their works] at any place of dramatic entertainment'. This Act covered 'any Tragedy, Comedy, Play, Opera, Farce, or any other Dramatic Piece or Entertainment'. Talfourd's definition borrowed this wording, though oratorio, and musical and scenic entertainment

[81] (1839) 8 LJ Ch 141.
[82] *Cox* v. *Land and Water Journal Co.* (1870) 18 WR 519.
[83] (1881) 17 Ch D 708.

were added (section 2).[84] No specific definition of musical composition was enacted, although there was venerable case law to show that musical compositions were included within the term 'book'.[85] By section 1 of this Act, the term mirrored the copyright term; life or twenty-eight years for printed and published pieces, or a perpetuity for unpublished works.

Talfourd sought to extend the right of representation in line with his proposed increase in copyright term. Early versions stipulated a term of life plus sixty years. The same issues arose with transitional provisions as for books: the 1837 and first 1838 versions specified reversion to the author after twenty-eight years in the case of an assigned subsisting copyright, whereas the 1839 version simply terminated the copyright in the hands of an assignee after twenty-eight years. These convolutions were rendered unnecessary by 1840. The clause was widened to cover musical compositions, and the term was defined simply by reference to the term of copyright in books.[86] The ability to register the right of representation was added in 1841, first public representation or performance to be deemed equivalent to first publication. Assignment of the copyright in a dramatic or musical work did not carry with it the right of representation unless the entry in the book of registry records this explicitly (section 22).

[84] On these definitions see also: *Russell* v. *Smith* (1848) 12 QB 217 at 236; *Duck* v. *Bates* (1884) 13 QBD 843.

[85] *Bach* v. *Longman* (1777) 2 Cowp 623; *Clementi* v. *Golding* (1809) 11 East 244; 2 Camp 25; *White* v. *Gerock* (1819) 1 Chit Rep 26.

[86] Unfortunately, some areas of uncertainty remained. The 1833 Act had granted a perpetuity to unpublished dramatic works. There were two possible interpretations of the 1842 Act. One was that although the right of representation had been extended to forty-two years (or life plus seven), the 1842 Act did not apply to dramatic works which had not been printed, so these retained the perpetual right under the 1833 Act. Alternatively it was argued that the 1842 Act applied both to printed and unprinted pieces, so that in spite of its expressed intention to 'extend' the term of the right, in fact it cut down the term for unprinted pieces, the right of representation now running for the same term for both printed and unprinted plays. For an unpublished play, the right of representation ran from its first performance in public. Scrutton suggested that the second interpretation would have been upheld in court, on the argument that the statute prevailed over the common law right to prevent publication: Scrutton, *Law of copyright*, pp. 72–3.

ENGRAVINGS AND OTHER ARTISTIC WORKS

The copyright position with regard to works of art was extremely unsatisfactory.[87] Engravings were the first artistic works to be protected, although paintings, drawings and photographs were not protected as such.[88] There was some statutory protection for sculptures, which had proved ineffective.[89] A review of these statutes would easily have justified Talfourd's decision to consolidate them as far as possible. However, provisions on engravings appeared only in the 1837 bill and were then dropped, the intention apparently being to include them in a new Act concerned with sculpture.[90] The 1837 draft provisions deserve a brief review nevertheless.

The previous Engravings Acts had given the artist a monopoly of engraving and printing his work for a term of twenty-eight years after first publication, provided his name and the date appeared on the original prints.[91] The artist was the person who, from his own original design, produced or caused to be produced an engraving, etching or work in mezzotinto or chiaroscuro of any historical print or prints, or any portrait, conversation, landscape or architecture, map, chart or plan, or any other print; alterna-

87 For trenchant criticism of this continuing state of affairs, see Delabere Roberton Blaine, *On the laws of artistic copyright and their defects* (1853), especially pp. 50ff.

88 At common law the owner of a work of art had the right to prevent its being copied, but he lost it as soon as it was published with his consent. This right was unaffected by Talfourd's Act: see (famously) *Prince Albert* v. *Strange* (1848) 13 Jur 45, on appeal (1849) 1 Mac & G 25; *Turner* v. *Robinson* (1860) 10 I Ch R 121, on appeal, ibid., 510. There was no specific protection until the Fine Arts Copyright Act 1862.

89 The first statutory protection for sculpture was the 1798 Act (38 Geo. 3 c. 71), passed to prevent the pirating of busts made and published by statuaries, and almost totally worthless. Lord Ellenborough observed that 'the statute seems to have been framed to defeat its own object': *Gahagan* v. *Cooper* (1811) 3 Camp 111. The Sculpture Copyright Act 1814 (54 Geo. 3 c. 56) admitted that the previous Act had been 'ineffectual for the Purposes thereby intended, namely, the Encouragement of Artists, and to secure to them the profits of and in their works, and for the advancement of said arts'. It gave fourteen years from date of first publication or putting forth (renewed for an extra fourteen if the owner was still alive at the end of the original term), provided that the proprietor's name and the date of publication were put on beforehand. It was of little commercial value at the time, but was not repealed until 1912.

90 Lowndes, *Sketch*, p. 84.

91 See *Newton* v. *Cowie* (1827) 4 Bing 234.

tively, instead of being the creator of the basic picture, he might be the person who carried out the actual engraving, etching or working, copying some existing picture.[92]

Talfourd's definition of engraving draws on these earlier models. He intended to leave subsisting interests unaltered, although with the benefit of the remedies given by the new Act. New engravings were to have the same term as books. The first engraver of a picture was not only to have had copyright in the engraving, but also an exclusive licence, any other licences to engrave the same picture being void. Consent of both painter and proprietor was required. However, although copyright in an engraving from a picture belonging to a public institution went to the engraver, this was subject to a proviso that other engravings could be made from the picture. Original engravings were specifically included. The engravings could be registered in the usual way, but only two deposit copies were required. It was prohibited to 'engrave, etch, work, print, copy or imitate, in whole or in part, for sale, or cause to be engraven, etched, worked, printed, copied or imitated, in whole or in part, for sale, any Engraving in which Copyright shall subsist' without the proprietor's consent. Similarly, import and knowing possession were prohibited. The remedies were as for book copyright.[93]

LECTURES

A curious provision appeared in the bills of 1838–9, extending the 1835 Lectures Copyright Act to 'all Sermons which after the passing of this Act shall be delivered in any church, chapel or place of religious worship authorised by law'.[94] The Lectures Act prevented the publication of lectures without consent, but only if various conditions as to notice had been complied with. Also, section 5 of the Act expressly excluded from its scope lectures 'delivered in any University or public school or college, or on any public foundation, or by any individual in virtue of or according to any gift, endowment, or foundation'. It is unclear what the real

[92] Engraving Copyright Act 1734, 8 Geo. 2 c. 13; Engraving Copyright Act 1766, 7 Geo. 3 c. 38; Prints Copyright Act 1776, 17 Geo. 3 c. 57; Prints and Engravings Copyright (Ireland) Act 1836.

[93] 1837 bill, s. 2 and ss. 20–26.

[94] See ch. 3, p. 54.

aim of this clause was. Talfourd had already sought to 'remove doubt' which had arisen concerning books written by 'spiritual persons', with a clause which gave them the right to sell their copyrights for profit, 'any law or usage to the contrary not withstanding'. If his intention was to remove doubts as to whether the clergy had rights in their delivered but unpublished sermons, the Lectures Act was perhaps never the best mechanism. Arguably, sermons delivered by clergymen of the Established Church, in endowed places of worship, were taken outside of the Lectures Act by the section 5 exception. Others, notably Scrutton, argued that the common law right in an unpublished manuscript was lost once a sermon had been delivered, 'being preached in edifices the doors of which are in theory open to all mankind'.[95] In any event, neither clause appeared in the 1840 bill.

REMEDIES AND RULES OF EVIDENCE

Talfourd proposed various changes to strengthen the plaintiff's hand in a copyright case. Although he did this with the best of intentions, he was regarded as far too presumptuous even by supporters of the central clauses of the bill.

Altogether, a plaintiff had three possible remedies. If the title was registered, statutory penalties were available, though few would bother to sue for these. The action on the case for damages was available regardless of whether the title was registered or not.[96] Proceedings in equity were often the first option. Originally, injunctions were not granted unless the plaintiff had clear legal title, but this approach later softened slightly. However, no injunction was given where the plaintiff's action at law was barred

[95] Copinger, *Law of copyright*, p. 35. Scrutton, *Law of copyright*, p. 68. See also *Caird* v. *Sime* (1887) 12 App C 326 (H.L.), *per* Lord Halsbury: 'it is intelligible that where a person speaks a speech to which all the world is invited, either expressly or impliedly, to listen, or preaches a sermon in a church, the doors of which are thrown open to all mankind, the mode and manner of publication negative, as it appears to me, any limitation [on the hearer's right to communicate it to others]'.

[96] *Beckford* v. *Hood* (1798) 7 TR 620 (above). Pirate copies became the property of the proprietor of the copyright.

as libellous or mischievous. There was effectively no copyright in any work regarded as obscene or immoral.[97]

Talfourd would have been extremely unwilling (and unwise) to interfere with this well-developed line of case law. He did, however, attempt to facilitate the use of injunctions in copyright cases. The power to grant injunctions was made much more flexible, and extended explicitly to 'the Supreme Courts of Judicature at Fort William, in Bengal, Madras or Bombay, and to any of the Supreme or Upper Courts of Judicature in any part of Her Majesty's British Dominions'. There was also a power to make an order for account of profits. This was all highly controversial, since the power of granting injunctions was exercised exclusively by the courts of equity. Godson explained that 'the object of the present clause was to enable [a plaintiff] to get both his injunction and his damages in the same court'. There was considerable opposition even from those who had supported the bill, and Gladstone intervened to suggest postponement of the clause (now clause 24), which was in fact deleted in the House of Lords.[98]

The plaintiff had no right to sue in respect of any infringement unless there was an entry in the book of registry. This entry was of crucial importance. At the end of 1838, a clause was added which attempted to prevent the defendant from impugning the plaintiff's title without giving adequate warning. It provided that a defendant had to give notice of the objections to title on which he intended to rely, and give the name of the person who he did consider to have title to the copyright. The clause remained unaltered, and became section 16 of the 1842 Act. It seems to have worked well and caused few problems.[99] A further clause was aimed at reducing piracy in the British Dominions of books published in the United Kingdom. The intention was to allow an officer of the Stationers' Company to certify that a particular book brought to him appeared to be a book printed in the United

[97] See *Fores* v. *Johnes* (1802) 4 Esp 97 (prints) and see also 2 Camp 511 (pictures); *Walcot* v. *Walker* (1802) 7 Ves Jun 1; *Hime* v. *Dale* (1803) 2 Camp 27n; *Du Bost* v. *Beresford* (1810) 2 Camp NPC 411; *Southey* v. *Sherwood* (1817) 2 Mer 435; *Lawrence* v. *Smith* (1822) Jac 471; *Murray* v. *Benbow* (1822) Jac. 474n; *Stockdale* v. *Onwhyn* (1826) 5 B & C 173.

[98] *Hansard, Parliamentary debates* (3rd series), lxii, 892 (20 April 1842).

[99] See for example *Leader* v. *Purday* (1849) 7 CB 4; *Boosey* v. *Purday* 10 Jur 1038; *Boosey* v. *Davidson* 4 D. & L. 147; *Chappell* v. *Purday* 1 D. & L. 458.

Kingdom and registered there. The stamped book would then have served as prima facie evidence of publication (and other registration details) in all courts in the British Dominions. However, this clause did not survive the House of Lords. A similar provision to control the mode of proving copyright in the colonial courts was likewise dropped. One addition in the House of Lords was a new version of the old rule that the defendant could plead the general issue and then give special matter in evidence, recovering his costs unless he lost.[100] Action on the statute normally had to begin within twelve months of the offence. However, Archbishop Howley once again sought to safeguard the interests of the deposit libraries by proposing an amendment exempting them from this limitation, and this was accepted.[101]

What, then, did Talfourd achieve with all these bills? The 1842 Act effected some significant changes to copyright law. The extension of term is the most famous of these, although the benefits for dramatic and musical works (including dramatic representation) are often forgotten. Less spectacular, but also important, are the attempts to improve and formalise arrangements for deposit and registration, and to clarify title to copyright in periodical articles. The new statutory presumptions as to matters of title can only have been helpful. Admittedly the Act did not achieve the consolidation which Talfourd had hoped for, though this was scarcely his fault: international copyright was taken out of his hands, and he was assured that engravings and other artistic works would be dealt with elsewhere also. On the matter of term, again, Talfourd was disappointed, although something was achieved.

The Act seems to have worked well enough for the remainder of the century. The 1911 Act was needed urgently to deal with copyright's growing international dimension, and in the process it did much that Talfourd had not been allowed to do. The

100 Copyright Act 1842, s. 26; cf. Copyright Act 1710, s. 8.

101 But see *Hogg* v. *Scott* (1874) LR 18 Eq 444 where the plaintiff author of *The fruit manual* and *British pomology – the apple*, did not realise for some time that the defendant's work *The orchardist* copied extensively, often verbatim, from his own works. The defendant's objection that section 26 applied to rule out any injunction more than twelve months after the offence was not accepted, and costs were awarded against him.

registration system maintained by the 1842 Act eventually approached the point of collapse, but this was a problem of volume rather than conception. Within the terms permitted to it, the 1842 Act produced a clear improvement in copyright law. To dwell on Talfourd's lack of political guile is to neglect his sensible and practical reforms, as well as to underestimate the vital publicity that copyright received as a result of his dogged efforts.

Appendix III

THE COPYRIGHT ACT 1842
5 & 6 Vict. c. 45

An Act to amend the Law of Copyright.

[1st July 1842]

Whereas is it expedient to amend the law relating to copyright, and to afford greater encouragement to the production of literary works of lasting benefit to the world: Be it enacted by the Queen's most Excellent Majesty, by and with the advice and consent of the Lords spiritual and temporal, and Commons, in this present parliament assembled, and by the authority of the same, that from the passing of this Act an Act passed in the eighth year of the reign of Her Majesty Queen *Anne*, intituled *An Act for the Encouragement of Learning, by vesting the Copies of printed Books in the Authors or Purchasers of such Copies during the Times therein mentioned*; and also an Act passed in the forty-first year of the reign of His Majesty King *George* the Third, intituled *An Act for the further Encouragement of Learning in the United Kingdom of* Great Britain *and* Ireland, *by securing the Copies and Copyright of printed Books to the Authors of such Books, or their Assigns, for the Time therein mentioned*; and also an Act passed in the fifty-fourth year of the reign of His Majesty King *George* the Third, intituled *An Act to amend the several Acts for the Encouragement of Learning, by securing the Copies and Copyright of printed Books to the Authors of such Books, or their Assigns*, be and the same are hereby repealed, except so far as the continuance of either of them may be necessary for carrying on or giving effect to any proceedings at law or in equity pending at the time of passing this Act, or for enforcing any cause of action or suit, or any right or contract, then subsisting.

2. Interpretation of Act

And be it enacted, that in the construction of this Act the word 'book' shall be construed to mean and include every volume, part or division of a volume, pamphlet, sheet of letter-press, sheet of music, map, chart, or plan separately published; that the words 'dramatic piece' shall be construed to mean and include every tragedy, comedy, play, opera, farce, or other scenic, musical, or dramatic entertainment; that the word 'copyright' shall be construed to mean the sole and exclusive liberty of printing or otherwise multiplying copies of any subject to which the said word is herein applied; that the words 'personal representative' shall be construed to mean and include every executor, administrator, and next of kin entitled to administration; that the word 'assigns' shall be construed to mean and include every person in whom the interest of an author in copyright shall be vested, whether derived from such author before or after the publication of any book, and whether acquired by sale, gift, bequest, or by operation of law, or otherwise; that the words '*British* Dominions' shall be construed to mean and include all parts of the United Kingdom of *Great Britain* and *Ireland*, the islands of *Jersey* and *Guernsey*, all parts of the *East* and *West Indies*, and all the colonies, settlements, and possessions of the Crown which now are or hereafter may be acquired; and that whenever in this Act, in describing any person, matter, or thing, the word importing the singular number or the masculine gender only is used, the same shall be understood to include and to be applied to several persons as well as one person, and females as well as males, and several matters or things as well as one matter or thing, respectively, unless there shall be something in the subject or context repugnant to such construction.

3. Endurance of term of copyright in any book hereafter to be published in the lifetime of the author; if published after the author's death

And be it enacted, that the copyright in every book which shall after the passing of this Act be published in the lifetime of its author shall endure for the natural life of such author, and for the further term of seven years, commencing at the time of his death, and shall be the property of such author and his assigns: provided always, that if the said term of seven years shall expire before the end of forty-two years from the first publication of such book, the copyright shall in that case endure for such period of forty-two years; and that the copyright in every book which shall be published after the death of its author shall endure for the term of forty-two years from the first publication thereof, and shall be the property of the proprietor of the author's manuscript from which such book shall be first published, and his assigns.

4. In cases of subsisting copyright, the term to be extended, except when it shall belong to an assignee for other consideration than natural love and affection; in which case it shall cease at the expiration of the present term, unless its extension be agreed to between the proprietor and the author

And whereas it is just to extend the benefits of this Act to authors of books published before the passing thereof, and in which copyright still subsists; be it enacted, that the copyright which at the time of passing this Act shall subsist in any book theretofore published (except as herein-after mentioned) shall be extended and endure for the full term provided by this Act in cases of books thereafter published, and shall be the property of the person who at the time of passing of this Act shall be the proprietor of such copyright: provided always, that in all cases in which such copyright shall belong in whole or in part to a publisher or other person who shall have acquired it for other consideration than that of natural love and affection, such copyright shall not be extended by this Act, but shall endure for the term which shall subsist therein at the time of passing of this Act, and no longer, unless the author of such book, if he shall be living, or the personal representative of such author, if he shall be dead, and the proprietor of such copyright, shall, before the expiration of such term, consent and agree to accept the benefits of this Act in respect of such book, and shall cause a minute of such consent in the form in that behalf given in the Schedule to this Act annexed to be entered in this Book of Registry herein-after directed to be kept, in which case such copyright shall endure for the full term by this Act provided in cases of books to be published after the passing of this Act, and shall be the Property of such person or persons as in such minute shall be expressed.

5. Judicial Committee of the Privy Council may license the republication of books which the proprietor refuses to republish after death of the author

And whereas it is expedient to provide against the suppression of books of importance to the public; be it enacted, that it shall be lawful for the Judicial Committee of Her Majesty's Privy Council, on complaint made to them that the proprietor of the copyright in any book after the death of its author has refused to republish or to allow the republication of the same, and that by reason of such refusal such book may be withheld from the public, to grant a licence to such complainant to publish such book, in such manner and subject to such conditions as they may think fit, and that it shall be lawful for such complainant to publish such book according to such licence.

6. Copies of books published after the passing of this Act, and of all subsequent editions, to be delivered within certain times at the British Museum

And be it enacted, that a printed copy of the whole of every book which shall be published after the passing of this Act, together with all maps, prints, or other engravings belonging thereto, finished and coloured in the same manner as the best copies of the same shall be published, and also of any second or subsequent edition which shall be so published with any additions or alterations, whether the same shall be in letter press, or in the maps, prints, or other engravings belonging thereto, and whether the first edition of such book shall have been published before or after the passing of this Act, and also of any second or subsequent edition of every book of which the first or some preceding edition shall not have been delivered for the use of the *British Museum*, bound, sewed, or stitched together, and upon the best paper on which the same shall be printed, shall, within one calendar month after the day on which any such book shall first be sold, published, or offered for sale within the bills of mortality, or within three calendar months if the same shall first be sold, published, or offered for sale in any other part of the United Kingdom, or within twelve calendar months after the same shall first be sold, published, or offered for sale in any other part of the *British* Dominions, be delivered, on behalf of the publisher thereof, at the *British Museum*.

7. Mode of delivering at the British Museum

And be it enacted, that every copy of any book which under the provisions of this Act ought to be delivered as aforesaid shall be delivered at the *British Museum* between the hours of ten in the forenoon and four in the afternoon on any day except *Sunday*, *Ash Wednesday*, *Good Friday*, and *Christmas Day*, to one of the officers of the said museum, or to some person authorized by the trustees of the said museum to receive the same, and such officer or other person receiving such copy is hereby required to give a receipt in writing for the same, and such delivery shall to all intents and purposes be deemed to be good and sufficient delivery under the provisions of this Act.

8. A copy of every book to be delivered within a month after demand to the officer of the Stationers Company, for the following libraries: the Bodleian at Oxford, the Public Library at Cambridge, the Faculty of Advocates at Edinburgh, and that of Trinity College, Dublin

And be it enacted, that a copy of the whole of every book, and of any second or subsequent edition of every book containing additions and alterations, together with all maps and prints belonging thereto, which after the passing of this Act shall be published, shall, on demand thereof in writing, left at the place of abode of the publisher thereof at any time within twelve months next after the publication thereof, under the hand of the officer of the Company of Stationers who shall from time to time be appointed by the said company for the purposes of this Act, or under the hand of any other person thereto authorized by the persons or bodies politic and corporate, proprietors and managers of the libraries following, (*videlicet*,) the *Bodleian* Library at *Oxford*, the Public Library at *Cambridge*, the Library of the Faculty of Advocates at *Edinburgh*, the Library of the College of the Holy and Undivided Trinity of Queen *Elizabeth* near *Dublin*, be delivered, upon the paper of which the largest number of copies of such book or edition shall be printed for sale, in the like condition as the copies prepared for sale by the publisher thereof respectively, within one month after demand made thereof in writing as aforesaid, to the said officer of the said Company of Stationers for the time being, which copies the said officer shall and he is hereby required to receive at the Hall of the said company, for the use of the library for which such demand shall be made within such twelve months as aforesaid; and the said officer is hereby required to give a receipt in writing for the same, and within one month after any such book shall be so delivered to him as aforesaid to deliver the same for the use of such library.

9. Publishers may deliver the copies to the libraries, instead of at the Stationers Company

Provided also, and be it enacted, that if any publisher shall be desirous of delivering the copy of such book as shall be demanded on behalf of any of the said libraries at such library, it shall be lawful for him to deliver the same at such library, free of expence, to such librarian or other person authorized to receive the same (who is hereby required in such case to receive and give a receipt in writing for the same), and such delivery shall to all intents and purposes of this Act be held as equivalent to a delivery to the said officer of the Stationers Company.

10. Penalty for default in delivering copies for the use of the libraries

And be it enacted, that if any publisher of any such book, or of any second or subsequent edition of any such book, shall neglect to deliver the same, pursuant to this Act, he shall for every such default forfeit, besides the value of such copy of such book or edition which he ought to have delivered, a sum not exceeding five pounds, to be recovered by the librarian or other officer (properly authorized) of the library for the use whereof such copy should have been delivered, in a summary way, on conviction before two justices of the peace for the county or place where the publisher making default shall reside, or by action of debt or other proceeding of the like nature, at the suit of such librarian or other officer, in any court of record in the United Kingdom, in which action, if the plaintiff shall obtain a verdict, he shall recover his costs reasonably incurred, to be taxed as between attorney and client.

11. Book of Registry to be kept at Stationers Hall

And be it enacted, that a Book of Registry, wherein may be registered, as herein-after enacted, the proprietorship in the copyright of books, and assignments thereof, and in dramatic and musical pieces, whether in manuscript or otherwise, and licences affecting such copyright, shall be kept at the Hall of the Stationers Company, by the officer appointed by the said company for the purposes of this Act, and shall at all convenient times be open to the inspection of any person, on payment of one shilling for every entry which shall be searched for or inspected in the said book; and that such officer shall, whenever thereunto reasonably required, give a copy of any entry in such book, certified under his hand, and impressed with the stamp of the said company, to be provided by them for that purpose, and which they are hereby required to provide, to any person requiring the same, on payment to him of the sum of five shillings; and such copies so certified and impressed shall be received in evidence in all courts, and in all summary proceedings, and shall be *primâ facie* proof of the proprietorship or assignment of copyright or licence as therein expressed, but subject to be rebutted by other evidence, and in the case of dramatic or musical pieces shall be *primâ facie* proof of the right of representation or performance, subject to be rebutted as aforesaid.

12. Making a false entry in the Book of Registry, a misdemeanor

And be it enacted, that if any person shall wilfully make or cause to be made any false entry in the Registry Book of the Stationers Company, or shall wilfully produce or cause to be tendered in evidence any paper falsely purporting to be a copy of any entry in the said book, he shall be guilty of an indictable misdemeanor, and shall be punished accordingly.

13. Entries of copyright may be made in the Book of Registry

And be it enacted, that after the passing of this Act it shall be lawful for the proprietor of copyright in any book heretofore published, or in any book hereafter to be published, to make entry in the Registry Book of the Stationers Company of the title of such book, the time of the first publication thereof, the name and place of abode of the publisher thereof, and the name and place of abode of the proprietor of the copyright of the said book, or of any portion of such copyright, in the form in that behalf given in the Schedule to this Act annexed, upon payment of the sum of five shillings to the officer of the said company; and that it shall be lawful for every such registered proprietor to assign his interest, or any portion of his interest therein, by making entry in the said Book of Registry of such assignment, and of the name and place of abode of the assignee thereof, in the form given in that behalf in the said Schedule, on payment of the like sum; and such assignment so entered shall be effectual in law to all intents and purposes whatsoever, without being subject to any stamp or duty, and shall be of the same force and effect as if such assignment had been made by deed.

14. Persons aggrieved by any entry in the Book of Registry may apply to a court of law in term or judge in vacation, who may order such entry to be varied or expunged

And be it enacted, that if any person shall deem himself aggrieved by any entry made under colour of this Act in the said Book of Registry, it shall be lawful for such person to apply by motion to the Court of Queen's Bench, Court of Common Pleas, or Court of Exchequer, in term time, or to apply by summons to any judge of either of such courts in vacation, for an order that such entry may be expunged or varied; and that upon any such application by motion or summons to either of the said courts, or to a judge as aforesaid, such court or judge shall make such order for expunging, varying, or confirming such entry, either with or without costs, as to such court or judge shall seem just; and the officer appointed by the Stationers Company for the purposes of this Act shall, on the production to him of any such order for expunging or varying any such entry, expunge or vary the same according to the requisitions of such order.

15. Remedy for the piracy of books by action on the case

And be it enacted, that if any person shall, in any part of the *British* Dominions, after the passing of this Act, print or cause to be printed, either for sale or exportation, any book in which there shall be subsisting copyright, without the consent in writing of the proprietor thereof, or shall import for sale or hire any such book so having been unlawfully printed from parts beyond the sea, or, knowing such book to have been so unlawfully printed or imported, shall sell, publish, or expose to sale or hire, or shall have in his possession, for sale or hire, any such book so unlawfully printed or imported, without such consent as aforesaid, such offender shall be liable to a special action on the case at the suit of the proprietor of such copyright, to be brought in any court of record in that part of the *British* Dominions in which the offence shall be liable to an action in the Court of Session in *Scotland*, which shall and may be brought and prosecuted in the same manner in which any other action of damages to the like amount may be brought and prosecuted there.

16. In actions for piracy the defendant to give notice of the objections to the plaintiff's title on which he means to rely

And be it enacted, that after the passing of this Act, in any action brought within the *British* Dominions against any person for printing any such book for sale, hire, or exportation, or for importing, selling, publishing, or exposing to sale or hire, or causing to be imported, sold, published, or exposed to sale or hire, any such book, the defendant, on pleading thereto, shall give to the plaintiff a notice in writing of any objections on which he means to rely on the trial of such action; and if the nature of his defence be, that the plaintiff in such action was not the author or first publisher of the book in which he shall by such action claim copyright, or is not the proprietor of the copyright therein, or that some other person than the plaintiff was the author or first publisher of such book, or is the proprietor of the copyright therein, then the defendant shall specify in such notice the name of the person who he alleges to have been the author or first publisher of such book, or the proprietor of the copyright therein, together with the title of such book, and the time when and the place where such book was first published, otherwise the defendant in such action shall not at the trial or hearing of such action be allowed to give any evidence that the plaintiff in such action was not the author or first publisher of the book in which he claims such copyright as aforesaid, or that he was not the proprietor of the copyright therein; and at such trial or hearing no other objection shall be allowed to be made on behalf of such defendant than the objections stated in such notice, or that any other person was the author or first publisher of such book, or the proprietor of the copyright therein, than the person specified in such notice, or give in evidence in support of his defence any other book than one substantially corresponding in title, time, and place of publication with the title, time, and place specified in such notice.

17. No person, except the proprietor, &c. shall import into the British Dominions for sale or hire any book first composed, &c. within the United Kingdom, and reprinted elsewhere, under penalty of forfeiture thereof, and also of 10*l*. and double the value; books may be seized by officers of customs or excise

And be it enacted, that after the passing of this Act it shall not be lawful for any person, not being the proprietor of the copyright, or some person authorized by him, to import into any part of the United Kingdom, or into any other part of the *British* Dominions, for sale or hire, any printed book first composed or written or printed and published in any part of the said United Kingdom, wherein there shall be copyright, and re-printed in any country or place whatsoever out of the *British* Dominions; and if any person, not being such proprietor or person authorized as aforesaid, shall import or bring, or cause to be imported or brought, for sale or hire, any such printed book, into any part of the *British* Dominions, contrary to the true intent and meaning of this Act, or shall knowingly sell, publish, or expose to sale or let to hire, or have in his possession for sale or hire, any such book, then every such book shall be forfeited, and shall be seized by any officer of customs or excise, and the same shall be destroyed by such officer; and every person so offending, being duly convicted thereof before two justices of the peace for the county or place in which such book shall be found, shall also for every such offence forfeit the sum of ten pounds, and double the value of every copy of such book which he shall so import or cause to be imported into any part of the *British* Dominions, or shall knowingly sell, publish, or expose to sale or let to hire, or shall cause to be sold, published, or exposed to sale or let to hire, or shall have in his possession for sale or hire, contrary to the true intent and meaning of this Act, five pounds to the use of such officer of customs or excise, and the remainder of the penalty to the use of the proprietor of the copyright in such book.

18. As to the copyright in encyclopædias, periodicals, and works published in a series, reviews, or magazines; proviso for authors who have reserved the right of publishing their articles in a separate form

And be it enacted, that when any publisher or other person shall, before or at the time of the passing of this Act, have projected, conducted, and carried on, or shall hereafter project, conduct, and carry on, or be the proprietor of any encyclopædia, review, magazine, periodical work, or work published in a series of books or parts, or any book whatsoever, and shall have employed or shall employ any persons to compose the same, or any volumes, parts, essays, articles, or portions thereof, for publication in or as part of the same, and such work, volumes, parts, essays, articles, or portions shall have been or shall hereafter be composed under such employment, on the terms that the copyright therein shall belong to such proprietor, projector, publisher, or conductor, and paid for by such proprietor, projector, publisher, or conductor, the copyright in every such encyclopædia, review, magazine, periodical work and work published in a series of books or parts, and in every volume, part, essay, article, and portion so composed and paid for, shall be the property of such proprietor, projector, publisher, or other conductor, who shall enjoy the same rights as if he were the actual author thereof, and shall have such term of copyright therein as is given to the authors of books by this Act; except only that in the case of essays, articles, or portions forming part of and first published in reviews, magazines, or other periodical works of a like nature, after the term of twenty-eight years from the first publication thereof respectively the right of publishing the same in a separate form shall revert to the author for the remainder of the term given by this Act: provided always, that during the term of twenty-eight years the said proprietor, projector, publisher, or conductor shall not publish any such essay, article, or portion separately or singly without the consent previously obtained of the author thereof, or his assigns: provided also, that nothing herein contained shall alter or affect the right of any person who shall have been or who shall be so employed as aforesaid to publish any such his composition in a separate form, who by any contract, express or implied, may have reserved or may hereafter reserve to himself such right; but every author reserving, retaining, or having such right shall be entitled to the copyright in such composition when published in a separate form, according to this Act, without prejudice to the right of such proprietor, projector, publisher, or conductor as aforesaid.

19. Proprietors of encyclopædias, periodicals, and works published in series, may enter at once at Stationers Hall, and thereon have the benefit of the registration of the whole

And be it enacted, that the proprietor of the copyright in any encyclopædia, review, magazine, periodical work, or other work published in a series of books or parts, shall be entitled to all the benefits of the registration at Stationers Hall under this Act, on entering in the said Book of Registry the title of such encyclopædia, review, periodical work, or other work published in a series of books or parts, the time of the first publication of the first volume, number, or part thereof, or of the first number or volume first published after the passing of this Act in any such work which shall have been published heretofore, and the name and place of abode of the proprietor thereof, and of the publisher thereof, when such publisher shall not also be the proprietor thereof.

20. The provisions of 3 & 4 W. 4. c. 15. extended to musical compositions, and the term of copyright, as provided by this Act, applied to the liberty of representing dramatic pieces and musical compositions

And whereas an Act was passed in the third year of the reign of his late Majesty, to amend the law relating to dramatic literary property, and it is expedient to extend the term of the sole liberty of representing dramatic pieces given by that Act to the full time by this Act provided for the continuance of copyright: and whereas it is expedient to extend to musical compositions the benefits of that Act, and also of this Act; be it therefore enacted, that the provisions of the said Act of his late Majesty, and of this Act, shall apply to musical compositions, and that the sole liberty of representing or performing, or causing or permitting to be represented or performed, any dramatic piece or musical composition, shall endure and be the property of the author thereof, and his assigns, for the term in this Act provided for the duration of copyright in books; and the provisions herein-before enacted in respect of the property of such copyright, and of registering the same, shall apply to the liberty of representing or performing any dramatic piece or musical composition, as if the same were herein expressly re-enacted and applied thereto, save and except that the first public representation or performance of any dramatic piece or musical composition shall be deemed equivalent, in the construction of this Act, to the first publication of any book: provided always, that in case of any dramatic piece or musical composition in manuscript, it shall be sufficient for the person having the sole liberty of representing or performing, or causing to be represented or performed the same, to register only the title thereof, the name and place of abode of the author or composer thereof, the name and place of abode of the proprietor thereof, and the time and place of its first representation or performance.

21. Proprietors of right of dramatic representations shall have all the remedies given by 3 & 4 W. 4. c. 15

And be it enacted, that the person who shall at any time have the sole liberty of representing such dramatic piece or musical composition shall have and enjoy the remedies given and provided in the said Act of the third and fourth years of the reign of his late Majesty King *William* the Fourth, passed to amend the laws relating to dramatic literary property, during the whole of his interest therein, as fully as if the same were re-enacted in this Act.

22. Assignment of copyright of a dramatic piece not to convey the right of representation

And be it enacted, that no assignment of the copyright of any book consisting of or containing a dramatic piece or musical composition shall be holden to convey to the assignee the right of representing or performing such dramatic piece or musical composition, unless an entry in the said Registry Book shall be made of such assignment, wherein shall be expressed the intention of the parties that such right should pass by such assignment.

23. Books pirated shall become the property of the proprietor of the copyright, and may be recovered by action

And be it enacted, that all copies of any book wherein there shall be copyright, and of which entry shall have been made in the said Registry Book, and which shall have been unlawfully printed or imported without the consent of the registered proprietor of such copyright, in writing under his hand first obtained, shall be deemed to be the property of the proprietor of such copyright, and who shall be registered as such, and such registered proprietor shall, after demand thereof in writing, be entitled to sue for and recover the same, or damages for the detention thereof, in an action of detinue, from any party who shall detain the same, or to sue for and recover damages for the conversion thereof in an action of trover.

24. No proprietor of copyright commencing after this Act shall sue or proceed for any infringement before making entry in the Book of Registry; proviso for dramatic pieces

And be it enacted, that no proprietor of copyright in any book which shall be first published after the passing of this Act shall maintain any action or suit, at law or in equity, or any summary proceeding, in respect of any infringement of such copyright, unless he shall, before commencing such action, suit, or proceeding, have caused an entry to be made, in the Book of Registry of the Stationers Company, of such book, pursuant to this Act: provided always, that the omission to make such entry shall not affect the copyright in any book, but only the right to sue or proceed in respect of the infringement thereof as aforesaid: provided also, that nothing herein contained shall prejudice the remedies which the proprietor of the sole liberty of representing any dramatic piece shall have by virtue of the Act passed in the third year of the reign of his late Majesty King *William* the Fourth, to amend the laws relating to dramatic literary property, or of this Act, although no entry shall be made in the Book of Registry aforesaid.

25. Copyright shall be personal property

And be it enacted, that all Copyright shall be deemed personal property, and shall be transmissible by bequest, or, in case of intestacy, shall be subject to the same law of distribution as other personal property, and in *Scotland* shall be deemed to be personal and moveable estate.

26. General Issue; limitation of actions; not to extend to actions, &c. in respect of the delivery of books

And be it enacted, that if any action or suit shall be commenced or brought against any person or persons whomsoever for doing or causing to be done any thing in pursuance of this Act, the defendant or defendants in such action may plead the general issue, and give the special matter in evidence; and if upon such action a verdict shall be given for the defendant, or the plaintiff shall become nonsuited, or discontinue his action, then the defendant shall have and recover his full costs, for which he shall have the same remedy as a defendant in any case by law hath; and that all actions, suits, bills, indictments, or informations for any offence that shall be committed against this Act shall be brought, sued, and commenced within twelve calendar months next after such offence committed, or else the same shall be void and of none effect; provided that such limitation of time shall not extend or be construed to extend to any actions, suits, or other proceedings which under the authority of this Act shall or may be brought, sued, or commenced for or in respect of any copies of books to be delivered for the use of the *British Museum*, or of any one of the four libraries herein-before mentioned.

27. Saving the rights of the universities, and the colleges of Eton, Westminster, and Winchester

Provided always, and be it enacted, that nothing in this Act contained shall affect or alter the rights of the two universities of *Oxford* and *Cambridge*, the colleges or houses of learning within the same, the four universities in *Scotland*, the college of the Holy and Undivided Trinity of Queen *Elizabeth* near *Dublin*, and the several colleges of *Eton*, *Westminster*, and *Winchester*, in any copyrights heretofore and now vested or hereafter to be vested in such universities and colleges respectively, any thing to the contrary herein contained notwithstanding.

28. Saving all subsisting rights, contracts, and engagements

Provided also, and be it enacted, that nothing in this Act contained shall affect, alter, or vary any right subsisting at the time of passing of this Act, except as herein expressly enacted; and all contracts, agreements, and obligations made and entered into before the passing of this Act, and all remedies relating thereto, shall remain in full force, any thing herein contained to the contrary notwithstanding.

29. Extent of the Act

And be it enacted, that this act shall extend to the United Kingdom of *Great Britain* and *Ireland*, and to every part of the *British* Dominions.

30. Act may be amended this session

And be it enacted, that this Act may be amended or repealed by any Act to be passed in the present session of parliament.

SCHEDULE to which the preceding Act refers

No. 1.

Form of minute of consent to be entered at Stationers Hall

WE, the undersigned, *A.B.* of the author of a certain book, intituled *Y.Z.* [or the personal representative of the author, *as the case may be*], and *C.D.* of do hereby certify, that we have consented and agreed to accept the benefits of the Act passed in the fifth year of the reign of Her Majesty Queen Victoria, Cap. , for the extension of the term of copyright therein provided by the said Act, and hereby declare that such extended term of copyright therein is the property of the said *A.B.* or *C.D.*

Dated this Day of 18 .

Witness (Signed) *A.B.*
C.D.

To the registering officer appointed by the Stationers Company.

No. 2.

Form of requiring entry of proprietorship

I *A.B.* of do hereby certify, that I am the proprietor of the copyright of a book, intituled *Y.Z.*, and I hereby require you to make entry in the Register Book of the Stationers Company of my proprietorship of such copyright, according to the particulars underwritten.

Title of book	Name of publisher, and place of publication	Name and place of abode of the proprietor of the copyright	Date of first publication
Y.Z.		*A.B.*	

Dated this Day of 18 .

Witness, *C.D.* (Signed) *A.B.*

No. 3.

Original entry of proprietorship of copyright of a book

Time of the entry	Title of book	Name of publisher, and place of publication	Name and place of abode of the proprietor of the copyright	Date of first publication
	Y.Z.	*A.B.*	*C.D.*	

No. 4.

Form of concurrence of the party assigning in any book previously registered

I *A.B.* of being the assigner of the copyright of the book hereunder described, do hereby require you to make entry of the assignment of the copyright therein.

Title of book	Assigner of the copyright	Assignee of the copyright
Y.Z.	*A.B.*	*C.D.*

Dated this Day of 18 .

(Signed) *A.B.*

No. 5.

Form of entry of assignment of copyright in any book previously registered

Date of entry	Title of book	Assigner of the copyright	Assignee of copyright
	[*Set out the title of the book, and refer to the page of the Registry Book in which the original entry of the copyright thereof is made.*]	*A.B.*	*C.D.*

BIBLIOGRAPHY

All places of publication are London unless otherwise indicated.

Abrams, H. B., 'The historic foundation of American copyright law: exploding the myth of common law copyright', *Wayne Law Review* 29 (1983), 1120–91

Ackroyd, Peter, *Dickens* (1990)

Acland, Alice, *Caroline Norton* (1948)

Adams, Thomas F., *Typographia: or, The printer's instructor* (Philadelphia, 1844; repr. 1981)

Address of the Journeymen Bookbinders of London and Westminster to the Trade Societies of Great Britain and Ireland on the conclusion of their struggle [1839–40?]

Allen, Christopher, *The law of evidence in Victorian England* (Cambridge, 1997)

Altick, Richard D., *The English common reader: a social history of the mass reading public, 1800–1900* (Chicago, 1957)

Anderson, J. Stuart, *Lawyers and the making of English land law, 1832–1940* (Oxford, 1992)

Anderson, Robert D., *Education and the Scottish people 1750–1918* (Oxford, 1995)

Andrews, Alexander, *The history of British journalism*, 2 vols. (1859)

Anon., 'The late Mr Justice Talfourd', *Law Magazine* 51 (1854)

A proposed new law of copyright; of the highest importance to authors, and to the inhabitants of Great Britain and Ireland in a letter addressed to Mr Serjeant Talfourd M.P. by a friend to authors

Areopagitica Secunda, or speech of the shade of John Milton on Mr Talfourd's Copyright Extension Bill (1838)

Arnold, Frederick, *The public life of Lord Macaulay* (1862)

Arnold, Thomas, *Miscellaneous works* (1845)

Thomas Arnold on education: a selection from his writings, with introductory material by Thomas W. Bamford (Cambridge, 1970)

Arnold's travelling journals, ed. Arthur P. Stanley (1852)

The life and correspondence of Thomas Arnold, ed. Arthur P. Stanley, 2 vols. (1844)

Arnould, Sir Joseph Arnold, *Lord Denman* (1873)

Aspinall, Arnold, *Lord Brougham and the Whig party* (Manchester, 1927)

Politics and the press, c. 1780–1850 (1949)
Atlay, James B., *The Victorian chancellors*, 2 vols. (1906–8)
Auchmuty, James J., *Sir Thomas Wyse* (1939)
Austen-Leigh, Richard Arthur, *The story of a printing house: being a short account of the Strahans and Spottiswoodes*, 2nd edn (1912)
Baines, Edward, *The life of Edward Baines, late M.P. for the borough of Leeds, by his son Edward Baines* (1851)
Bamford, Thomas W., *Thomas Arnold* (1960)
Barber, Giles, 'Galignani and the publication of English books in France from 1800 to 1852', *The Library*, 5th ser., 6 (1961), 267–86
Barnes, James J., *Authors, publishers and politicians: the quest for an Anglo-American copyright agreement, 1815–54* (1974)
'Depression and innovation in the British and American booktrade, 1819–1839', in eds. Robin Myers and Michael Harris, *Economics of the British booktrade 1605–1936* (Cambridge, 1985)
Free trade in books: a study of the London book trade since 1800 (Oxford, 1964)
'Galignani and the publication of English books in France: a post-script', *The Library*, 5th ser., 25 (1970), 294–313
Beattie, William, *Life and letters of Thomas Campbell*, 3 vols. (1849)
Belanger, Terry, 'From bookseller to publisher: changes in the London book trade, 1750–1850', in ed. Richard G. Landon, *Book selling and book buying: aspects of the nineteenth-century British and North American book trade* (Chicago, 1978)
Bellamy, Joyce M. and John Saville, *Dictionary of labour biography* (1972)
Bentham, Jeremy, *Collected works*, ed. James H. Burns (1968–)
An introduction to the principles of morals and legislation, in *Collected works*, eds. James H. Burns and Herbert L. A. Hart (1970)
Birrell, Augustine, *Seven lectures on the law and history of copyright in books* (1899)
Blackstone, Sir William, *Commentaries on the laws of England* (Oxford, 1765–70)
Blagden, Cyprian, 'Booksellers' trade sales, 1718–1768', *The Library*, 5th ser., 5 (1951), 243–57
The Stationers' Company: a history, 1403–1959 (1960)
Blaine, Delabere Roberton, *On the laws of artistic copyright and their defects* (1853)
Blainey, Ann, *The farthing poet* (1968)
Blanchard, Laman, 'Memoir of Mr. Serjeant Talfourd, M.P.', New Monthly 51 (1837), 213
Blunden, Edmund Charles, *Leigh Hunt: a biography*, 2nd edn (1930)
Leigh Hunt's 'Examiner' examined (1928)
Boas, Guy H. S., *The Garrick Club, 1831–1947* (1948)
Bond, Richmond P., 'John Partridge and the company of Stationers', *Studies in Bibliography* 16 (1963)
Bourne, Henry R. F., *English newspapers*, 2 vols. (1887)
Bowes, Robert, *The Philo-Union, or Cambridge Literary Society, 1826–1888. A record*. Printed for private circulation (Cambridge, 1890)

Bowker, Richard Rogers, *Copyright: its history and its law* (1912)
Bowring, Sir John, *Autobiographical recollections* (1877)
Brabrook, Sir Edward William, *The Royal Society of Literature: a brief account of its origin and progress*, 2nd edn (1879)
Briggs, Asa (ed.), *Essays in the history of publishing in celebration of the 250th anniversary of the House of Longman* (1974)
Brock, Michael, *The Great Reform Act* (1973)
Bromhead, Peter A., *Private members' bills in the British parliament* (1956)
Brougham, Henry, *Works of Henry, Lord Brougham*, 11 vols. (Edinburgh, 1872)
Browne, Charles T., *Life of Robert Southey* (1854)
Browning, Robert, *The poetical works of Robert Browning*, eds. I. Jack, Rowena Fowler and Margaret Smith (Oxford, 1983–91)
Bugbee, B. W., *Genesis of American patent and copyright law* (Washington, DC, 1967)
Bundock, Clement J., *The story of the National Union of Printing, Bookbinding and Paper Workers* (Oxford, 1959)
Burke, Peter, *Supplement to Godson's Practical treatise on the law of patents . . .* (1851)
Popular culture in early modern Europe (1978)
Camic, Charles, *Experience and enlightenment: socialization for cultural change in eighteenth-century Scotland* (Edinburgh, 1983)
Campbell, John C., *Life of John, Lord Campbell*, ed. the Hon. Mrs Hardcastle, 2 vols. (1881)
The lives of the Chief Justices of England, 3 vols. (1849–57)
Campbell, Thomas, *History of our own times*, 2 vols. (1843)
Canning, Hon. Albert Stratford George, *Lord Macaulay, essayist and historian* (1882)
Cannon, John, *Parliamentary return, 1640–1832* (Cambridge, 1973)
Carlyle, Thomas, *Critical and miscellaneous essays: collected and republished*, 7 vols. (1872)
The collected letters of Thomas and Jane Welsh Carlyle, ed. Charles R. Saunders, 15 vols. (Durham, NC, 1970)
Chambers, William, *Memoir of William and Robert Chambers*, 13th edn (Edinburgh, 1884)
Chambers, William and Robert Chambers, *Brief objections to Mr Talfourd's new Copyright bill* (Edinburgh, 1838)
Chancellor, Valerie, *The political life of Joseph Hume, 1775–1855* (1986)
Chapman, John, *Cheap books, and how to get them* (1852)
(ed.), *A report of the proceedings of a meeting (consisting chiefly of authors), held May 4th, at the house of Mr J. Chapman, 142 Strand, for the purpose of hastening the removal of the trade restrictions on the Commerce of Literature* (1852)
Charvat, William, *The profession of authorship in America, 1800–1870; the papers of William Charvat*, ed. Matthew J. Bruccoli (Columbus, OH, 1968)
Literary publishing in America 1790–1850 (Philadelphia, 1959)

Chester, Sir Norman, *The English administrative system, 1780–1870* (Oxford, 1981)

Chilcott, Tim, *A publisher and his circle; the life and work of John Taylor, Keats' publisher* (1972)

Chitnis, Anand C., *The Scottish Enlightenment and Early Victorian English society* (1986)

Christie, William Dougal, *A plea for perpetual copyright in a letter to Lord Monteagle* (1840)

Clarke, Martin Lowther, *George Grote: a biography* (1962)

Clayden, Peter William, *Samuel Rogers and his contemporaries*, 2 vols. (1889)

Clements, H. G. J., *Lord Macaulay, his life and writings* (1860)

Clive, John L., *Scotch Reviewers: the 'Edinburgh Review'; 1802–15* (1957)

Thomas Babington Macaulay: the shaping of the historian (1973)

Clowes, William, *Family business* (1953)

Cockburn, Henry, *Journal of Henry Cockburn 1831–54: being a continuation of the memorials of his time* (Edinburgh, 1874)

Coleman, Donald Cuthbert, *The British paper industry, 1495–1860* (Oxford, 1958)

Coleridge, Hartley, *Letters*, eds. Grace and Earl L. Griggs (1936)

Coleridge, Samuel Taylor, *The collected letters of Samuel Taylor Coleridge*, ed. Earl L.Griggs (Oxford, 1956)

Literary remains, ed. Hartley N. Coleridge, 4 vols. (1836–39)

Notebooks, ed. Kathleen Coburn (1957)

Collet, Collet Dobson, *History of the taxes on knowledge, their origin and repeal*, 2 vols. (1899)

Collins, A. S., *Authorship in the days of Johnson* (1927)

The profession of letters: a study of the relation of author to patron, publisher and public, 1780–1832 (1928)

Cooper, John James, *Some worthies of Reading* (1923)

Copinger, Walter Arthur, *The law of copyright in works of literature and art*, 1st edn (1870)

Cornish, William R., *Intellectual property*, 2nd edn (1989)

Cornish, William R. and Geoffrey de N. Clark, *Law and society in England, 1750–1950* (1989)

Cottle, Joseph, *Reminiscences of Samuel Taylor Coleridge and Robert Southey* (1847)

Cowie, George, *Printer's pocket-book and manual*, 3rd edn (c. 1836–7)

Crawfurd, John, *Taxes on knowledge: a financial and historical view of the taxes which impede the education of the people* (1836)

Cross, Nigel, *The common writer: life in nineteenth-century Grub Street* (Cambridge, 1985)

Curtis, George Ticknor, *A treatise on the Law of Copyright in Books, Dramatic and Musical compositions, Letters and other Manuscripts, Engravings and Sculpture, as enacted . . . in England and America; with some notices of the history of literary property* (1847)

Curwen, Henry, *A history of booksellers* (1874)

Dicey, Albert V., *Lectures on the relationship between law and public opinion in England during the nineteenth century* (1905)

Dickens, Charles, *The letters of Charles Dickens*, eds. Madeleine House and Graham Storey (Oxford, 1965–)

Dramatic Authors' Society, *Catalogue of dramatic pieces, the property of the members of the Dramatic Authors Society* (1865)

Duman, Daniel, *The judicial bench in England 1727–1875: the reshaping of a professional elite* (1982)

Duncombe, Thomas Slingsby, *Life and correspondence*, ed. Thomas H. Duncombe, 2 vols. (1868)

Eardley-Wilmot, Sir John E., *Acts and bills [of Lord Brougham' and Vaux] from 1811 to the present time, now first collected and arranged, with an analytical review showing their results upon the amendment of the law* (1857)

Edgeworth, Maria, *Chosen letters*, introduction by F. V. Barry (1931)

Letters from England, 1813–44, ed. C. Colvin (Oxford, 1971)

Edwards, John L. J., *The law officers of the Crown: a study of the offices of Attorney-General and Solicitor-General of England, with an account of the office of the Director of Public Prosecutions of England* (1964)

Eilenberg, Susan, 'Mortal pages: Wordsworth and the reform of copyright', *ELH: A Journal of English Literary History* 56 (1989), 351–75

Epstein, James and Dorothy Thompson (eds.), *The Chartist experience: studies in working-class radicalism and culture, 1830–60* (1982)

Erskine May, Thomas, *A treatise upon the law, privileges, proceedings and usage of parliament* (1844)

Feather, John, *A history of British publishing* (1988)

'Publishers and politicians: the remaking of the law of copyright in Britain 1775–1842. Part I: Legal deposit and the battle of the library tax', *Publishing History* 24 (1988), 49–76

'Publishers and politicians: the remaking of the law of copyright in Britain 1775–1842. Part II: The rights of authors', *Publishing History* 25 (1989), 45–72

Publishing, piracy and politics: an historical study of copyright in Britain (1994)

Fifoot, Cecil H. S., *Law and history in the nineteenth century* (1956)

Findlay, Joseph J., *Arnold of Rugby: his school life and contributions to education* (Cambridge, 1897)

Finlayson, Geoffrey B. A. M., 'The politics of municipal reform, 1835', *English Historical Review* 81 (1966), 673–92

Fonblanque, Albany E., *The life and labours of Albany Fonblanque*, ed. by his nephew, Edward Barringont de Fonblanque (1874)

Forster, John, *The life of Charles Dickens*, ed. J. W. T. Ley (1928)

Walter Savage Landor. A biography, 2 vols. (1869)

Foucher, Victor, *De la propriété littéraire et de la contrefaçon* (Paris, 1836)

Fox, William Johnson, *Memorial edition of collected works*, 12 vols. (1865–8)

Francis, George Henry, *Henry, Lord Brougham and Vaux: a critical biography* (1853)

Fraser, Derek (ed.), *The new poor law in the nineteenth century* (1976)

Fraser, Peter, 'The growth of ministerial control in the nineteenth-century House of Commons', *English Historical Review* 75 (1960), 444–63

Fredeman, William E., 'Emily Faithfull and the Victoria Press: an experiment in social bibliography', *The Library* 29 (1974)

Gash, Norman, *Pillars of government and other essays on state and society c.1770–c.1880* (1986)

Politics in the age of Peel: a study in the technique of parliamentary representation 1830–50 (1953)

Reaction and reconstruction in English politics 1832–52 (Oxford, 1965)

George, Eric Beardsworth, *The life and death of Benjamin Robert Haydon, 1786–1846* (1948)

Gettmann, Royal Alfred, *A Victorian publisher: a study of the Bentley papers* (Cambridge, 1960)

Gladstone, William E., *Gleanings from past years*, 7 vols. (1879)

Godard, John George, *George Birkbeck: the pioneer of popular education. A memoir and a review* (1884)

Godson, Richard, *A practical treatise on the law of patents for inventions and of copyright*, 1st edn (1823), 2nd edn (1840–4)

A supplement to a practical treatise on the law of patents for inventions, with suggestions of many alterations in that law; and an abstract of the laws in force in America, Spain, Austria, Netherlands, and France (1832)

Godson, Richard, *A supplement to Godson's treatise on the law of patents, and of copyright in literature, &c.*, by Peter Burke, (1851)

Goodrich, Samuel Griswald, *Recollections of a lifetime; or, men and things I have seen* (New York 1857)

Goodway, David, *London Chartism 1838–1848* (Cambridge, 1982)

Gosden, Peter H. J. H., *Self-help: voluntary associations in the 19th century* (1973)

Grant, James, *Portraits of public characters* (1841)

The newspaper press, 2 vols. (1871)

Walks and wanderings in the world of literature, 2 vols. in 1 (1839)

Greenwood, Thomas, *Edward Edwards, the chief pioneer of municipal public libraries* (1902)

Greville, Charles Cavendish Fulke, *The Greville memoirs, 1814–60*, eds. Lytton Strachey and Roger Fulford, 8 vols. (1938)

Griggs, Earl L., *Hartley Coleridge, his life and work* (1929)

Grobel, Monica C., 'The Society for the Diffusion of Useful Knowledge 1826–46' (unpublished MA thesis, London, University College, 1933)

Grote, George, *Shall we overturn the coach? or, what ought the radicals to do?, discussed in a letter to George Grote, from a Radical Member of the House of Commons*, 2nd edn (1839)

Grote, Harriet, *The personal life of George Grote* (1873)

Haight, Gordon S. *George Eliot & John Chapman; with Chapman's diaries* (New Haven, 1940)

Halévy, Elie, *A history of the English people in the nineteenth century,* translated from the French by Edward I. Watkin and Donald A. Barker, with an introduction by Ronald B. McCallum (1949–52)

Thomas Hodgskin, ed. in translation, with an introduction, by Arthur J. Taylor (1956)

Hawes, Francis, *Henry Brougham* (1957)

Haydon, Benjamin Robert, *Autobiography and memoirs, 1786–1846*, ed. A. P. D. Penrose (1927)

Hepburn, James, *The author's empty purse and the rise of the literary agent* (1968)

Heyck, Thomas W., *The transformation of intellectual life in Victorian England* (1982)

[Hickson, William Edward], *Mister Spring Rice and his penny stamp* [1836]

Hickson, William Edward, *Taxes on knowledge: reduction or abolition of the newspaper stamp-duty* [1836]

Hillard, George S. (ed.), *Life, letters and journals of George Ticknor*, 2 vols. (London and Boston, 1876)

Hills, Richard L., *Papermaking in Britain 1488–1988: a short history* (1988)

Hindle, Wilfred, *The Morning Post* (1937)

Hollis, Patricia, *The pauper press: a study in working-class radicalism of the 1830s* (Oxford, 1970)

(ed.), *Class and conflict in nineteenth-century England, 1815–50* (1973)

Hodgson, Norma and Cyprian Blagden, *The notebook of some aspects of book trade practice* (1953)

Holdsworth, Sir William, *A history of English law*, 16 vols. (1903–52)

Holmes, Richard, *Coleridge* (Oxford, 1982)

Holt, Raymond V., *The Unitarian contribution to social progress in England*, 2nd edn (1952)

Horne, Richard H., *The dreamer and the worker: a story of the present time*, 2 vols. (1851)

Exposition of the false medium and barriers . . . excluding men of genius from the public (1833)

A new spirit of the age, 2 vols. (1844)

The Poor Artist; or, seven eye-sights and one object (1850)

Hostettler, John, *Thomas Wakley: an improbable radical* (Chichester, 1993)

Hotten, John Camden, *Literary copyright, seven letters addressed by permission to the Right Honourable The Earl Stanhope* (1871)

Howarth, Patrick J. F., *Questions in the House; the history of a unique British institution* (1956)

Howe, Ellic (ed.), *The London compositor: documents relating to wages, working conditions and customs of the London printing trade, 1785–1900* (1947)

Howe, Ellic and J. Child, *The Society of London Bookbinders* (1952)

Howe, Ellic and Harold E. Waite, *The London Society of Compositors . . . a centenary history* (1948)

Hudson, Derek R., *A poet in Parliament: the life of W. M. Praed, 1802–1839* (1939)

Hunt, Felicity, 'Opportunities lost and gained: mechanization and women's work in the London bookbinding and printing trades', in ed. Angela V. John, *Unequal Opportunities: women's employment in England 1800–1918*, (Oxford, 1986)

Hunt, Frederick Knight, *The fourth estate: contributions towards a history of newspapers, and of the liberty of the press*, 2 vols. (1850)

Hunt, James Leigh, *Autobiography*, ed. R. Ingpen, 2 vols. (1903)

Correspondence, ed. by his eldest son T. Hunt, 2 vols. (1862)

James, Louis (ed.), *Fiction for the working man 1830–1850*, revised edn (1974)

Print and the people, 1819–1851 (1976)

Jeffreys, James B., *Story of the engineers, 1800–1945* (1946)

Jerdan, William, *Autobiography, with his literary, political, and social reminiscences and correspondence of the last fifty years*, 4 vols. (1852–3)

The plan of a National Association for the Encouragement and Protection of Authors, and Men of Talent and Genius (1839)

Men I have known (1866)

Jerrold, Walter, *Thomas Hood: his life and times* (1907)

Johnson, Leonard George, *General T. Perronet Thompson (1783–1860), his military, literary and political campaigns* (1957)

Jones, Andrew, *The politics of reform: 1884* (Cambridge, 1972)

Kaplan, Benjamin, *An unhurried view of copyright* (New York, 1967)

Kay-Shuttleworth, James, *Four periods of public education* (1862)

Kelly, Thomas, *George Birkbeck: pioneer of adult education* (Liverpool, 1957)

Kennedy, William F., 'Lord Brougham, Charles Knight and *The rights of industry*', *Economica* 29 (1962), 56–71

Knight, Charles, *The newspaper stamp and the duty on paper viewed in relation to their effects upon the diffusion of knowledge* (1836)

The old printer and the modern press (1854)

Passages of a working life during half a century, 3 vols. (1864–5)

Shadows of the old booksellers (1865)

Koss, Stephen, *The rise and fall of the political press in Britain* (1990)

Landon, Richard G. (ed.), *Book selling and book buying: aspects of the nineteenth-century British and North American book trade* (Chicago, 1978)

Landor, Walter Savage, *Letters and other unpublished writings*, ed. Stephen Wheeler (1897)

Letters, private and public, ed. Stephen Wheeler (1869)

Lang, Andrew, *Books and Bookmen* (1887)

The life and letters of John Gibson Lockhart, 2 vols. (1897)

Leavis, Queenie D., *Fiction and the reading public* (1932)

Le Marchant, Sir Denis, *Memoir of John Charles, Viscount Althorp, 3rd Earl Spencer* (1876)

Leys, Colin, 'Petitioning in the nineteenth and twentieth centuries', *Political Studies* 3 (1955), 44–64

Lochhead, Marion Cleland, *John Gibson Lockhart* (1954)

Lockhart, John Gibson, 'The copyright question', *Quarterly Review* 69 (1841), 186–227

Memoirs of the life of Sir Walter Scott, Bart., 7 vols. (Edinburgh 1837–8)

Longman, *Index to archives of the House of Longman 1794–1914*

Lowndes, John James, *An historical sketch of the law of copyright with remarks on Sergeant Talfourd's Bill* (1840)

Ludlow, John M., and Lloyd Jones, *Progress of the working class, 1832–1867* (1867)

Macaulay, Thomas Babington, *Legislative Minutes*, selected with an introduction by C. D. Dharkar (Madras, 1946)

The letters of Thomas Babington, Baron Macaulay, ed. Thomas Pinney, 6 vols. (Cambridge, 1974–81)

Maccoby, Simon, *English radicalism*, 6 vols. (1935–61)

MacDonagh, Oliver, *Early Victorian government, 1830–70* (1977)

MacDonald, J. Ramsay (ed.), *Women in the printing trades: a sociological study* (1904)

Macready, William C., *Diaries, 1833–1851*, ed. William Toynbee, 2 vols. (1912)

Maginn, William and Daniel Maclise, *A gallery of illustrious literary characters (1830–38)*, ed. William Bates (1873)

Mandler, Peter, *Aristocratic government in the age of reform: Whigs and Liberals 1830–1852* (Oxford, 1990)

Marryat, Florence, *Life and letters of Captain Marryat*, 2 vols. (1872)

Marryat, Fredrick, *A diary in America, with remarks on its institutions*, 6 vols. (1839)

Martineau, Harriet, *A history of the thirty years' peace*, 4 vols. (1878)

Harriet Martineau's autobiography, 3 vols. (1877)

Maugham, Robert, *A treatise on the laws of literary property . . .* (1828)

May, Thomas Erskine, *A treatise upon the laws, privileges, proceedings and usage of parliament* (1844) [Facsimile] (Shannon, 1971)

McCalman, Iain, *Radical underworld: prophets, revolutionaries and pornographers in London, 1795–1840* (Cambridge, 1988)

[McCulloch, John Ramsey], *Observations, illustrative on the practical operation and real effect of the duties on paper, showing the expediency of their reduction or repeal* (1836)

McCulloch, John Ramsey, *Principles of political economy*, 2nd edn (1830)

McFarlane, Gavin, *Copyright: the development and exercise of the performing right* (Eastbourne, 1980)

McGilchrist, James, *Life and career of Lord Brougham* (1868)

McKitterick, David, *Cambridge University Library: a history: the eighteenth and nineteenth centuries* (Cambridge, 1986)

Merriam, Harold G., *Edward Moxon, publisher of poets* (New York, 1939)

Mill, John Stuart, *The earlier letters of John Stuart Mill, 1812–48*, ed. Francis E. Mineka, 2 vols. (Toronto, 1963)

The later letters of John Stuart Mill, 1849–73, eds. Francis E. Mineka and Dwight N. Lindley, 4 vols. (Toronto, 1972)

Miller, Thomas, *Geodfrey Malvern; or, the life of an author*, 2 vols. (1842)

Millgate, Jane, *Scott's last edition* (Edinburgh, 1987)

Milton, John, 'Areopagitica, A Speech of Mr John Milton for the liberty of unlicenc'd printing, to the Parlament of England', *Complete Prose Works of John Milton*, general ed., Don M. Wolfe, 8 vols. (New Haven and London 1953–82), II, ed. Ernest Sirluck.

Mineka, Francis E., *The dissidence of dissent: the Monthly Repository, 1806–38, under the editorship of Robert Aspland, W. J. Fox, R. H. Horne, & Leigh Hunt; with a chapter on religious periodicals, 1700–1825* (Chapel Hill, NC, 1944)

Mitford, Marg Russell, *Elizabeth Barrett to Miss Mitford: the unpublished letters of E. B. Barrett to M. R. Mitford*, ed. and introduced by Betty Bergson Miller (1954)

Letters of M. R. Mitford, ed. H. Chorley, 2nd ser., 2 vols. (1872)

Letters, selected with an introduction by R. Brimley Johnson (1925)

The friendships of Mary Russell Mitford, as recorded in letters from her literary correspondents, ed. Alfred G. l'Estrange, 2 vols. (1882)

Monkhouse, William Cosmo, *Life of Leigh Hunt*, 2nd edn (1893)

Moore, M. C., 'The history of the agitation against the stamp duty on newspapers 1830–55', (unpublished MA Thesis, London, King's College, 1935)

Moore, Thomas, *Journal of Thomas Moore, 1818–41*, ed. Peter Quennell (1964)

Memoirs, journal and correspondence, ed. the Rt Hon. Lord John Russell, 8 vols. (1853–56)

Poetical works, collected by himself, 10 vols. (1840–41)

The journal of Thomas Moore, ed. Wilfred S. Dowden (Newark and London, 1983–91)

Moorman, Mary, *William Wordsworth; a biography*, 2 vols. (Oxford, 1957–65)

Morley, Edith J., *The life and times of Henry Crabb Robinson* (1935)

Mumby, Frank A., *The romance of book selling: a history from the earliest times to the twentieth century* (1910)

Munford, William A., *Edward Edwards, 1812–86: portrait of a librarian* (1963)

William Ewart, M.P., 1798–1869: portrait of a radical (1960)

Musson, Albert E., *The Typographical Association: origins and history up to 1949* (1954)

Trade union and social history (1974)

Myers, Robin, *The Stationers' Company archive: an account of the records, 1554–1984* (Winchester, 1990)

Myers, Robin and Michael Harris (eds.), *Bibliophily* (Cambridge, 1986)

Development of the English booktrade, 1700–1899 (Oxford, 1981)

Economics of the British booktrade 1605–1939 (Cambridge, 1985)

Spreading the word: the distribution networks of print, 1550–1850 (Winchester, 1990)

Napier, Macvey, *Selection from the correspondence of the late Macvey Napier*, ed. by his son Macvey Napier (1879)

New, Chester William, *The life of Henry Brougham to 1830* (Oxford, 1961)

Newdick, Robert Spangler, *The first life and letters of Charles Lamb: a study of Thomas Noon Talfourd as editor and biographer* (Columbus, OH, 1935)

Newdick, Robert Spangler, 'Studies in the literary works of Sir Thomas Noon Talfourd, D.C.L.' (unpublished thesis, Harvard University, 1926)

Nichols, John, *Literary anecdotes of the eighteenth century*, selected and ed. Colin Clair (1967)

Norton, Caroline, *The letters of Caroline Norton to Lord Melbourne*, eds James O. Hoge and Clarke Olney (Ohio, 1974)

Nowell-Smith, Simon Harcourt, *International copyright law and the publisher in the reign of Queen Victoria* (Oxford, 1968)

Noyes, Russell, 'Wordsworth and the Copyright Act of 1842: Addendum', *Proceedings of the Modern Language Association of America* 24 (1961), 380–3

Objections to and remarks upon Mr Serjeant Talfourd's scheme (1841)

Observations on the Law of Copyright; in reference to the bill introduced into the House of Commons by Mr Serjeant Talfourd: in which it is attempted to prove that the provisions of that Bill are opposed to the Principles of English Law; that Authors require no additional protection, and that such a Bill would inflict a heavy blow on Literature, and prove a great discouragement to its diffusion in this country (1838)

Oliphant, Margaret, *Annals of a publishing house, William Blackwood and his sons, their magazine and friends*, 2 vols. (Edinburgh, 1897)

Packer, Maurice, *Bookbinders of Victorian London* (1991)

Partridge, Robert C. B., *The history of the legal deposit of books throughout the British Empire* (1938)

Paston, George, *At John Murray's: records of a literary circle, 1843–1892* (1932)

Patterson, Lyman Ray, *Copyright in historical perspective* (Nashville, TN, 1968)

Pearl, Cyril Altson, *Always morning: the life of Richard Henry 'Orion' Horne* (Melbourne, 1960)

Peel, Sir Robert, *Memoirs by the Right Hon. Sir Robert Peel*, 2 vols. (1856)
Private Letters . . ., ed. George Peel (1920)

Peterson, M. Jeanne, *The medical profession in mid-Victorian London* (1978)

[Petheram, John], *Reasons for establishing an author's publication society: by which literary labour would receive a more adequate reward and the price of all new books be much reduced* (1843)

Phillips, Charles Palmer, *The law of copyright* (1863)

Pickering, William, *Booksellers' monopoly* (1832)

Pierce, Edward L., *Memoir and letters of Charles Sumner*, 4 vols. (1878–93)

Place, Francis, *The autobiography of Francis Place, 1771–1854*, ed. Mary Thale (Cambridge, 1972)

Polson, Archer, *Law and lawyers; or, sketches and illustrations of legal history and biography*, 2 vols. (1840)

Pope-Hennessy, James, *Monckton Milnes: the years of promise, 1809–51* (1951)

Pope-Hennessy, Una, *Three English women in America* (1929)
Proceedings at a meeting of the booksellers and publishers of London and Westminster, held at the London Coffee-House, Friday, January 18, 1839 (1839)
Prothero, Iorwerth J., *Artisans and politics in early nineteenth-century London: John Gast and his times* (Folkestone, 1979)
Pryme, George, *Autobiographic recollections of George Pryme*, ed. Alicia Bayne (Cambridge, 1870)
Pugh, Martin D. *The making of modern British politics, 1867–1939* (1982)
Radzinowicz, Leon, *A history of English criminal law* (1948)
Ramsden, Charles, *Bookbinders of the United Kingdom (outside London) 1780–1840* (1956, reprinted 1987)
London bookbinders 1780–1840 (1956, reprinted 1987)
Raven, James, *Judging new wealth: popular publishing and responses to commerce in England, 1750–1800* (Oxford, 1992)
Read, Donald, *Press and people, 1790–1850: opinion in three English cities* (1961)
Redding, Cyrus, *Literary reminiscences and memoirs of Thomas Campbell*, 2 vols. (1860)
Reed, Mark, 'Two letters of William Wordsworth to Richard Monckton Milnes', *Notes and Queries* 209 (1964), 18–20
Reid, Sir Thomas Wemyss, *The life, letters and friendships of Richard Monckton Milnes*, 2nd edn, 2 vols. (1890)
Renouard, Augustin-Charles, *Traité des droits d'auteurs dans la littérature, les sciences et les beaux-arts*, 2 vols. (Paris, 1838–9)
Rivington, Septimus, *The publishing family of Rivington* (1919)
Robinson, Henry Crabb, *Correspondence with the Wordsworth circle, 1806–66*, ed. Edith J. Morley, 2 vols. (Oxford, 1927)
Diary, reminiscences and correspondence of Henry Crabb Robinson, ed. Thomas Sadler, 2 vols. 2nd edn (1869)
On books and their writers, ed. Edith J. Morley, 3 vols. (1938)
Roebuck, John A., *Life and letters of J. A. Roebuck, with chapters of autobiography*, ed. Robert E. Leader (1897)
Rose, Mark, *Authors and owners: the invention of copyright* (1993)
'The author as proprietor: *Donaldson v. Beckett* and the genealogy of modern authorship', *Representations* 23 (1988), 51–85
Rowe, David John (ed.), *London radicalism, 1830–43; a selection from the papers of Francis Place* (1970)
Sadleir, Michael, *Bulwer and his wife . . . 1803–1838* (1933)
Saunders, David, *Authorship and copyright* (1992)
Saunders, John Whiteside, *The profession of English letters* (1964)
Sawyer, C. J., *Dickens v. Barrabas, Forster intervening* (1972)
Scott, Sir Walter, *Journal 1825–32*, revised by J. G. Tait, 3 vols. (Edinburgh 1939–46)
The letters of Sir Walter Scott, ed. Herbert J. C. Grierson, 12 vols. (1932–37)
Scrope, George Poulett, *Memoirs of the life of the Rt Hon. Charles Lord Sydenham, G.C.B., with a narrative of his administration* (1843)

Scrutton, Thomas E., *The law of copyright*, 2nd edn (1890)

Shannon, Richard Thomas, *Gladstone* (1982)

Shaylor, Joseph, *The fascination of books, with other papers on books and bookselling* (1912)

Simpson, A. W. Brian (ed.), *Biographical dictionary of the common law* (1984)

Skone James, Edmund P., *et al.*, *Copinger and Skone James on copyright*, 14th edn (1998)

Smiles, Aileen, *Samuel Smiles and his surroundings* (1956)

Smiles, Samuel, *A publisher and his friends: memoir and correspondence of the late John Murray*, 2 vols. (1891)

Smith, Francis B., *The making of the second Reform Bill* (Cambridge, 1966)

Southey, Charles C., *The life and correspondence of Robert Southey*, 6 vols. (1849–50)

Southey, Robert S., 'An inquiry into the Copyright Act', *Quarterly Review* 21 (1819), 196–213

New letters of Robert Southey, ed. Kenneth Curry, 2 vols. (1965)

Selections from the letters of Robert Southey, ed John W. Warter, 4 vols. (1856)

Sir Thomas More: or, Colloquies on the progress and prospects of society (1829)

Spicer, A. Dykes, *The paper trade* (1907)

Sprigge, Samuel Squire, *The life and times of Thomas Wakley* (1897)

Stephen, Leslie, *The English utilitarians*, 3 vols. (1900)

Stern, Madeleine B., *Books and book people in nineteenth-century America* (1978)

Stewart, Robert, *Henry Brougham 1778–1868: his public career* (1986)

Strömholm, Stig, *Le droit moral*, 2 vols. (Stockholm, 1966–73)

Sutherland, Gillian (ed.), *Studies in the growth of nineteenth-century government* (1972)

Sutherland, John Andrew, *Victorian novelists and publishers* (1976)

Swinfen, David A., 'Henry Brougham and the Judicial Committee of the Privy Council', *Law Quarterly Review* 90 (1974) 396–411

[Talfourd, Thomas Noon], 'The late Mr Justice Talfourd', *Law Magazine* 51 (1854)

Talfourd, Thomas Noon, *Final memorials of Charles Lamb; consisting chiefly of his letters not before published with sketches of some of his companions* (1848)

A speech delivered in the House of Commons May 18, 1837, on moving for leave to bring a Bill to consolidate the Law relating to Copyright (1837)

Speech for the Defendant, in the prosecution of the Queen v. Moxon, for the publication of Shelley's works. Delivered in the Court of Queen's Bench, 23 June 1841 (1841)

Three speeches delivered in the House of Commons (1840)

Vacation rambles and thoughts 1840–43, 2 vols. (1845)

Tebbel, John, *A history of book publishing in the United States* (1972)

Tegg, Thomas, *Extension of Copyright proposed by Serjeant Talfourd [A Letter to Lord John Russell]* (1840)

Remarks on the speech of Sergeant Talfourd, on moving for leave to bring in a Bill to consolidate the Laws relating to copyright (1837)

[Review of Talfourd's speech in House of Commons and remarks], *Monthly Review* 1, 52–62

Tholfsen, Trygve R., *Working class radicalism in mid-Victorian England* (1976)

Thomas, William, *The philosophic radicals* (Oxford, 1979)

Thompson, Thomas Perronet, *Exercises, political and others*, 6 vols. (1842)

Thorogood, Peter, 'Thomas Hood: a nineteenth-century author and his relations with the book trade to 1835' in eds. Robin Myers and Michael Harris, *Development of the English book trade 1700–1899*, (Oxford, 1981), pp. 106–72

Ticknor, George, *Cost books of Ticknor and Fields and their predecessors, 1832–58*, eds. William Charvat and Warren Tryon (New York, 1949)

Timperley, Charles H., *Encyclopaedia of literary and typographical ancedote* (1839) (2nd edn, 1842)

Todd, William B., *A directory of printers and others in allied trades, London and vicinity, 1800–40* (1972)

Tompson, Richard S., 'Scottish judges and the birth of British copyright', *Juridical Review* 37 (1992), 18–42

Trades Societies and Strikes. Report of the committee on Trades' Societies appointed by the National Association for Promotion for Social Science . . . (1860)

Trevelyan, Sir George O., *The life and letters of Lord Macaulay*, 2 vols. (1876)

Trevor, Meriol, *The Arnolds: Thomas Arnold and his family* (1973)

Trewin, John Courtenay and King, Evelyn M., *Printer to the House: the story of 'Hansard'* (1952)

Turberville, Arthur S., *The House of Lords in the age of reform, 1784–1837* (1958)

Vincent, David, *Bread, knowledge and freedom: a study of 19th century working class autobiography* (1981)

Literacy and popular culture: England 1750–1914 (Cambridge, 1989)

Wakley, Thomas, *A letter to the people of England, on the new project for gagging the press i.e. A Bill to consolidate the laws relating to stamp duties*, (1836)

Wallas, Graham, *The life of Francis Place 1771–1864* (1898)

William Johnson Fox (1786–1864) (1924)

Walpole, Spencer, *The life of Lord John Russell*, 2 vols. (1889)

Ward, William S., 'An early champion of Wordsworth: Thomas Noon Talfourd', *Proceedings of the Modern Language Association of America* 68 (1953), 992–1000

Wardroper, John, *Kings, lords and wicked libellers; satire and protest, 1760–1837* (1973)

Watson, Vera, *Mary Russell Mitford* (1949)

'The journals of Thomas Noon Talfourd', *Times Literary Supplement*, 8 February 1957, p. 88

Watts, Alaric Alexander, *Alaric Watts: a narrative of his life*, 2 vols. (1884)

Webb, Robert Keifer, *Harriet Martineau* (1960)

Webb, Sidney James and Beatrice Webb, *The history of trade unionism*, revised edn (1920)

Weiner, Joel H., *A descriptive finding list of unstamped British periodicals, 1830–1836* (1970)

The war of the unstamped (Ithaca, NY, and London, 1969)

Wheatley, Vera, *The life and work of Harriet Martineau* (1957)

Whitridge, Arnold, *Dr Arnold of Rugby* (1928)

Wickwar, William H., *The struggle for the freedom of the press, 1819–1832* (1928)

Williams, David, *Claims of literature* (1802)

Woodmansee, Martha, *The author, art, and the market: rereading the history of aesthetics* (New York, 1994)

'The genius and the copyright: economic and legal conditions of the emergence of the "author"', *Eighteenth-century studies* 17 (1984) 425–48

Woodmansee, Martha and Peter Jaszi (eds.), *The construction of authorship: textual appropriation in law and literature* (Durham, NC, and London, 1994)

Worboise, Emma Jane, *Life of Thomas Arnold D.D.* (1859)

Wordsworth, William, *The letters of William and Dorothy Wordsworth*, 2nd edn, revised arranged and ed. Alan G. Hill from the 1st edn (ed. Ernest De Selincourt), 7 vols. (Oxford, 1969–88)

Letters of the Wordsworth family 1787–1855, collected and ed. William A. Knight, 3 vols. (Boston, 1907)

The prose works of William Wordsworth, eds. Warwick J. B. Owen and Jane W. Smyser (Oxford, 1974)

Wordsworth and Reed: the poet's correspondence with his American editor, ed. Leslie Nathan Broughton (Ithaca, NY, 1933)

Zall, Paul M., 'Wordsworth and the Copyright Act of 1842', *Proceedings of the Modern Language Association of America* 70 (1955), 135–44

INDEX

www.ingramcontent.com/pod-product-compliance
Lightning Source LLC
LaVergne TN
LVHW090311210926
848480LV00001B/208
* 9 7 8 0 5 2 1 1 7 4 5 0 3 *